Fighter Pilots in World War II

HURRICANE 1940

Just twisted scrap thrown on a dump
Strips of wing and a Merlin sump
Old Fighter plane
Your flight is done
Your landings made and Victories won

Gun barrels scorched and motors tired
Your masters fought as men inspired
Old Fighter plane
They trusted you
Who faithfully served the Gallant Few

Casually now they fly around
Jet propelled at speed of sound
New Fighter planes
Fierce in your power
Spare thought for those who had their hour

BIGGIN HILL, JULY, 1947

On Weald of Kent I watched once more
Again I heard that grumbling roar
Of fighter planes; yet none were near
And all around the sky was clear
Borne on the wind a whisper came
"Though men grow old, they stay the same"
And then I knew, unseen to eye
[illegible]less Few were sweeping by

THE RIGHT HONOURABLE LORD BALFOUR OF INCHRYE, P.C., M.C., UNDER SECRETARY OF STATE FOR AIR, GREAT BRITAIN

Balfour of Inchrye
(from Sunday Times)

Three kings, from left to right, the Duke of Windsor – formerly Edward VIII – George V and George VI.

Fighter Pilots
in
World War II

Bruce Barrymore Halpenny

Pen & Sword
AVIATION

First published in 1986 by
Patrick Stephens Limited, London as *Fight for the Sky.*

Republished in Great Britain in 2004 by
Pen & Sword Aviation
An imprint of
Pen and Sword Books Ltd
47 Church Street,
Barnsley,
South Yorkshire
S70 2AS

ISBN 1-84415-065-8

A CIP record for this book is available from the British Library

Printed by CPI UK

For a complete list of Pen & Sword titles please contact
PEN & SWORD BOOKS LIMITED
47 Church Street, Barnsley, South Yorkshire, S70 2AS, England
E-mail: enquiries@pen-and-sword.co.uk
Website: www.pen-and-sword.co.uk

Contents

Glossary

AACS Anti-Aircraft Co-op School.
Ace An aeroplane combat pilot who has brought down at least five enemy aircraft.
Ack-ack Anti-aircraft gun or its fire.
ADGB Air Defence of Great Britain.
AEAF Allied Expeditionary Air Force.
AFC Air Force Cross.
AFS Advanced Flying School.
AI Aircraft interception.
Ammo Ammunition.
Angels 7 Enemy aircraft at 7 o'clock.
AOC Air Officer Commanding.
AOC-in-C Air Officer Commanding-in-Chief.
AP Armament Practice (Bomb).
ARW Air Raid Warden.
AVM Air Vice Marshal.

Bandit Enemy aircraft.
Base Home aerodrome.
Belly landing To crash land an aeroplane with wheels up.
Bf Bayerische Flugzeugwerke (Messerschmitt).
Blood wagon or **meat wagon** Ambulance.
Bought it Killed or shot down.

'Cab rank' Small formations of patrolling fighters and fighter-bombers on immediate call for close tactical support.
CD Canadian Forces Decoration
Chiefy Flight Sergeant.
'Circus' Code name for an operation by bombers or fighter-bombers, escorted by fighters and designed primarily to bring enemy fighters into action.
C&M Care and Maintenance.
CO Commanding Officer.

'Crossbow' The offensive and defensive measures to counter the V-weapon attacks.

DCM Distinguished Conduct Medal.
D-Day 6 June 1944, code name 'Overlord'. Allied armies began landing in Normandy with support from both Tactical and Strategic Air Forces.
DFC Distinguished Flying Cross.
DFM Distinguished Flying Medal.
DI Daily Inspection.
'Diver' The code name given to the FZG76, the V1 (flying bomb).
DROs Daily Routine Orders.
Duff No good.
DZ Dropping Zone.

EFTS Elementary Flying Training School.
'Erk' An Aircraftman or Aircraftwoman in the Royal Air Force.

F Fighter.
FB Fighter Bomber.
Fighter 'Roadsteads' Code name for low level attacks on ships, whether at sea or in the harbour.
Flak Anti-aircraft fire.
FR Fighter Reconnaissance.
Fw Focke-Wulf Flugzeugbau.

GCI Ground Controlled Interception.
'Gong' Medal.
GP General Purpose (Bomb).
GSU Group Standardization Unit.

He Heinkel.
HE High Explosive.
'Hercules' Projected German invasion of Malta in 1942. (The Italian code name was C-3.)
HQ Headquarters.
Hurri Hurricane.

IAF Indian Air Force.
IAS Indicated Air Speed.
i/c In charge.
Intruder Operations Offensive night patrols over enemy territory intended to destroy enemy aircraft and disrupt flying.

'Kipper Patrols' Protecting fishing fleets in the North Sea.
Kite Aeroplane.

Lighters Flat bottomed boat or barge that is mainly used for unloading or loading ships not lying at wharves.

Mae West Life saving waistcoat inflated if wearer falls into the sea, a name derived from its resemblance to the bust of the famous actress.
MC Military Cross; Medium Case (Bomb).
Me Messerschmitt AG.
MO Medical Officer.
MT Motor Transport.

NAAFI Navy, Army and Air Force Institute.
NCO Non-Commissioned Officer.
'Noball' V-weapon launching sites, storage and manufacturing centres.

OBE Order of the British Empire.
Ops rest Non-operational duties.
OTU Operational Training Unit.

PoW Prisoner of War.
Props Propellers.
PRU Photographic Reconnaissance Unit.

RAAF Royal Australian Air Force.
RAF Royal Air Force.
RAFVR Royal Air Force Volunteer Reserve.
'Ramrod' Code name for an operation similar to 'Circus' except that its principal objective was the destruction of a specific target in daylight and the fighters used cannon.
RCAF Royal Canadian Air Force.
Recce Reconnaissance.
RFC Royal Flying Corps.
'Rhubarb' Code name for low-level strike operation mounted in cloudy conditions against enemy fringe targets in occupied countries by pairs of aircraft against road and rail traffic.
'Rodeo' Code name for fighter sweeps over enemy territory without bombers.
RN Royal Navy.

RNZAF Royal New Zealand Air Force.
R&R Refuelling and rearming.
R/T Radio-Telephone.

SAAF South African Air Force.
Scramble An immediate operational take-off.
SFI Senior Flying Instructor.
SFTS Service Flying Training School.
Sortie Operational flight by a single aircraft.
Spit Spitfire.
Sprog pilot Inexperienced pilot.
Square bashing Drill on the square or parade ground.
Stuka Sturzkampfflugzeug, ie Ju 87 dive bomber.

Tannoy The public address system.
Tiffie Typhoon aircraft.
Trade Enemy, from the phrase 'looking for trade'.

USA United States of America.
U/T Under training.

VC Victoria Cross.

WD War Department.
WDAF Western Desert Air Force.
Winco or **Wingco** Wing Commander.
'Window' Metallized strips dropped from aircraft to simulate aircraft echoes to disrupt enemy radar systems.

Introduction

Following the huge success of my Bomber Command book *To Shatter the Sky* (now entitled *Bomber Aircrew in World War II*), I am anxious to place on record an authoritative and factual account of the activities of those who served in Fighter Command on fighter airfields during World War II. This book contains the story of those days and I have based it on the first-hand experiences of those who were there – many were unsung heroes, all were proud to have served. The aircraft are as varied as the tasks they performed and include the Spitfire, Hurricane, Beaufighter, Mosquito, Typhoon and Tempest.

The sheer determination to be a fighter pilot is clearly shown by Squadron Leader 'Jake' Coupland in the chapter 'Typhoon Pilot'. His 1934 Christmas School Report was a stinker! His house master's note regarding his application to studies read, 'It is not that he cannot, rather that he will not.' His uncle, an Honours graduate from Queen's (Belfast) and Oxford Universities, blew his top. The *Boy's Own Annual* that he received for Christmas 1934 had in it an interesting chapter that gave an exciting description of the life and golden opportunities open to any boy lucky enough to be accepted into the Royal Air Force as an Aircraft Apprentice or Boy Entrant. 'It fired my imagination', he said. 'I could become another Mannock or Ball! But my uncle being a realist snorted, "With your maths, you couldn't pass the Entrance Exams". He engaged a maths tutor to see that I did! Obviously he wanted out too!'

On 4 June 1935, 3,000 boys selected from throughout the United Kingdom sat the Royal Air Force Apprentice Entrance Examinations of which 300 were accepted. On 21 September 1935, 28 fresh-faced young boys started twelve tough months of training at the Royal Air Force School of Photography, one of those young boys was Coupland.

All fighter airfields were much the same. Some were all grass, a few had runways – all had tarmacadam taxyways. Nissen huts were standard and accommodation varied from luxurious to rundown. The permanent fighter stations had excellent quarters. On wartime stations the officers were usually quartered in requisitioned manor-type houses nearby the airfield. For example at Warmwell the officers stayed in a lovely house on a large estate and Robert Morrow remembers it well: 'I do not recall the name but after the war I saw the house featured in a book on outstanding English country homes. I think we tried to treat these buildings with reasonable care, but no doubt the owners after the war had much legitimate complaint. Another was at Gerrards Cross where I attended War Staff College, the house was the estate of the famous Judge Jefferies. Sad to relate at these quarters we shared three officers to a hut, sleeping quarters in Nissen huts. My companions were excellent and great fun; Guy Gibson (of dambusting fame) and George Jumper, a Colonel in the 8th Air Force. Staff College was interesting beyond description. I suppose there were about forty officers in the class, all Colonels and Wing Commanders. We had lectures from just about everybody, Eisenhower, Ernest Bevin, Attlee to name a few. We were also briefed on what was to come, ie V1s and V2s, the latest in aircraft and so on. Foodwise we fared not so badly and better than most. The English country folk were always able to set aside a few "goodies" for the Air Force such as eggs and the like, which were otherwise unobtainable – nor do I recall any great shortage of liquor – in retrospect we lived a life of considerable privilege. The United States Air Force was in a class by itself – thanks to such as George Jumper. The Americans were really well organized and in one aspect far better than the Royal Air Force – in that all aircrew shared the same Mess. It was very embarrassing at a dispersal hut to have the officers' food delivered almost on silver, whilst the Sergeant Pilots had theirs arrive in a pail. Naturally there was sharing but still it was embarrassing and, to my mind, not a proper arrangement.'

For the airmen and the 'erks' of Fighter Command the Fighter Stations were crowded, and those in brick billets were envied by those living in huts or tents. On the whole, the food was good, and meals were taken in shifts – early, main or late – according to work pattern. The NAAFI and other canteens were always well patronized and they did their best to satisfy, even under difficult conditions. One canteen had its windows blown out and no electric power, but the NAAFI girls still managed to provide beef puddings and chips!

'Achtung, Schpitfeuer!' The Luftwaffe pilots cried that many times – often for the last time – over the Kent countryside in the autumn of 1940. The enemy soon realized that Fighter Command was wide

A large house at Southend that was requisitioned during the war and used as an Officers' Mess.

awake and active, for the German pilots could be heard calling to each other over their wireless phones 'Achtung, Schpitfeuer!'

The Battle of Britain was the first great air battle in history. It is true that aircraft frequently met in combat in the First World War; but they did so in numbers very small when compared with those which were engaged over the fields of Kent and Sussex, the rolling country of Hampshire and Dorset, the flat lands of Essex and the sprawling mass of London. Moreover, from 1914 to 1918 fights took place either between individual aircraft or between small formations and an engagement in which more than a hundred aircraft on both sides were involved was rare.

'Tallyho' – enemy sighted ... and the battle was on. With information fed to them, the Controllers then set the pieces on the wide chess-board of the English skies and made the opening moves. Flexibility was their motto. Without this system of central control, no battle, in the proper sense of the word, would have taken place. Squadrons would have gone up haphazardly as and when enemy raids were reported. Eight hundred aircraft were used by the Luftwaffe in a most determined effort to destroy or temporarily put out of action the airfields at Biggin Hill, Debden, Duxford, Detling, Kenley, Hornchurch, Lympne, Northolt and North Weald. During this period George Williams was at North Weald: 'For me as an eighteen-year-old, North Weald as a fighter airfield was the most exciting eight months of my RAF Service,' he said 'I saw my first German aircrew there. The all clear had not sounded, and he came down by parachute right next to No 25 Squadron dispersal. There were no shortage of groundcrew to escort him and he was very arrogant. I also saw my first land mine at North Weald, lucky for us, it hadn't been fuzed.'

It was a very hectic period with fighter squadrons continually on the move. Most of the German aircraft came over at heights above 15,000 ft in sunny skies which made the task of the Observer Corps very difficult. There were dogfights all over Kent. The air was for some minutes – never for very long – vibrant with machine-gun fire. People on the ground stood and watched. Many times the watchers would see the blue field of the sky blossom suddenly with the white flowers of parachutes. The countryside was soon littered with the wrecked carcases of aircraft. Jack Strachan was a young Armourer and he was called out many times: 'The incidents over this period of time were not recorded and accepted as routine, such as crashes we attended to remove armaments' he said. 'Specific details of pilots' names etc, have long passed out of the mind, although the smell of burnt flesh, glycol and oil, and the usual sounds from the burnt-out wreckage remain for ever.'

Edward (Herb) Curotte arrived from Canada with No 1 (Fighter) Squadron, Royal Canadian Air Force, and his itinerary was as follows; Liverpool, Middle Wallop, then to Croydon where he experienced his first bombing, on to Northolt for the duration of the Battle of Britain, Prestwick, Castletown, Driffield, thence to Digby from where he was reposted to Canada.

'For me, I have many lovely lovely wartime memories' he said. 'Memories of Lincoln Cathedral – pleasant afternoon teas in a small shop in Lincoln. The friendliest pub within walking distance of the station. Rolling countryside where one could get "fresh" eggs from motherly farmers' wives who somehow circumvented the rationing system. We in turn would smuggle tea to them …

'I look back on my stay at Northolt and Digby with pleasant nostalgic memories of Service pals, friendly pubs, brave civilians … the bulldog tenacity of the Brits. I have seen at the height of the

A controller at work plotting the enemy.

Controllers in touch with the fighters.

London Blitz, ladders with a numerous number of the AFS go down into the flames, to be replaced within minutes by more men, and I often wonder if New York, Montreal or other North American cities could endure. It's not cities that create courage, it's population with courage that makes cities ... this the population of London, Coventry and others had! Can one say more!'

Winston Churchill, wartime British Prime Minister, immortalized the Allied pilots with his rich phrases in the House of Commons while the Battle of Britain still raged: 'Never in the field of human conflict was so much owed by so many to so few.'

The gallant pilots of Fighter Command hit the Nazi war machine very hard. The young Luftwaffe pilots had swept across Europe from Poland to the English Channel, and they expected to sweep over Britain, subdue her people and prepare the way for an invading army. Death and disillusion awaited them. The German pilots showed qualities of courage and tenacity. Of the morale of the British pilots and, not forgetting the Polish and Czech pilots who took their full share in the battle, little need be said – the facts are eloquent. They only had to see the enemy to engage him immediately. However, the Battle of Britain was not achieved without cost ...

Wing Commander the Honourable Max Aitken, DFC was in action throughout that phase, and after a short period in the Air Ministry was later given command of a night-fighter squadron. He was one of the 64 fighter pilots drawn by the artist Cuthbert Orde.

These were official drawings and Orde spent a year with the pilots of Fighter Command. 'He is a person with a very forceful personality and great charm', said Orde when he drew the then Squadron Leader Max Aitken. 'I found his company interesting and entertaining. I admire him because, in spite of all the influence which he could no doubt bring to bear, he stays in the front line.' Max Aitken stayed in for the duration of the war and was a very successful fighter pilot. Sir Max, the President of Express Newspapers, died at the age of 75 on 30 April 1985.

On the fortieth anniversary of the Battle of Britain, Wing Commander David Cox, an ex Battle of Britain Spitfire pilot, had his final sortie in a fighter aircraft when he took to the air in a Lightning at RAF Binbrook in Lincolnshire. A different era, but no doubt the memories of those hectic wartime 'scrambles' came flooding back.

The big turning point of World War II was Malta. It was the key. Feldmarschal Kesselring said: 'Failure to carry out Operation Hercules would seriously jeopardize the success of overall operations in the Mediterranean'. The difficulty was that Hitler could not accept the importance of the Malta operation. He let Italy take the initiative, despite the fact that it was German, not Italian, soldiers who were going to their death on the way to Africa because British warships and aircraft based at Malta were sinking the troop transport, all too often left to fend for themselves by their Italian escort ships. Hitler had made it clear to his Italian ally that the Armed Forces High Command intended to carry out Operation Hercules, either alone or jointly with Italy, but he could not bring himself to recognize its urgency. It is certain that Hitler's aversion to the operation, like Göring's was influenced by the fear that it could result in paratroop losses as high as those suffered in taking Crete.

Generaloberst Student's original force, constantly reinforced from the air, would probably have been sufficient to take Malta. It would have been much easier than Crete, for there the landing force had operated at three widely separated points of attack; in Malta there was only one and the ultimate goal, La Valetta, was only about six miles away from the initial landing area. Because of the relatively short distance between Malta and the base operations in Sicily, the Luftwaffe could even have established an airlift if it had been necessary. But in the end the Luftwaffe bombardment of Malta was in vain. The fruit was ripe, but it was never plucked. This made it a whole new ball game for the island, which regarded its escape as a miracle, and it soon recovered. Facilities were restored to the point where British aircraft could land and British ships could utilize its harbours.

If Malta had been taken in 1942 it would have been a very different story – Rommel might not have suffered defeat and the Allied landing in North Africa, if tried at all, would have come to a sticky end in the mountains of Algeria. Also, it would have lifted civilian morale in the Axis nations! As it turned out, however, the fruit was not plucked and therefore Tunisia capitulated, Sicily was lost, then came the forced resignation of Benito Mussolini (Il Duce), and the complete eclipse of the Fascist Junta. Italy called it a day and withdrew from the war, Naples was lost – and with it the airfields at Pomigliano and Foggia in southern Italy, then came Rome, and finally in April 1945 came the collapse of Germany's operations in the Italian theatre of war. Victory in Malta would have prevented this string of catastrophies.

The Royal Air Force in the Western Desert had a very difficult task – what may be called the cinema impression of a desert is nothing like the Western Desert. The sandstorms so often mentioned are more frequently choking clouds of dust rather than sand. Vast stretches are hard, firm going (except after rain), and resemble flat rock more than anything else. There are practically no features in the landscape, other than occasional shallow depressions which allowed tanks to get into hull-down positions. Among the more disagreeable features are the flies. They are a filthy, pertinacious, excruciating pestilence. When General von Ravenstein, commander of the 21st German Armoured Division was captured he said 'The desert is the tactician's paradise, but the quartermaster's hell!'

The Desert Air Force worked with the 8th Army and one of the Flying Desert Rats was Group Captain Bert Houle, DFC and Bar, CD: 'We had a feeling that the breakthrough at El Alamein was indeed the first yards on the invasion of Germany itself', he said. 'We were right and history has proved it.'

Those in the Desert Air Force had more than just the heat of the battle to contend with and it is a great pity that more medals were not forthcoming in this theatre of war – it is certain that many were well and truly earned, but 'gongs' were in short supply. This is unfair when you take into consideration that when the Headquarters of the North-west African Air Forces merged into those of the Mediterranean Air Command to become Headquarters Mediterranean Allied Air Forces, the number of squadrons available was 267 of which 146 were American and 121 British. The

Americans predominated in heavy and medium bombers and transport aircraft, the Royal Air Force was stronger in fighters and fighter-bombers. A single Tactical Air Force, to which both Allies contributed, had been created and was to render support to two armies fighting side by side.

The fighters were there in force to cover the D-Day landings on 6 June 1944, and a total of 171 squadrons of day fighters and fighter-bombers were available for fighter protection and direct support. All squadrons maintained a state of readiness to protect their own airfields. Twelve squadrons were retained by ADGB on home defence. The fighters were also out in force to combat the flying bomb menace. The Allies refused to accept information concerning the V1s. The 'V' designation originally denoted Versuchmuster (experimental model) and the change to Vergeltungswaffe was made purely for propaganda purposes. Germany had been working on rocket-propelled vehicles for many years and in 1933 Hitler had visited the army experimental rocket station.

Beginning in December 1943, bombing attacks began against the 'secret weapon' firing sites in northern France and in the next six months some 25,150 sorties and 36,200 tons of bombs were expended by the American 8th Air Force, AEAF, and RAF Bomber Command. The campaign cost 150 aircraft and 770 aircrew members. The fighters then took over with anti-Diver patrols. One of the fighter pilots was Flight Lieutenant 'Buck' Feldman flying a Tempest aircraft at the time. Those hectic wartime days are still clear in his mind. From 1956 until the time of writing Buck Feldman has been an Air Traffic Control Specialist with the Federal Aviation Administration and has resided in Albuquerque, New Mexico, USA. He retains his wartime link with a small Royal Air Force Museum at his home where he has on display his RAF memorabilia.

These first-hand accounts will give the reader some idea of the background to wartime conditions on a fighter airfield – the men, machines and the airfields. It is not just the story of the pilots, though they get a large slice of the book, but also about the groundstaff whose job it was to 'mend 'em for the pilots to bend 'em'.

The dedication and devotion to duty of those who served on fighter airfields during World War II should not be forgotten. 'The wartime atmosphere created was great and it's a great pity that the spirit did not prevail in this day and age', said Jack Strachan. Our fighters pulled us through – they fought alone in the skies. This book is about those who served on fighter airfields.

To the reader I present the chaps …

To the chaps I raise my glass … 'Scramble!'

Acknowledgements

I would very much like to thank the many people who have given me invaluable assistance during the preparation of this book. Special mention must be given to my old friend Ted Evans of Lincoln who made this book possible. During my illness Ted stepped in to help in many ways – a true friend – thank you.

Special mention also to my Canadian friend (ex-Chiefy) Edward (Herb) Curotte, ARW, Campbellton, New Brunswick, Canada. Over the years he has supplied me with much material from his wartime diary, which makes fascinating reading, and many excellent photographs that are published here for the first time. His note with his last batch for this fighter book was: 'It's difficult to obtain good prints from forty year old negs. Similarly good stud service from old airmen.' Herb closed his letter with the following postscript:

> *'Two old fighter pilots are chatting at the fortieth anniversary of the Battle of Britain.*
>
> *'First old Vet "Do you remember, Barry, the pills they would give us so we would not be too wild after women in wartime service?"*
>
> *'Barry "Yes, I do recall the pills."*
>
> *'First old Vet "Methinks they are starting to work ... must check with the nurse."'*

Even decades after the war Herb, and many others like him, still have a fine sense of humour.

My thanks also go to:

Airforce Magazine, Ottawa, Canada for help with my request for material; George D. Aitken (Ex-416 RCAF (Fighter) Squadron), Edmonton, Canada for material and photographs. It took a long time to prise it out of him but was well worth the wait; my old friend Brian Ayre for help with copies of photographs and drinking all my Italian coffee.

Ian Baines, Christchurch, New Zealand (ex-Mohawk pilot) for Mohawk material and photographs; Gerry Beauchamp, Gloucester, Canada for help with Mohawk material; Ken Border for his help with airfield research; Robert Brett, Christchurch, New Zealand who was most helpful but whose material I could not use because it was from

World War I. It was very interesting and one anecdote is worthy of mention: During the 1914–18 war an aircraft force landed in a field adjacent to, and south of the railway at Bleasby, and a crew was sent out to start it up again; a source of untaxed entertainment for the villagers who inevitably gather on such occasions. The pilot kept singing out 'contact' as the mechanic unrewardingly swung on the airscrew and being a young man of expensive education, his vowels were a little exaggerated. After several repetitions of his starting-drill, a large lady (a Mrs Clayton, if you must know) in the congregation turned to her companion and announced wisely 'It can't act'!; Joy Burrows for transporting material for typing.

Canadian Government Photo Centre, Ottawa, Canada; Air Vice Marshal Sir Bernard Chacksfield, KBE, CB, CEng, FRAeS, RAF (Ret), L. Choles, formerly 549351 Corporal Fitter with Nos 5 and 146 Squadrons during Mohawk period for help with material and two Mohawk servicing photographs.

My special friend, ex-Flight Lieutenant Len Devonshire, Lincoln for Far East airfield material. Len was chased out of Singapore by the Japs and walked out of Burma still hotly pursued by the same 'yellow peril'; Hon Walter Dinsdale, Brandon-Souris MP, Manitoba, Canada. Sadly, Walter died in November 1982. He was an eminent Canadian who won the Distinguished Flying Cross for his service as a Mosquito night-fighter pilot with the Royal Canadian Air Force in World War II. A good friend for many years, the story 'They shot down the first Mistel' is in Walter Dinsdale's memory; Director General, Information National Defence Headquarters, Ottawa, Canada; The Dodo Bird Club (Flight-Sergeants), Canada for their help and newsletters.

'Buck' Feldman (ex-RAF Flight Lieutenant, DFC) Albuquerque, USA for his help with material and photographs. In June 1985 he made a pilgrimage to his old haunts which included a visit to the 'Black Bull' inn at Newchurch where he spent many wartime hours relaxing from the air battles; Beatrice Foster, Canada.

John Gillies; G. Greenough, Kentville, Canada.

Mr R. S. Heath, BEM for his help with fighter servicing. He served with Nos 46 and 151 Squadrons. The first aircraft he worked on were Hurricanes in 1940s and the last were Jaguars in 1976; Dr Hofmann, Bundesarchiv, Koblenz, Germany for the two Mistel photographs; Air Vice Marshal H. A. V. Hogan, CB, DFC; Albert U. Houle (ex-Wing Commander) Manotick Canada for his help with Desert Rats material and photographs; my friend George Hubbert.

My thanks to my friend James Kinlay, Associate Editor, *Sunday Express* London for sorting material regarding Sir Max Aitken and for the photograph and permission to publish, same also to the *Express* for permission to quote their 1940 articles; Elliott Klein, McKeesport, Pennsylvania.

Hon Gilles Lamontagne, Lieutenant-Governor, Quebec City, Canada for his unending help while Defence Minister, sorting and helping with photographs and other material; My good friend Jim Lown, Healing, Grimsby for photographs and overseas material.

Reg W. Mack, Photograph Section, Royal Air Force Museum, London and Flight Lieutenant James Nicolson for helping to check some facts; Godfrey Mangione, Malta for his help with the map; my special friend of many years, Mario Medoro, Italy; Bill Miles; Doug Mills, Nottingham for his desert airfield material and photographs which were excellent, my good friend Robert E. (Bob) Morrow, QC, Montreal, Canada for all his material and photographs over the years.

My old friend Patrick Otter for sorting out material and *Grimsby Evening Telegraph* for permission to quote from Battle of Britain articles by Patrick; Palmer Oliver of Rapid City, South Dakota.

Public Record Office, Kew, London for squadron history records.

Ronald J. Regan (ex-501 Squadron). He stayed with 501 Squadron RAuxAF until February 1957 when the Royal Auxiliary Air Force was disbanded. He relinquished his commission in 1981 as a Flight Lieutenant and is now Civilian Instructor; *Royal Air Force News* for help with request for material and reaching many ex-servicemen; Royal Canadian Legion, Ottawa, Canada for publishing my request letter for material.

Ray Sellers (ex-Sergeant pilot No 46 Squadron (Hurricane)) for material and photographs; Ex-Squadron Leader Allan J. Simpson DFC, CD for permission to quote from his article 'The Tank Busters' and for his photographs. Also his help in locating one or two members; Bud Stevenson Canada for help with some photographs; Jack Strachan for material regarding Armourers' duties and for photographs.

Mr George Williams.

Finally a special thank you to my valued friend and UK assistant, Margaret Morris of Lincoln, who again spent many hours of typing and retyping. A very special mention and a big thank you for my wife and my son Baron for their many hours of proof-reading.

Bruce Barrymore Halpenny
Rome, Italy
November 1985

Chapter One

Fighter Airfields

British Army Aeroplane No 1, a large biplane constructed at Farnborough, made its first recorded flight on 16 October 1908 but, although the flight was successful, the great cost of aeroplanes caused all work on them to be stopped for a while. Eventually their potential military value was realized, work recommenced and the Air Battalion, Royal Engineers formed from the Balloon Section on 1 April 1911.

The early aeroplanes flew from open spaces conveniently situated near the garrison areas of Aldershot and Salisbury Plain, men and machines being housed under canvas. Several photographs exist of these first flying fields, and the canvas hangars appear to have been almost as flimsy as the aeroplanes they were intended to shelter. In the spring of 1912 the Royal Flying Corps was formed and the flying fields began to be developed into permanent aerodromes at which the units of this new Corps could

Early aeroplane sheds with a Bristol Monoplane.

be based. The tented camps were replaced by hutted accommodation for the personnel and some of these old huts still survive at the Wiltshire airfields of Upavon and Netheravon, two of the original Salisbury Plain aerodromes. Wooden 'Aeroplane Sheds' were erected, looking rather like a series of garden sheds stood side by side, in which the aeroplanes were kept; most of these original wooden sheds were demolished within a few years and it is unlikely that there are any still in existence.

When World War I started in 1914 there was still only a handful of military aerodromes in the United Kingdom but it soon became obvious that many more would be required to train the large number of pilots needed by the expanding RFC. Several new aerodromes were opened and an improved type of aeroplane shed was brought into use, one of which may still be seen at Manston having amazingly survived being moved from its original site at another aerodrome during World War I and the furious attacks of the German Air Force in World War II which destroyed most of the buildings at Manston except this shed and one other nearby of a slightly later vintage. By the middle of World War I a standard layout had been adopted for military aerodromes using a completely new, purpose designed type of hangar – the 1915 pattern Aeroplane Shed constructed of timber with both ends covered by large sliding doors to allow easy access for the aeroplanes. This type was superseded by the 1917 GS Shed (often called the Belfast hangar because of the wooden Belfast trusses upon which the roof was supported) which was a substantial brickwalled building similar in general outline to the 1915 pattern.

It was not until the Germans started to bomb British targets that there was a need for any home-based fighter aeroplanes, and the first home-defence fighters operated from makeshift fighter aerodromes that were often little more than areas of pastureland. That sufficed in the beginning for the fighter aeroplanes for they were little more than modified scout or spotter aeroplanes. The fighter aeroplane was designed primarily to secure control of the air by destroying enemy aircraft in combat. Almost any piece of pastureland was good enough to be a fighter airfield. However, by the last years of the war a few home defence aerodromes had been planned and construction started. One of these was Bekesbourne, four miles south-east of Canterbury, which was a 6th Brigade Squadron Station housing No 50 Squadron, equipped with 24 Sopwith Camel fighters. It covered an area of almost a hundred acres of undulating land in a strip adjoining the South Eastern and

Chatham Railway. It had two aeroplane sheds, one of which (a 1917 GS Shed) still survives and on the western end of the landing ground there were also MT sheds, workshops, hutted accommodation for about 260 men and women, and all the other facilities necessary to support a fighter squadron.

Some of these early fighter aerodromes had not been completed by the time the war ended and during the ensuing rundown of the infant Royal Air Force most of them were closed and the land returned to the former owners. Within two or three years the government accepted that the rundown had been too drastic and had left the country virtually defenceless against attack from the air, so it was decided to expand the RAF by fifteen squadrons. To house the new fighter units several additional aerodromes were needed particularly in the area around London, and a survey was carried out of the sites of former aerodromes to assess their suitability. Bekesbourne was rejected as unsuitable but in Essex the site of the former Sutton's Farm aerodrome was repurchased only a year or so after most of its buildings had been demolished, and a few miles to the north the old North Weald aerodrome was also selected for development.

This new generation of fighter aerodromes were still only small grass fields but they had substantial barrack blocks and other buildings grouped neatly nearby behind the aeroplane sheds. These were of a new pattern, the 'A' type which had been designed in 1924 as the standard general purpose hangar for RAF aerodromes, and were much larger than the wartime hangars, having a width of 120 ft and a length of 250 ft. The 'A' type had a steel frame with brick walls and a multi-ridged roof covered with toughened asbestos sheeting; four massive steel doors slid to cover each end and offices

A Gloster Gauntlet II of No 46 Squadron at Kenley.

were usually built against the side walls. Two of these hangars were built at both Hornchurch (as Sutton's Farm was renamed) and North Weald, and they were widely spaced leaving room for a third hangar to be constructed between them at a later date to complete a shallow arc. This practice was followed at later fighter stations but the third hangar was rarely built, Hornchurch being somewhat unusual in that it did get a third permanent hangar but this was of a later design, the 'A' type having been superseded by the time it was built.

These substantial hangars were complemented by the permanent workshops, barrack blocks and other buildings that were erected on these aerodromes; severe the survivors may look to modern eyes but they were a vast improvement on the hutted accommodation standard on most RAF stations at that time. A large landing circle was dug into the turf and packed with chalk to make the aerodromes conspicuous and in some instances the name was displayed, either within the circle as at Hawkinge or below it. There was so little traffic in the sky that flying control barely existed; the day of the control tower had not yet arrived and such control as there was lay in the hands of the duty pilot who was usually provided with a hut in front of the hangars. The fighters were all biplanes not vastly different from those in front line service at the end of World War I little over a decade earlier except that the drab camouflage had been replaced by an overall silver scheme with brightly coloured squadron markings. Much of the equipment was also from the wartime period with ageing Crossley tenders much in evidence and the airmen still wore uniforms with high buttoned necks, the pattern introduced shortly after the formation of the Royal Air Force.

For several years life at our handful of fighter aerodromes proceeded at a gentle peacetime pace with no great modernization of equipment or facilities. A new type of general service aeroplane shed was designed to supersede the 'A' and was rather like an enlarged version of that pattern; this was the 'C' type (Gabled), so called because of the gable ends to the roof sections. Very few of this type were constructed but one was built at Hornchurch between the two 'A' types to complete the arc of hangars and it was the only nine-bay version erected in this country, the remainder being intended for use by larger aircraft than fighters and therefore being twelve bays long.

Events in Germany in the early 1930s finally convinced the government of the day that our air defences were still woefully inadequate and the first of a series of expansion programmes was approved for the Royal Air Force. A completely new range of

The RAF uniform with the high buttoned neck.

buildings was designed for the new airfields planned under the expansion scheme and also for modernizing the existing bases. It proved to be a particularly well-designed range of purpose-built structures for all the wide variety of facilities required by an operational military airfield and very many of them are still in use at front-line RAF bases half a century after their plans were drawn up. The 'C' type (Gabled) hangar was updated to the 'C' type (Hipped), the most obvious difference being that the ends of the roof sections were hipped, ie sloped inwards, on the revised model and this became the standard hangar built on the permanent airfields constructed under the expansion schemes. It was steel framed with brick (or occasionally stone) walls containing large windows for most of their length and each end was covered by six massive sliding steel doors. Although they conformed to a basic design there was considerable variety in the number and type of offices that were built on the side walls, particularly those adjacent to the landing grounds, and they were also built to several different lengths. Generally the twelve-bay, 300 ft-long version was constructed on those airfields planned as bomber bases or maintenance units while the nine-bay model was erected at fighter airfields, interestingly space was invariably left at the latter to enable the extra three bays to be added later if required.

The fighter airfields constructed, or in several cases reconstructed on the sites of former aerodromes, during the mid-1930s were provided with a pair of the nine-bay 'C' type (Hipped) hangars at each end of an arc, and the support facilities were units from the new range of airfield buildings, modified where necessary to suit local conditions. The sites were landscaped and trees were planted, partly to placate local residents who were none too pleased to have an airfield constructed in the district and partly for the purpose of camouflage. The very substantial buildings were still closely grouped together like a small township with even the married quarters near the administrative and technical sites, and there was a new type of building – the watch office or control tower. No longer was the duty pilot relegated to a hut or bungalow, he now had a specially-designed building on the edge of the airfield, the 1934 design being a brick single-storey box-like building with a tower on it giving a fair view of the airfield. Many of these early watch offices have been demolished, either by enemy action during World War II or to make way for more modern buildings but the example on the former fighter station at Digby was still there (albeit disused) until recently and others may still be seen at airfields like Cosford, Catterick and Bicester. The fighter airfields were still grass surfaced with the fighters housed in the squadron's hangar but they were gradually preparing for the war that many were now convinced was inevitable. The landing circles were not laid out on the new airfields and new equipment was beginning to appear, including a new range of motor transport to replace the last of the veterans from World War 1.

As the Royal Air Force Expansion Programmes built up there came a need to economize in both money and other resources and this became apparent on the later airfields to be constructed under those programmes as some of the rather lavish designs were replaced by more austere patterns. Thus the attractive pseudo-Georgian style buildings gave way to plainer, and arguably equally attractive, structures with flat roofs utilizing a greater proportion of concrete. Finally, by 1938 further economies were brought in so that airfields could be made available as quickly as possible in view of the ever worsening international situation and some airfields were brought into service with hutted accommodation – a reversion to World War 1 conditions! Even the 'C'-type hangar was a victim of austerity and was redesigned to produce an economy version – the 'C1' which used a frame similar to the 'C' but lacked the prominent end brickwork. It was also available in either nine- or twelve-bay lengths but only three of the shorter model were erected,

Winter comes to Biggin Hill, January 1942.

all at the fighter airfield of Kirton-in-Lindsey which thus became unusual in actually receiving all three of the permanent hangars planned for the fighter stations – Debden was another exception, having three 'C'-type hangars two of which were demolished in 1979 after the site had been transferred to the Army Department. By 1938 the old 'dog collar' uniforms had been discontinued and had been replaced by the pattern to become so familiar to thousands of airmen as their 'best blues'. Most of the gaily-coloured biplanes had been superseded by drab camouflaged monoplane fighters.

When war was finally declared in September 1939 it found the squadrons of Fighter Command based at a few recently-built airfields such as Debden and Church Fenton, some old airfields that had been reconstructed to operate fighters, eg Digby and Wittering, the handful of early expansion fields at North Weald, Hornchurch etc, and several old World War 1 aerodromes like Biggin Hill and Tangmere that had undergone several rebuilding programmes but still retained many of their original buildings. Each had a technical

North Weald in spring 1942. This shows clearly the fighter blast pens. The walls were mounds of earth which gave some protection from blast to the fighters. The fighter coded S-M inside the pen is that of Wing Commander Scott-Malden, RAF. The other aircraft are those of No 403 Squadron, RCAF.

site containing the hangars with practically all the other buildings nearby making them a tempting target for hostile bombers. Grass surfaces were the norm with paved runways being laid on only a tiny number of RAF airfields, a mistake that had to be corrected at a later date. The planned satellite airstrips had not been opened.

The lull during the opening months of the war enabled the fighter airfields to be put on to a war footing by the completion of facilities, construction of dispersal hardstandings around the perimeter tracks, installation of air raid defences and the opening of some satellites. At Debden, for instance, two runways were constructed as were dispersals, and Castle Camps was opened as a satellite airfield to which the Debden squadrons could be dispersed. On the main airfields some of the dispersal hardstandings were provided with aircraft pens, walls backed by earth which gave some protection from blast to the fighters which were pushed into them. Dispersal huts of many different types appeared, some looking like refugees from an allotment garden, to give shelter to the pilots and ground crew, and the humble bicycle became a necessity to commute between the barrack blocks and these distant flight huts.

By the summer of 1940 Fighter Command had concentrated most of its front line strength on to a band of airfields around London

An excellent view of an early wartime fighter airfield showing the 'Blister' hangar. In the fore is a Nissen hut and in the background behind the 'Blister' hangar on the left is a 'T2' type hangar.

and the southeast coast area, the majority of them being of pre-war origin but also including one or two that had been civil airfields prior to 1939 and had been taken over by the RAF as satellites. They had little or no military facilities and the personnel either lived under canvas or were billeted with families in nearby villages. By this time also, the shortages of resources and the need to get more airfields into service had caused great alterations to be made to the buildings planned to be constructed on the new sites. For a short time the RAF clung to the idea of permanent hangars and introduced the 'J' type as a replacement for the 'C1'; it was steel framed and clad with metal sheeting but it appeared on very few of the fighter airfields built early in the war.

Before the war the RAF had placed orders for numbers of transportable hangars of various patterns and some of these had been erected, usually at second-line airfields. The most common type was the 'Bellman' which was steel framed with corrugated iron cladding, some of the early examples reputedly having canvas doors although the vast majority had six steel sliding doors at each end. Bellman hangars were erected at several of the fighter airfields built during the opening phase of World War 2 but the low angle of pitch on the roof of this pattern made them vulnerable to damage by heavy falls of snow and they were superseded by the 'T' family of transportable sheds designed by the Teesside Bridge and Engineering Works. These were quite similar to the Bellman but they had a steeper slope to the roof. More than 900 were produced between 1940 and the end of the war, most of them being the 'T2' type. This version had a clear door height of 25 ft and a clear width of 113 ft 6 in. It comprised a number of 10 ft 5 in long bays; the standard length was 23 bays but there were numerous variations, particularly on the airstrips constructed in the Highlands and Northern Islands where short thirteen bay hangars were common to present smaller targets to the high winds.

Even more numerous than the 'T2' was the 'Blister' hangar which originated in 1941 and was produced in great numbers. There were several varieties of which the most common were the Miskins 'Over' and 'Enlarged Over' types giving clear widths of 65 ft and 69 ft respectively, each being 45 ft long although two, or even three, were sometimes joined end to end. As the name suggests, these hangars were curved with no separate side walls, the steel frame supporting corrugated iron cladding. Both ends were open but they had provision for canvas curtains to be fitted, and they were excellent utility shelters with a low profile that made them far less conspicuous than most other aeroplane sheds.

Mud and tins mark the dispersal area at Prestwick in October 1940. The tents gave very little protection from the icy winds.

After the last of the pre-war-designed fighter airfields had been built the next generation began to reflect the lesson of dispersal that had been learnt at such a high price and no longer were all the buildings grouped together in neat, orderly rows. The technical site was still on the edge of the airfield and usually had a large hangar for major servicing, probably a 'T2' or the smaller 'T1', but the remainder of the facilities were dispersed around the surrounding countryside making use of hedges and thickets to provide natural cover. Living accommodation was provided on dispersed domestic sites, some of which were considerable distances from the airfield, and the buildings were of two main types – the Nissen huts and Maycrete buildings. Nissen huts originated in World War I and comprised semicircular steel frames with corrugated iron cladding with a concrete base and either wooden or brick ends while the Maycrete buildings were made of brick and concrete, purpose-designed for a whole range of duties from guard hut to gymnasium.

Fighters at Castletown airfield.

Over forty years after they were erected, many can still be seen at former airfield sites throughout the United Kingdom. Many of them are derelict but some are still in use and have been converted into a wide variety of farm or industrial buildings by their new owners. Most of these wartime fighter airfields had a box-like brick building on the edge of the landing area, this was the watch office or control tower from which the air traffic controller had a good view of the airfield and nearby were usually a shelter for the crash tender and a hut for the duty crew, plus the signals square in which was displayed the airfield identification letters and any necessary signals indicating landing restrictions, etc. By now some of the hard-standings dispersed around the perimeter of the airfields had been equipped with Blister hangars to give some shelter from the weather to the parked aircraft and to the groundcrew responsible for keeping them serviceable. Metal tracking also began to appear about this time, one of the earliest types being Sommerfeld Tracking, and this was laid in large quantities to form runways and additional hardstandings on those airfields that had not been provided with adequate permanent facilities.

By 1942 it had been realized that several additional fighter airfields would be needed in southern England when the planned invasion of German-occupied Europe was mounted, and a large number of sites were surveyed. It was not considered necessary to construct elaborate airfields, and anyway the resources were not available, so more than twenty very basic strips were built. These had Sommerfeld Track runways at first although this had to be replaced by more substantial tracking in many instances when it became damaged by heavy use, and they had little accommodation other than three or four 'Blister' hangars, the personnel either living

A 1914–18 airfield? No, this is a forward airfield at Gare, Holland, in October 1944. This picture clearly shows the condition the pilots and groundcrew had to work under on forward airfields.

Makeshift conditions on a forward airfield. DH Mosquito NF Mk XIII MM466 of No 409 (Night Fighter) Squadron is serviced on a frosty January morning at Vendeville, France.

in tents or being billeted in houses requisitioned for the purpose. These Advanced Landing Grounds played a vital role in the months prior to and during the landings but as soon as airstrips had been secured in France they became redundant. Most were derequisitioned during the latter part of 1944 and now show few traces of their short but hectic life as operational fighter airfields.

After the Allied landing in Normandy in 1944, fighters moved into France and made do with makeshift airfields for many captured airfields were bombed to pieces. The military engineers of World War 2 faced and mastered problems on a scale and often of a character previously not experienced. Because airpower was the deciding factor, airfields and airstrips had to be built, usually in great haste, frequently under fire. The construction and maintenance of forward airfields was a major problem for the engineers and a variety of rapid airfield surfacing materials were developed, the American Pierced Steel Planks being the most successful. For combined operations in the Pacific, floating airfields, consisting of prefabricated sections bolted together, were developed.

A method of forward fighter airfield site selection in the North Africa campaign consisted of a preliminary recce carried out by an RE officer accompanied, whenever possible, by an RAF Liaison Officer. In any event, the site was always finally approved and the runway sited by the senior RAF Liaison Officer. It was the practice to survey sites ahead of requirements, but, in case of urgency, work usually started within two days of recce.

Forward Airfield Engineers also had to take training for removal of mines and booby traps for some of the commitments of Engineer Units were employed in 'delousing' airfields, such as with Benghazi and Tripoli airfields.

Considerable research was carried out in all countries on substitute reinforcement materials for use in concrete. Woods, grasses, plastics, and asbestos were all tried with no real success. In Norway in 1940 a landing strip was cut out and levelled, then the whole length of the strip was covered with coconut matting, held down with wire mesh. However, it was not a success and it only lasted ten days. Difficulties were numerous and similar in all cases. The chief problem being in bonding between the reinforcement and the concrete. This gave trouble due to the need to protect the wood or other substitute from insects and to inhibit moisture absorption during curing of the surrounding concrete. In Italy and Japan bamboo found favour due to a claimed tensile strength of 28,250 psi and a modulus of elasticity of 2.55 x 106 psi. In India experiments were carried out to prevent moisture absorption and swelling of the bamboo causing cracking of the green concrete and a complete breakdown of bond. Suffice it to say that they fulfilled their function in part.

Sommerfeld Track was used with success as a fighter runway. The only failures were small and local in character. Portions were threaded with coir camouflage, but this was subsequent to the wet weather. The good results were no doubt due to thorough grading which shows in the following report for a fighter runway:

'(1) Nature of soil – a sandy loam. Rather light texture on surface but very good natural drainage.

'(2) The ground carefully graded and thoroughly compacted by rolling, but prior to laying the Sommerfeld Track the top two inches had become pulverized by fighter aircraft. No soil stabilization was carried out.

'(3) There were a few patches of grass prior to laying the track, but not of great extent. Under the protection of the steel track and influence

Hawker Typhoon Mk Ib RB407, *coded F3-T, of No 438 (FB) Squadron taxys into a wet dispersal at Eindhoven, Holland in February 1945.*

of the wet season (which followed laying the track) practically the entire surface became covered with a thick mat of grass. No artificial underlay was used.

'(4) Rainfall for the period in question (November to March) was 38.43 in. Heaviest fall 3.09 in in 24 hours. Surface proved satisfactory even after heavy rain.

'(5) No artificial drainage except one small area. A crossfall of 1 ft throughout the length of the strip.'

In New Guinea Pierced Steel Plank was laid on natural soil and mud oozed through. The runway was slippery but usable. The most suitable sites for landing strips in New Guinea were those where patches of grassland (Kuni) exist near streams, as they have considerable sand and gravel deposits, and drainage is good. The construction of the landing strip was carried out by natives who cleared the strip with knives and by burning. A glide angle of 1 in 40 was desirable and in average jungle with scattered large trees, the average for this type of clearing was 200 sq yd per native per day.

The runway length for a minimum strip was 2,400 ft, with surface width of 60 ft and cleared width of 4,000 ft. A first class strip would have a runway length of 5,000 ft. All strips were limited to about 150 landings at the most in dry weather before it was necessary to close the strip and effect repair work. In wet weather as few as six landings could result in a very rough and dangerous surface. This was overcome by compacting with a 10 or 11 ton roller, tractor drawn. Experience on all airfields showed that gravel with up to fifty per cent clay mixed did not consolidate with traffic alone and in fact made the surface worse instead of improving it. Filling holes and ruts with gravel, and rolling with a heavy roller was effective.

For the construction of forward airfields it was often necessary to airlift light items of plant and labour to lift sections of heavier items that could be reassembled on the ground. Great advances were made

Some groundcrew stroll down the main street of what they called 'Shanty Town', Petit Brogel, Belgium, March 1945.

in the science of soil stabilization and although the engineering tasks varied in size in these operations, they were basically similar.

As the war progressed the need for fighter airfields in the United Kingdom decreased and few new ones were opened in the last year or two of the war. When the war ended there began another run-down of the Royal Air Force which resulted in a very large proportion of its airfields being closed within a short period, busy airstrips becoming deserted and unwanted almost overnight. Many of the wartime temporary buildings were 'liberated' by enterprising farmers and others, some being moved to new sites so Bellman, 'T2' and Blister hangars may still be seen at locations far from any present or former airfield.

The introduction of jet engines on fighter aircraft meant the end of the grass-surfaced fighter airfield, including those with temporary steel planking runways, and several well-known fighter stations such as Hawkinge and Digby were either closed or retasked. As always, there were exceptions and the long-established fighter base of Duxford had its first permanent runway constructed several years after the war had ended, but generally the small post-war fighter force was concentrated on a handful of airfields which had permanent hangarage and other facilities plus substantial runways.

For several years the fighters were to be seen in natural metal finish with colourful unit markings, motor transport reverted to its pre-war RAF blue paintwork and the Service appeared to have settled into a peacetime routine. However, international tensions were responsible for the fighters to once more be camouflaged and for the progressive toning down of their unit and national markings; this was followed by the application of drab colours to vehicles and to many of the airfield buildings.

With the increased performance of the new generations of jet fighter aircraft there had gone an increase in their requirements for runway strength and length, and also for more complex support facilities. Most fighter airfields in Great Britain were rebuilt with one long, all-weather runway, any other existing runways usually being either abandoned or used only in emergency. This runway extension programme also entailed laying new lengths of taxyways to link the ends with the old perimeter tracks and in some cases it also necessitated constructing completely new control towers to obtain a view over the extended airfield. Many other new buildings have appeared at fighter airfields since the war ended, ranging from additional technical blocks to estates of married quarters but the well-proven pre-war 'expansion period' buildings still remain the core of most of the current fighter airfields.

CHAPTER TWO

Operational Fighter Pilots

Contrary to popular belief you could not tell a wartime fighter pilot from a bomber pilot. There was, of course, a great difference between the lives they led, for the fighter must be ready to 'Scramble' at a moment's notice, while the bomber knows that he will not fly operationally until early evening; so their routine and habits were entirely different.

Each fighter squadron was self-contained and run by the Squadron CO, no two squadrons were run on the same lines, each had their own little ways. Anyone put on a charge came up in front of their own Squadron CO. It had to be very serious to bring in the Station Commander.

'Scramble' – No 402 Squadron RCAF at Digby race towards their fighters – 1941.

The most striking thing about the operational fighter pilots was their ordinariness. The source of supply was so varied that it provided the variety of temperaments that made the required mixture. A fighter squadron could be divided into three groups: natural leaders and fighters at the top; then the main body containing the germ of leaders of the future, those whose qualities developed with experience or under pressure; and then the few who never quite made it but nevertheless pulled their weight. Then there was always the exception to the rule and the rare bird would stand head and shoulders above the rest. He had to be a good pilot, good shot, able to keep his squadron together in the air and look after the stragglers, for the straggler was always picked out and picked off.

Many of the fighter pilots wore a scarf or sweater instead of a collar as the pilot had to continually turn his head so that he was not taken unawares by the enemy. 'Red Section! Scramble!' and they were away. The whole squadron of twelve fighters could be in the air within three minutes of hearing the word 'scramble'. Many were airborne in $2\frac{1}{2}$ minutes. Because of this the fighter pilots lived a very unsettled life. When on the ground it was hard to concentrate very much because at any moment the word 'Scramble' might be sounded, sending them into the air and into battle. So about the huts and dispersal point there was an atmosphere of restlessness.

The pilots just stood around, some playing cards, others reading the newspaper, smoking a cigarette or cat-napping in a chair. The casual visitor might well have asked, 'Why don't they do something?' At the word 'Scramble' they did. They dropped what they were doing and ran as fast as possible to their fighters. The moment the pilot was strapped in he would taxy into the wind, each pilot getting himself into his correct position in the formation. The moment they had got into formation the Squadron Leader

Jenk relieves the tension of waiting with his pipe and newspaper. No 402 (Fighter) Squadron at Digby, 1941.

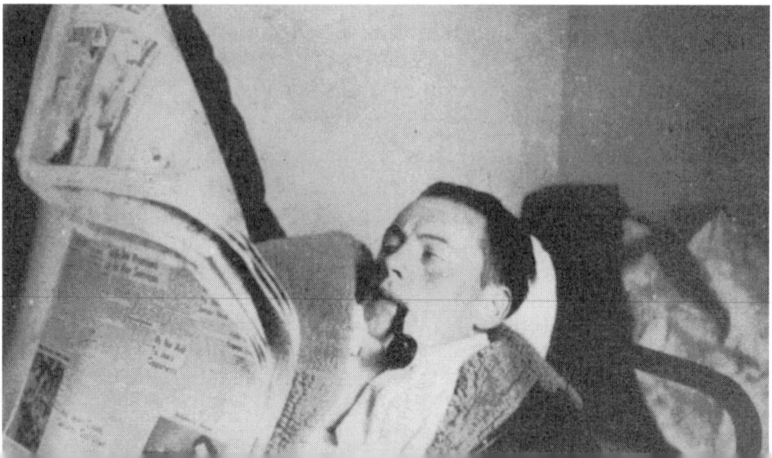

The Fighter Directional Aerial System equipped with a cabin on the aerial structure which housed both the transmitter and the receiver.

opened up his engine and the whole bunch would roar across the airfield and climb into the sky.

Generally speaking, a formation was composed of sections of three or four aircraft in some definite arrangement, with a further section acting as 'weavers'. The job of these weavers was to protect the squadrons from being pounced on by the enemy. They were the look-out men, who spent their time in twisting and turning their necks and their machines in every direction so that the main body of the wing or squadron might feel secure against surprise attack. The squadron was controlled from the ground by wireless. At the time of the 'scramble' the fighters had no orders at all; they received their orders when they were in the air.

Waiting on the airfield for the squadron to come back, the groundcrews stood by to refuel and rearm each fighter as soon as it had landed. Should the squadron appear in strict formation the groundcrews knew no contact had been made; but if the fighters returned singly or in twos or threes it was certain they had been in action. As they taxied to their dispersal points, a quick glance at the leading edge of their wings would tell which aircraft had been in a fight, for there would be eight holes visible where the first shots fired had blown off the fabric patches that covered the mouths of the gun barrels. Before the pilot had time to climb from his cockpit two mechanics would be on the wings to ask what happened and to see if everything had worked satisfactorily. Then would follow debriefing with the Intelligence Officer and then once more back to await another 'scramble'.

Night fighters were like day fighters who worked in reverse. The night fighters came to readiness at dusk instead of dawn and spent the night-time in the sky. They made airworthy flights during the daytime to check their equipment and aircraft. As darkness fell the night fighter went to the dimly-lit dispersal hut to await orders.

Fighter Command Ops Room at Bentley Priory – 1940.

One of the early night fighters was Squadron Leader Maxwell Aitken, the thirty-year-old elder son of Lord Beaverbrook, Minister for Aircraft Production. He flew Hurricanes with No 601 (County of London) Squadron at Biggin Hill. On 16 May 1940 a flight went to Merville, France and two days later Squadron Leader Aitken downed two Heinkel 111s near Brussels. He was a born fighter: 'Night fighting is a fascinating game', he said. 'It is like a game of rather noisy hide and seek, or better still, it is like a game my brother and I used to play some years ago. We used to climb down into a large maze of stone quarries near our home and start stalking each other. Our ammunition was sharp stones, and the loser the first to be hit. We used to play for hours, wriggling on our stomachs, slowly gaining a good position, and then a hard throw.

'The other night at midnight the operational phone rang and I received orders to patrol a certain line. As I ran out to my fighter plane I could hear the sirens wailing in a neighbouring town. There was no moon and quite a lot of cloud. I took off and climbed through the clouds. I was excited, for I had waited for this chance for the previous three nights, sitting in a chair all night dressed in my flying clothes and yellow-painted rubber life jacket which we call "Mae West".

'I climbed to the height ordered and remained on my control line. After about an hour, I was told by wireless that the enemy were at a certain spot flying from north-west to south-east.

Spitfires of No 411 (F) Squadron at Digby, Lincolnshire in October 1941. Two WAAF groundcrew help the pilot in DB-R.

'Luckily, I was approaching that spot myself. The searchlights, which had been weaving about beneath light cloud, suddenly all converged at one spot.

'They illuminated the cloud brilliantly, and there silhouetted on the cloud, flying across my starboard beam were three enemy aircraft. I turned to port and slowed down slightly. One searchlight struck through a small gap and showed up the whole of one plane, I recognized it as a Heinkel 111.

'One of the enemy turned to port, I lost sight of the other. I fastened on the last of the three, I got about 100 yd behind and below, where I could clearly see his exhaust flames. As we went out of the searchlights and crossed the coast he went into a shallow dive.

'This upset me a bit, for I got rather high almost directly behind him, but I managed to get back and opened my hood to see better. I put my firing button to fire and pressed it. Bullets poured into him. It was at point blank range; I could see the tracer disappearing inside but nothing seemed to happen except that he slowed down considerably. I almost overshot him, but put the propellor into the full 'fine' pitch and managed to keep my position. I fired again in four bursts, and then noticed a glow inside the German machine. We had been in a shallow dive, and I thought we were getting near the sea; so I fired all the rest of my ammunition into him. The red glow got brighter. He was obviously on fire inside. At 500 ft I broke away to the right and tried to follow, but overshot so I did not see him strike the water.

Group Captain Max Aitken DSO, DFC and Bar, Czech War Cross – fighter ace. He flew from the first day of the war right through to the last day.

'I climbed and at 1,000 ft pulled off a parachute flare. As the flare fell towards the sea I saw the Heinkel lying on the water. A column of smoke was blowing from his rear section. I circled twice, but there was no movement; no one tried to climb out so I turned and flew for home.'

Squadron Leader Aitken then attacked and destroyed two Heinkel 111s, a Messerschmitt 110 and two Junker 88s, all within the space of a few days. On one occasion Aitken chased an enemy aircraft more than 20 miles, almost at ground level, before destroying it.

Max Aitken joined the Auxiliary Air Force in 1935, as a Volunteer Reserve, and when war broke out, he was flying Blenheims with No 601 Squadron. The first operational sortie was on 27 November

The gyro gunsight. This was introduced in late 1943 and it greatly improved the standard of aerial marksmanship for the average pilot. All the pilot had to do was set the control on his sight's panel to the span of the enemy aircraft's wings, and then follow the enemy aircraft into a turn. The pilot then adjusted the size of the graticule to match the enemy's apparent diameter and the gyro mechanism in the sight produced the right deflection for the range and rate of turn, so that when the pilot had the enemy in the right-sized graticule, his fire would hit the target.

1939, when Flying Officer Aitken led a section which strafed aircraft in the water at the enemy seaplane base at Borkum. This was the first fighter strike of the war into enemy territory. All aircraft returned safely to base.

After their brief spell at Merville, the flight returned to England. From Tangmere, Aitken shot down two more enemy aircraft, a Heinkel and a Junkers, and received his first Distinguished Flying Cross from King George VI at Buckingham Palace. He also took over Command of No 601 Squadron in June 1940. In August 1940, Aitken began to form No 68 Squadron, a night-fighter unit equipped with Beaufighters and they became operational in January 1941. In 1942 when his squadron of night fighters pulverized a German formation Aitken received a telegram from Prime Minister Churchill saying: 'Renewed congratulations to your squadron and personally to you'. When Max Aitken was awarded the Distinguished Service Order in August 1942, the citation read: 'A brilliant pilot and gallant leader, this officer has set a most inspiring example.'

With his total kills at fourteen, Aitken was posted to Headquarters of Fighter Tactics in the Middle East as a Wing Commander. While with No 46 Squadron on 5 March 1944, he shot down two Ju 52s to bring his final total to 16½ kills. Aitken was then promoted and posted to Banff, Scotland, as Commanding Officer of a Mosquito wing of Coastal Command. Group Captain Max Aitken led the strike wing and the losses were great, out of his six squadron commanders, four were killed on operations. Aitken remained with the Mosquito wing until the end of the war. Post-war he was CO of his old 601 Squadron which had destroyed more than 200 enemy aircraft but half the auxiliary pilots had lost their lives.

In June 1944, No 149 Wing arrived at Zeals, Wiltshire, and took over the two Mosquito squadrons. Squadron Leader March and Flight Lieutenant Eyolfson, 410 Squadron, Royal Canadian Air Force, destroyed an Me 410; the Form 'F' Personal Combat Report reads:

'*Pilot*: Squadron Leader March, RCAF
Navigator: Flight Lieutenant Eyolfson, RCAF

We took off from Zeals at 23:55 hours and set course for Pool 2 where we were controlled by 21 Sector GCI. A freelance contact was picked up at 01.05 hours while Yardley controller was busy with Jungle 28 (Flight Lieutenant Huppert, Flying Officer Christie) who was in the process of baling out after shooting down an enemy

A fighter at the receiving end. Thankfully it is a friendly encounter during a training exercise on fighter affiliation.

A night-fighter Mosquito shows its devastating fire power.

aircraft which I saw fall in flames at approx 15 miles north of Pointe de la Percée. Our contact was obtained at a range of $1\frac{1}{2}$ miles, well below, crossing port to starboard, while we were on a vector of 100. We turned after it and informed control. A very long chase ensued during which the enemy aircraft was taking violent evasive action at very high speed. For the first part of the chase the enemy aircraft maintained a mean southerly course. He then dropped several batches of 'Window' and turned in an easterly direction. At this point the range, after it had been closed considerably, increased to 7,000 ft. The violent evasive action decreased. I believe this was due to the fact that the enemy aircraft, having known that he was being followed, presumed that he had shaken off pursuit. A visual was obtained at 1,800 ft on four bright exhausts. Height, approx 3,000 ft. We closed the range to 300 ft and with the help of Ross night glasses we identified the aircraft as an Me 410. We pulled up astern and fired a burst from approx. 600 ft. Strikes were observed at several points on the port side and wing of the enemy aircraft. He broke off to starboard and turned to port. We came in again behind and delivered another burst from approx. 600 ft. Strikes were observed and pieces flew off enemy aircraft, whereupon he put on his navigation lights (of which he only had two – tail and starboard), and fired a recognition cartridge which burst into approx. five white stars. I then fired another burst which caused an explosion and a large fire in port wing and engine. The glare from the fire made it possible to see the black cross on the port side of the fuselage and blue-green camouflage. The enemy aircraft spun to port with the whole port side of the aircraft blazing furiously. It crashed into the ground with a terrific explosion lighting up the surrounding countryside – which appeared to be the dispersal area of an aerodrome. Position of combat was believed to be approx. over the south-west outskirts of Paris. We then flew west for a considerable period, climbing to 6,000 ft, before I could contact Yardley by R/T. I set course for base as my port engine had overheated and was running rough. Landed at base at 02:20. I claim one Me 410 as destroyed.'

In June 1940, days after the last British troops had been evacuated from Dunkirk, Sergeant Nicholls was posted to the sector station at Kenley, Surrey. There he was due to join No 616 Squadron flying the very latest Spitfire. It was a posting he was looking forward to with some relish. He was already an accomplished Spitfire pilot, though still to be blooded in battle. 616 was a prestigious unit and Kenley was bound to be in the front line when, in the parlance of the day, the balloon finally went up. However the Germans got to Kenley first and by the time Sergeant Nicholls arrived, the airfield was pitted with bomb craters and 616 Squadron had moved to Church Fenton in Yorkshire. That was the last chance Sergeant Pilot Doug Nicholls had to fly Spitfires, for the next four years at least. Instead he went into the replacement pool and from there was posted to Debden with 85 Squadron, operating the more pedestrian Hurricane.

'There was most certainly a feeling that you were going into an aircraft which was inferior,' said Doug Nicholls, 'but you got over that quick enough and all the pilots came to look on the Hurricane with great affection. It was not as fast as the Spitfire, but, my goodness, it was a lot tougher and we came to bless that sturdy undercarriage when we needed to get down in a rough field', he went on.

In those days there were no conversion units and Sergeant Nicholls, who had trained on Spitfires in Cheshire, had to convert to Hurricanes on the squadron. He stayed in the South-east until August 1940, just as what Churchill came to call the Battle of Britain was warming up. Up until that time he had been busy learning the art of a fighter pilot and particularly lesson number one – not to do anything rash. The squadron was operating mainly on convoy protection patrols and their brief was to stick with the ships and not allow themselves to be drawn into running fights over the Channel.

In August No 85 Squadron was sent on rest to the North and Nicholls, being very much the new boy, was deemed to be fresh enough to continue operational flying and was posted to Coltishall to join the legendary Douglas Bader in No 242 Squadron. This was up in 12 Group territory and, like No 85, No 242 Squadron was flying defensive patrols but this time over the area north of the Thames, operating for much of the time out of Duxford, just south of Cambridge. Nicholls was with the squadron for little more than a month before being posted yet again, this time nearer home. His new squadron was No 151, which had just moved itself from North Weald to Digby, midway between Lincoln and Sleaford. This was another squadron which spent a lot of time away from its home base, operating out of Wittering, a fighter station familiar to everyone who travelled on the Great North Road.

It was with 151 Squadron that Nicholls was to register his only score of the Battle of Britain, a half share in a Ju 88 shot down by a pair of Digby Hurricanes into the sea off Mablethorpe. We can be

Canadian fighter pilots of the Kenley Wing – 1943.

forgiven for thinking that, to a young pilot involved in the greatest aerial battle the world had ever seen this brief incident must have been the highlight of his service career. Here was a youngster at the controls of a modern fighter aircraft helping shoot down an enemy intruding over the very county in which he had been raised. But Doug Nicholls, did not, and still does not, look at it that way. 'It was a job which, unfortunately, had to be done', he said. 'When you were firing your guns, you didn't think that there were people on the other end, just an aircraft which as far as we were concerned, had no right to be there in the first place.'

The Junkers incident, however, did not have fatal consequences for its crew. They crash landed in the sea and the circling Hurricanes saw them safely into their dinghy before heading back for Lincolnshire. It was only after he had landed back at Digby that Nicholls realized how near he had come to joining the Germans in the sea. During the brief engagement, a bullet from the German aircraft had pierced the oil tank in the Hurricane's Merlin engine. 'I noticed the oil pressure dropping all the way back, but it wasn't until I landed that I found out why', he said.

Handful of aces, from left to right: Group Captain 'Sailor' Malan (Station Commander), Squadron Leader Jack Charles (CO 611 Squadron) and Wing Commander 'Al' Deere (Biggin Hill Wing Leader). The photograph was taken in May 1943 after the 1,000th victory by Biggin Hill-based aircraft.

During this period the major air battles were raging over the South-east coast, the Thames estuary and London itself and Sergeant Nicholls was not alone in No 151 Squadron in wondering what it was doing up in Lincolnshire, chasing off the occasional intruder, while 200 miles away seemingly the rest of Fighter Command was engaged in a struggle which meant life or death to Britain.

Doug Nicholls' squadron was one of those selected to switch to the night role. Starting only on moonlit nights, the Hurricanes began patrolling 'boxes' under direction of ground controllers. But despite the advent of radar, albeit in a very rudimentary form, it was still like looking for a dark needle in a black haystack. It was a frustrating time, too, for the pilots engaged in this deadly game of hide-and-seek. As the bombers came over to pound cities in the Midlands, the Hurricane pilots flew box searches as the controllers gave approximate positions for the bombers.

'But what the radar they had then couldn't give them was the height', said Nicholls. 'The fighters would be stacked up, one on top of the other with the hope that someone would catch the Germans. There were one or two pilots on the new squadron who

Brad Walker, royal Canadian Air Force – a born leader.

actually shot something down, but the only glimpse I got of a German bomber in several months of these operations was a quick blurr as one flew over me one night.'

The only action he was involved in during this period happened at the end of one patrol – and Nicholls found himself on the receiving end. 'I was on my final approach into Wittering wheels and flaps down and lights on when I suddenly began to wonder why the exhaust sparks were going the wrong way. Then I realized I was being attacked by a German intruder', he said. 'I don't mind saying that I rapidly pulled everything up and went round looking for the German but he had gone.'

Nicholls then joined No 258 Hurricane Squadron, with which he was to serve with distinction both in Britain and the Far East. After a spell at Martlesham Heath, again on convoy patrols, the squadron was on the move again, and this time it was a long move. The pilots were embarked on to a troop ship at Gourock and told they were earmarked for Malta, then beseiged by both German and Italian bombers. In Gibraltar all the pilots went on board *Ark Royal* which promptly sailed to within 100 miles of Malta before they flew off to bolster the depleted fighter units on the island. *Ark Royal* then turned back for Gibraltar to pick up the remainder of the squadron. And this was where fate stepped in again for Doug Nicholls.

'She was torpedoed and sunk and instead we were told we were going to the Far East', he said. 'But there was no escape from a carrier take-off for us. We were flown across Africa to Port Sudan and embarked on *Indomitable*. The crated Hurricanes were assembled and we were told to fly off 100 miles from Java.' Doug Nicholls survived both the take-off from the carrier and the war. He was awarded the Distinguished Flying Cross for his exploits in the Far East.

As the war clouds gathered over Europe Harry Cook was soon to change his beloved motor bike for a fighter aircraft. He and his cousin Fred Margarson tried to enlist as dispatch riders at the RAF VR centre in Victoria Street, Grimsby. 'They didn't want any motor cyclists,' he said. 'But the recruiting officer asked us if we had ever thought about flying. To be truthful, I don't think either of us had, but he gave us some pamphlets and explained how much flying pay we would get and then I think we started to show a bit of interest.'

And so, on 6 August 1939, Harry Cook took to the air and by the end of the month he had 21 hours 55 minutes in his flying log-book. 'To be honest, I didn't enjoy it as much as riding the motor bike, except at low level. There was no sensation of speed and half the time you seemed to be standing still' said Harry Cook. But things were soon to change, and by the time war had been declared on 3 September 1939, the Royal Air Force Volunteer Reserve had been fully mobilized. Harry Cook was in uniform – well almost. 'The trouble was there were not enough uniforms to go round and when we did finally get them there were so many sergeants [the rank allotted to pilots in training in Grimsby, you couldn't get hold of any stripes', he said.

After his initial training at Hastings, there was more flying training at Hamble, Kinloss and Cranfield before, on 21 June 1940, Sergeant Pilot Harry Cook was finally awarded his Wings. Then followed a conversion course on Spitfires at Hawarden in Cheshire before he joined his first squadron, No 266 at Wittering at the end of August. Cook was destined to spend only a fortnight with the squadron, during which time he flew two or three operational sorties in Douglas Bader's famous 'big wing', the massed formation of 12 Group squadrons which generally arrived too late to affect the issue in the battles raging further south. On 12 September he was on the move again, this time right into the front line, when he was posted to No 66 Squadron at Gravesend.

By now Harry Cook realized he was really in the thick of the battle. He spent the first couple of days getting used to the routine of his new squadron – 'it really was like the newsreels, pilots sitting round in deck chairs waiting for the "scramble" alarm' – before flying his first operational sortie with them on 15 September, the day the Battle of Britain reached its climax.

Squadron Leader (later Group Captain Stanley Percival Turner, pilot of No 242 Squadron with Hurricanes. He enlisted in December 1938 and at the end of the war his kills numbered at least fourteen. On 25 May 1940 he shot down three Me 109s over Dunkirk. He received the DSO, DFC and Bar, Czech War Cross and Czech Medal for Valour.

It was a day when the sky over Gravesend was criss-crossed with the vapour trails of hundreds of aircraft, both British and German, as Göring finally tried to neutralize the Royal Air Force. The RAF claimed 175 Germans shot down during the day. Post-war research indicated the actual figure was nearer 57. From that day's total Harry Cook got half a kill although he didn't bother to put in a claim for it.

Cook was on patrol over Kent when 66 Squadron Spitfires were fortunate enough to catch some unescorted Heinkel 111s. The Spitfire's normal role was to take on the Messerschmitt 109s. 'One of the other pilots shot an engine out of one of the bombers and I went in and finished him off', said Cook. 'The Heinkel crash landed on West Malling airfield and I landed alongside, pinched the pilot's binoculars and took off again.' Trophy hunting like this was one of the 'sports' of Fighter Command of the day and Harry Cook, though he lost the binoculars later, was eager to join in.

Day after day the Spitfires of 66 Squadron were thrown into the battle as the Luftwaffe began switching its assault from the airfields in the South-east to London. On 24 September Harry Cook got the first of the three 'probables' credited to him during the Battle of Britain (at the time, the Royal Air Force insisted on independent verification of claims if the aircraft was not fitted with a camera). It was a Bf 109 which Cook shot down into the English Channel. His Spitfire didn't carry a camera and no one else saw the Messerschmitt hit the water, so it only counted as a 'probable'.

Three days later there were plenty of people around to see his second victory, this time a twin-engined Me 110. 'When we came across this pack of Me 110s they were flying in one of their defensive circles. The idea was that if they flew in this formation you couldn't get on the tail of one and shoot him down', said Cook. 'But being barely twenty and a bit carefree, I rather stupidly joined the circle,

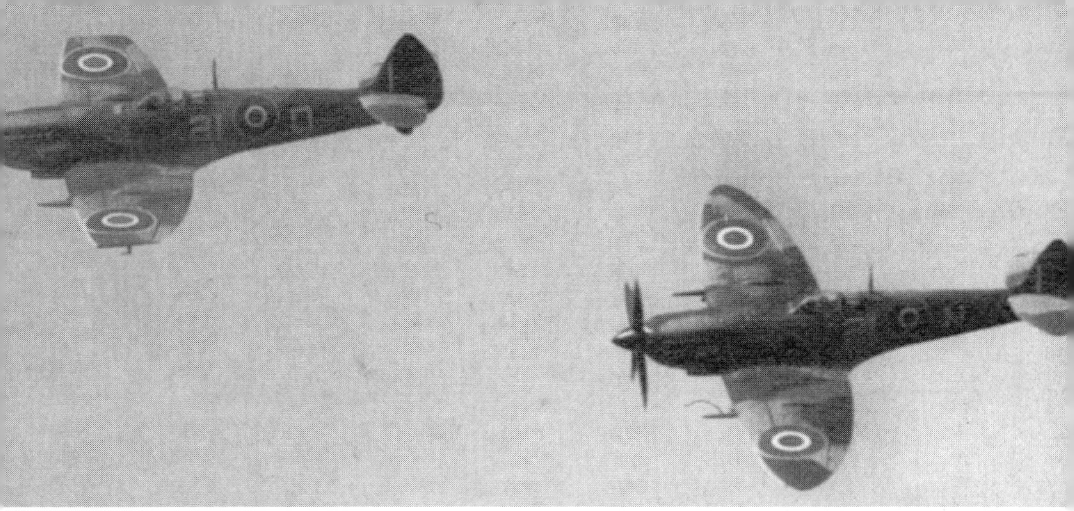

Supermarine Spitfire Mk XVIes, coded 21-D and 21-N, of No 443 (F) Squadron RCAF. This illustrates the variation in wing plan between the clipped and standard configurations.

but flew the other way round so, while they couldn't shoot at me for fear of hitting one of their colleagues, I could shoot at them.'

On 30 September another Me 109 went down into the sea off Dover before Sergeant Cook's guns and again it had to go down as a 'probable'. 'Most of the time we were fighting at 25,000 ft and there were not many occasions when you were able to follow the other chap down', he said. 'I just don't know how a lot of these other fighter pilots had time to make sure their "kills" were confirmed. I know I didn't.

'This time when I did see the Me 109 go down I got one hell of a rocket from our CO, Squadron Leader Rupert Lee. If anyone kept me alive in those days, he did. On this occasion he gave me a right rollicking. He told me that if I concentrated on the one going down, the one still flying would get me. His idea was to hit them like hell and get out as quick as you could.'

It was one squadron theorist, however, who almost cost Harry Cook his life a few days later. 'He had this idea that we should always attack the Jerries head-on', said Cook. 'That way, or so he argued, they would be forced to break and we would be left with an easy target. But when I tried it the Jerry I picked had obviously never heard of this theory. He didn't break and, right at the last second, I was forced to pull away. There was a hell of a bang and I later found he had put a cannon shell right in the middle of the spinner. The engine was all right but the reduction gear on the prop was shot to hell and I had to put the Spit down just outside Hornchurch in a bit of a hurry.' Hornchurch was on the opposite side of the Thames Estuary to Gravesend and, with communications

Bristol Beaufighter TF Mk Xc NE355, *coded EE-H, of 404 (CF) Squadron.*

Boulton Park Defiant Mk If V1123, *coded RA-R, of No 410 (F) Squadron while the unit was based at Drem, Scotland.*

North American Mustang Mk I AM251, *bearing the RCAF operational roundel in its proper location ahead of the wing leading edge. Aircraft 'O' served with No 414 (FR) Squadron based at Ashford, Kent in September 1943. Although the North American P-51 Mustang was produced in smaller numbers than the P-47 Thunderbolt it established itself as the principal Allied strategic fighter. It eventually re-equipped all but one 8th Air Force Thunderbolt group. Nineteen RAF squadrons flew the Mustang.*

difficult to say the least, Cook was posted as missing in action. When he turned up everyone was so relieved he got a 48-hour pass.

In the sixteen days Sergeant Cook was in action in September he flew 22 interceptor patrols and in October a total of 41, ranging from 35-minute dogfights almost over their own airfield to 90-minute patrols in which they didn't fire their guns in anger. His score for that month was four damaged and a 'probable' which later became a confirmed – another Bf 109, an 'Emil' from Adolph Galland's Ace of Spades unit which he shot down in a battle fought in the rarefied air at 31,000 ft.

There was a thrill for his family the next month when, after one successful action in which he took part with a Canadian pilot, he was first interviewed by the BBC and then filmed by Gaumont British News. 'My mother went to see it at the old Savoy Cinema in Victoria Street, Grimsby and was thrilled to bits', he said. 'We were living life at an enormous pace, our diet seemed to consist of nothing but corned beef and tinned carrots served from a cookhouse in a bell tent.'

As the battle finally petered out Cook was posted back to Hawarden, this time as an instructor, and it was here that he came closer to death than at any time during the Battle of Britain. Cook was flying one of two Miles Masters in formation when the other pilot, having 'lost' his leader, committed the cardinal sin of looking for it in his blind spot. The result was that the prop on the upper Master chopped off part of Sergeant Cook's aircraft tail and then cut through the canopy, through his flying helmet and just nicked his skull before pulling clear. His problems, however, were still not over. The pupil sitting behind him, having seen the other aircraft coming, had fainted and slumped over the controls, pushing the stick forward. Harry Cook had to unstrap himself, wriggle through to the rear seat, push the pupil clear and then get back to regain control of the aircraft before it hit the ground.

During a leave in 1940, Sergeant Harry Cook married Dorothy Westcott, the girl he had left behind when war broke out. The following year he was commissioned and he was back on operations flying Spitfires from Portreath in Cornwall with No 234 Squadron, which later moved to Perranporth, Cornwall, where they continued the fighter sweeps over France. The squadron was also engaged escorting American B-17s on their daylight raids on the Channel and Biscay ports.

After a spell in the Orkneys, then followed a 'terrifying' spell with the Merchant Ship Fighter Unit – the famous Camships, which involved firing an elderly Hurricane from the bows of a merchant ship in mid Atlantic to harry the reconnaissance Condors.

This fighter only made it to the beach. The wreckage of a Republic P-47, which crashed during the D-Day invasion, lies on the battle-scarred beach at St Aubin-sur-Mer. This was on 'Juno' beach where the Canadians landed, photographed on 22 June 1944. Very little has changed since the day the Canadians swept by.

After a brief spell practising flying on to the first aircraft carrier merchant ship, HMS *Activity*, Harry Cook was posted to No 41 Squadron flying the powerful Spitfire XII. Their role included attacking road convoys, troop concentrations and 'Diver' patrols. During his period with 41 Squadron, Harry Cook got the strangest 'kill' of all time for a fighter pilot – a German destroyer. He surprised it coming out of a Biscay harbour early one morning, and was as astonished as anyone that, after one burst of cannon fire the destroyer suddenly turned and ran on to a clump of rocks.

When Harry Cook was demobbed in 1946 he had exactly 1,152 hours 5 minutes flying time in his logbook and he had flown nine different types of aircraft. His 'kills' included three confirmed, three probables and four damaged aircraft, a V1, a train, two armoured vehicles, twenty other types of vehicles, 47 road convoys attacked – and his destroyer.

Fred Margarson who joined the RAF VR at the same time as Harry Cook also became a fighter pilot but he was not so lucky. He was shot down over Singapore and spent three and a half painful years as a Prisoner of War at the hands of the Japanese.

These were a few of our operational fighter pilots, ordinary chaps doing an extraordinary thing – and they did it well.

CHAPTER THREE

Fighter Groundcrew

Everyone on a fighter airfield was essential, whatever their job, but the actual groundcrew attached to an aircraft were a race apart. The working day for groundcrew could be a long one, especially if the squadron was on 'stand by' or 'readiness', and could start before first light.

A Flight Rigger (afterwards known as a Flight Mechanic Airframe) was a Group 2 trade, whereas an MT Driver was a Group 5. The highest rank that one could attain as a Flight Rigger was Leading Aircraftman. If one wanted to be an NCO it was necessary to take further training and become a Fitter in a Group 1 Trade. The chances of anyone on an Operational Squadron being sent on a course in the early days of the war were very remote.

Avro Tutor at Duxford in 1939. It was in this type of aircraft that Ronald Regan had his first flight.

World War I groundcrew.

Petty unserviceability or light battle damage was usually dealt with in the late evening and, if there was hangar accommodation available, overnight. During operations the aircraft had to be turned round and rearmed as soon as the pilot shut down his engine, ready for the next sortie. Even if the airfield was under attack it was still the job of the groundcrew to get the fighter back into the air! To 'turn round' the fighter meant refuelling, rearming, replenishment of the air and oxygen systems, rectification of minor snags, wheel changes, etc, and there was the ever-present problem of radio serviceability. Every effort was made to keep to the servicing pattern laid down for the aircraft, ie periodic servicing by flying hours, provided the aircraft survived that long.

The Maintenance Flight personnel carried out the major tasks such as engine changes, the replacement of components of the airframe – wings, undercarriage, control surfaces, etc – and battle damage repairs, of which there were plenty! Very badly damaged aircraft were taken by road to Repair Depots, both Service and civilian, where the repairs and replacements were carried out. The aircraft were then reissued as available and squadron code markings were hurriedly painted on.

At 21:30 hours Ronald Regan arrived at RAF Kenley in Surrey, with No 501 squadron. 'It was 18:00 hours before we were moving,' he said, 'HQ Fighter Command didn't give you much time.' Regan had just moved in from Gravesend. He had joined 501 as an Auxiliary Air Force Metal Rigger U/T on 9 May 1938. He was just seventeen years of age and apart from having a couple of flights in a Wallace, Hind and an Avro Tutor and helping to push aircraft around, that was his sum total of getting near aircraft. The first aircraft that he worked on was a Hurricane as an AC2 trained Airframe Fitter (in those days he was classed as a Fitter 11A). He was to stay with 501 Squadron until 1942, when he was then posted to the Far East.

Contact. Early World War II groundcrew at work.

Hurricane at Filton – August 1939. Ron Regan is sitting on the wing. The unit only had three aircraft with constant speed props, the rest were two bladed 'Watts' airscrews.

At Kenley one evening, Spitfires from Hawkinge arrived. Their airfield had taken a battering and they had been unable to land there, so they were diverted to Kenley. 'This was the first Spitfire I had worked on,' said Regan, 'and I was told to do the DI [Daily Inspection].

'The Rigger was responsible for the oxygen cylinder, and this had to be changed. To reach this there was a door in the rear fuselage, and to change this was a difficult job. You needed to be small or deformed to do this, and the carrier had to be wire locked. I changed this, opened the bottle, checked for control cables etc, then completed the rest of the DI. I arrived then at the cockpit, and checked the controls. The only hydraulics on a Spitfire I was the undercarriage; this was locked, but I wanted to check the flap operation. I found a lever marked flaps on the starboard side of the instrument panel, and operated the flaps. I was out of the cockpit in next to no time. The flaps operated by air pressure and the noise they made when they went down, I thought the undercart had operated as well. Dixie Dean who was the engine bod was down off the wing quicker than a flash. I inspected the flaps, and now was the time to get them back up. I moved the lever to the up position nothing happened, only the noise of the relief valve getting rid of the air from the two jacks, then the assistor springs took over, and again, I was out of the cockpit wondering what else I'd done. I carried out the Instrument Daily Inspection which we could do, and signed up for the Airframe and Instrument Daily Inspection. When 501 Squadron received Spitfires at Colerne in June 1941 I had no problems, but never forgot the first Daily I done on a Spitfire. The squadron of Spitfires that came to us at Kenley was Mungo Parks' squadron.'

After the aircraft had received its Daily Inspection, and been signed for, the groundcrew then played cards in the shelter pen, at the back of which was a concrete air raid shelter running the full length of the two fighter pens and the Armourers kept the .303 rounds of ammunition in this shelter. To keep warm the groundcrew had a bucket of sand on which petrol was poured and then lit, giving off quite a bit of heat (this method was used in the Western Desert for brewing up). One night in November 1940 Ron Regan was on duty when suddenly the fire went out in their shelter. 'So someone took the oil can for some more petrol', he said. 'They brought it in, made sure there was no flame, and poured it on the sand. This vapourized – then one of us struck a match – the ensuing explosion and sheet of flame which ran the full length of the shelter had to be seen to be believed. We came out minus eyebrows, eyelashes, the nap off our uniforms, and hair singed which wasn't under our caps. The Corporal didn't know whether to charge us, or send us to the Station Sick Quarters, lucky for us all he didn't do anything. However, for us, that was the end of "instant heat".'

The duties of the airframe 'erk' were twofold – he worked with the Engine Fitter and he also helped the Rigger. The complete airframe, hydraulics, pneumatic system, undercart etc, was the Rigger's responsibility. The cowlings which had to be removed were a two-handed job. The pneumatic system was operated by an engine driven compressor, and this had to be 'topped up' with castor oil and the water trap drained. If the air pressure was below 80 psi you had to get the foot pump out and charge the system by Schraeder valve to approximately 120 lb, the compressor would then take over and charge the system to the correct pressure, the brakes operated by air pressure. The Maintenance Flight carried out the primary and full maintenance but wheel changes and brake changes were all done by the Airframe Fitter.

Bob Corbett of 402 Squadron nosed over after landing in bad weather at Coleby Grange.

When the Squadron was at 'readiness' or 'stand by', the groundcrew had to remain on the airfield, but on 'release' there was a rush to the local pub. If you didn't go out you either read, played cards or went to the NAAFI. At Kenley, 'A' Flight had a good arrangement. They did not go out via the Guard Room, but under the wire. The Irish Guards carried out the guard duties and when 'A' Flight were on stand by at night at dispersal, they plied the Irish Guards with cocoa and when they wanted to go out of camp, or come back in, the groundcrew only had to whistle and the Irish Guards would hold up the wire and let them in or out.

In the autumn of 1940 there were two squadrons at Kenley, No 501 took over from 66 Squadron. The code names for the two squadrons were Mandrel and Furnace. So you would hear over the tannoy: 'Mandrel Squadron will come to readiness and Furnace Squadron will scramble' or 'Both squadrons scramble'. The Fitter would be in the cockpit, some pilots would leave their parachutes on the wing tip or tail plane while others would leave them in the cockpit. Once the pilot was in the cockpit the Fitter or the Rigger would put the straps over the pilot's shoulders, his helmet would be over the reflector sight. However, this was frowned on because the grease from the helmet would smear the glass. 'Once the pilot was strapped in the two of you would stand by to pull the chocks away,' said Regan, 'we would then walk to each wing tip to marshal him out. On landing after a sortie he would taxy into the pen, stop his engine, then it was two-six to turn him round and push him back into the pen. The bowser would then turn up for refuelling, the tanks were filled, oil checked, air pressure, oxygen cylinder changed, an in-between-flight inspection carried out for damage etc, this was visual. The canopy was cleaned and polished, aircraft checked, then it was time for a smoke.'

After square bashing at South Cerney and then a course on Flight Rigger training on Hawker Harts, Gladiators etc at St Athan in South Glamorgan, with No 4 School of Technical Training, George

Saved by the hedge!

Groundcrew at work on Spitfires.

Williams arrived as a Flight Rigger at Fighter Command and his first fighter airfield was Northolt. He recalls his first fighters: 'They were Blenheims, the short-nose type, which had been converted to fighters by strapping four .303 Brownings under the belly.'

Early in 1940 Rigger Williams moved to North Weald, he was just eighteen. He well remembers his first sight of Hurricanes: 'At North Weald we had two crack Hurricane squadrons and when there was a "scramble" it was really something to watch them take off in mass formation. By the same token it wasn't good when you saw some of them crash when landing.'

Williams took every opportunity to go up for a trip but his first flight was not until 14 February 1940. He went up as the Air Gunner, with no flying gear other than the helmet that was plugged into the intercom. He was frozen solid for the weather in 1940 was the worst for 45 years according to the weather experts. At this particular time, being early days of the war, any airman on a ground trade could act as Air Gunner after two weeks' training. On successful completion of the training they received 9d a day extra and they wore a little brass bullet on their sleeve. Later on Air Gunners were given three stripes and made permanent aircrew. A lot of groundcrew were not too keen on this and they opted to stay in their own jobs.

During his eight-month stay at North Weald the squadron had a detachment at Martlesham Heath and on 9 May 1940 Williams flew

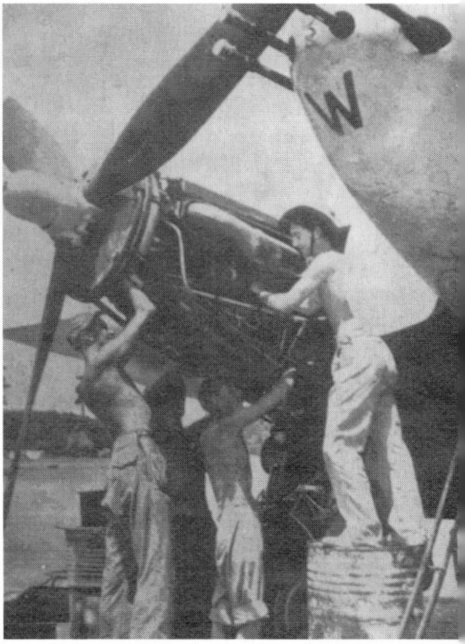

Servicing a Mosquito's engine in Burma. RAF Mosquitoes worked round the clock attacking Japanese strong-points, infantry, and motor transport. This picture shows the groundcrew who helped to keep the aircraft airworthy.

there with some spare parts for their detachment. All the groundcrew had a couple of weeks there in turn. 'It was so different from North Weald,' said Williams, 'you had the hit-and-run-type Jerry there, as against the mass raids at North Weald.'

Rigger Williams enjoyed his work and he served on many airfields and worked on many aircraft, one being a Beaufighter. This fighter aircraft had three groundcrew, a Rigger and two Flight Mechanics, one for each engine. The Beaufighter had twin engines and a crew of two. Gun armament was four 20 mm cannon and six or seven 0.303 in machine guns. The Mk Xf also had eight 60 lb or 90 lb rocket projectiles. All marks had a top speed of well over 300 mph. For example, the Mark II had a maximum speed of 337 mph at 22,000 ft and a still air range of 1,770 statute miles.

'The Beaufighter was a beautiful aircraft,' said Williams, 'although a bit tricky to fly. Our Commanding Officer at Dyce was killed in a Beaufighter. I, as a Rigger, supervised the starting up and marshalling of the aircraft. We had the same aircrew as much as possible and we had our own aircraft. We had a good relationship with the crew although we did have the odd drop out. Other airmen who had access to our aircraft were the Electrician, Wireless

The remains of Kemps fighter. A Rigger gives it the once over. 402 Squadron RCAF at Digby.

Groundcrew preparing a Hurricane for patrol duty.

Mechanic and Instrument Basher, no one else, and when they had done their bit they went on to the next aircraft.'

Also at Northolt during the same period as Rigger Williams were the Canadians and one small elite unit was the Instrument Section which consisted of one Corporal and two LACs, all instrument men. The Senior Corporal in charge was 'Herb' Curotte who worked under the Engineering Officer. Curotte had joined the Royal Canadian Air Force via the auxiliary route in Montreal with 115(F) Squadron in May 1938. Ever since his teens he had been interested in engines and involved in racing outboard hydroplanes. His next greatest interest was motor cycles. Because of this love and ambition he had tried to join the Auxiliary Air Force as a Fitter (as then called 'Aero Engine'). In the words of Curotte:

'I still recall the recruiter, no less than at the time Air Vice Marshal Frank McGill, a World War 1 pilot who returned to active service in World War 2, in any event, he was at the time forming the 115(F) in Montreal.

'When it came my turn for interview I outlined my wishes … unfortunately I was informed the establishment for Aero Engine was filled. Perusing my employment record which was typewriter, adding machine and calculator repair man, the AVM enlisted me as the Squadron's Instrument Maker so called … the establishment calling for just one. I was to reap the benefit of his decision as the years went on.

'Summer of 1938 I duly went to Borden, Ontario taking basic training on all aspects of aircraft, engines, rigging. . .there was an excellent cadre of instructors. Thereafter the squadron was operating out of St Hubert near Montreal. We would devote evenings, weekends

A groundcrew member marshalling in a fighter to its dispersal point.

etc with the usual enthusiasm when one is in love with engines and airplanes.

'The squadron was equipped with de Havilland Tiger Moths as fleets... Having little instrument work to do I plunged in with the Fitters who to my everlasting appreciation let me take full part in aircraft servicing ... P. 30 as the periodic checks were called. DIs, Daily Inspection etc.... so that after many months one was well versed in aircraft maintenance from all aspects. This also proved a great benefit later.

'Finally September 1939 ... war declared and the squadron placed on full time basis. I left my civilian occupation with enthusiasm looking forward to full time service life. We were then amalgamated with No 1(F) regular force squadron which was equipped with the two-bladed

An early Air Gunner – the rear gunner in a Fairey Battle – 1939. Note that the airman is wearing the winged brass bullet badge on his tunic sleeve.

Herb Curotte and a Tiger Moth in 1938 at Borden, Ontario, Canada.

Hurricanes. They located in St Hubert where 115 lost its identity and pilots and personnel became part of No 1(F) RCAF.'

By this time Curotte had reached the exalted rank of Corporal and been given charge and responsibility of the Squadron's Instrument Section under the Engineering Officer. Eventually they proceeded overseas as No 1(F) Royal Canadian Air Force. As a unit, they were self supporting, bringing their own motor transport, stores and all other sections. From then on Corporal 'Herb' Curotte remained in charge of the Instrument Section of No 1(F) Squadron RCAF. His responsibility under the Squadron Engineering Officer was of course the smooth and efficient operation of this section. He continues:

'I structured the section as follows: Corporal Anderson to remain at hangar workshop. LACs Trimble and Milne to 'A' and 'B' Flights at dispersal. This proved to be very efficient for they were excellent types, reliable as well as knowledgeable. Throughout the following months they proved their worth.

'Compared to other sections, the Instrument Section was easy ... in that instruments were either serviceable or not. Obviously no repairs were carried out at squadron level. If any instrument was faulty it meant replacement. This could be carried out at hangar level, or, depending on circumstances, at the flight area. This was my responsibility.

'In order to check instrument performance the engine of course had to be run up. Navigational instruments such as Gyro Horizon etc, were

vacuum operated only when the power plant was on. According to strict "gen" only Fitters were permitted to run up engines. But when one had shown sufficient knowledge, and shown responsibility, this was overlooked. A full run up required usually two men sitting or leaning on the tail, blast and flying bits of debris were not the most comfortable features of their situation.

When I said the Instrument Section was "easy", I meant compared to Fitters and Riggers. There were engine changes, prop removal, plugs to change and, all of this a Fitter's work ... So they put in many additional hours ... Riggers repairing landing gear, hydraulics etc ... needless to say the Armourers ... speed with them was the essence when operations became acute.

'However, the crucial element of the Instrument Section was the supply of oxygen. One simply could not run out. The Hurricane carried one 750 litre bottle of oxygen. At section level these bottles were refilled from a large cylinder through a transfer unit. The 750 litre bottle had a major defect in that the shut-off valve would stick. The valve body was brass to brass and could become stuck or impossible to operate. (I did submit a modification to Air Ministry but left before it was approved.) Transfer of oxygen had a certain danger element, for under high pressure oxygen cannot be exposed to oil as it will explode. So constant care and surveillance was of the essence.'

Under the ever watchful eye of Curotte the Instrument Section carried out the individual daily inspection of aircraft. This was done by the LACs and other 'erks'. After each sortie this was again performed, usually requiring a 'fresh' bottle of oxygen. If perchance the fighter had been hit by Jerry, obviously the inspection had to be more detailed, involving the aircraft to be moved into the hangar

Filling oxygen bottles.

Hurricane Mk II Z3658 coded YO-N, with servicing panels removed, is run up by fitters of No 401 (F) Squadron RCAF. Two groundcrew sit on the tail as ballast.

where it was inspected by either Curotte or Corporal Anderson. When an aircraft arrived as replacement for one lost or damaged it was again thoroughly inspected at the hangar before being assigned to the flight.

Even in wartime you still had the sneak thief and the Instrument Section was no exception as Curotte explains: 'At one time the theft of navigational clocks became a serious problem. This was done somewhere in transit. It was then decided the clock would not be installed on the panel but tied neatly in the tail section! The first time we hunted like hell to find the clock ... wired some message

Sergeant Curotte, RCAF stands on the wing of a Hurricane coded YO-E of No 1 (F) Squadron while the groundcrew are at work. It was cold work, out in the open in the freezing wind. YO-E had served throughout the Battle of Britain and you can see the many patches. The photograph was taken at Castletown, December in 1940.

a classic photo – airmen sitting on tail of Hurricane BE483 to hold it down on engine run-up.

to the Distribution Unit where we were advised of the location. Another scheme designed to avoid pilfering of the clock was to solder the nuts! These of course were at the back of the panel screwing on the attaching screws! So you see war does not necessarily produce all honest people regardless of their patriotism!

'The wonders of war came home to us daily and a few days after we had arrived at Northolt I stood to watch the arrival of a replacement 'Hurri'. It stopped close to the hangar on the tarmac … helmeted figure stepped out … I thought it rather a feminine form, but I thought surely it's my subconscious need of female company … but no, lo and behold, removing the regulation helmet a cascade of beautiful blond hair fell on the shoulders of a most attractive female pilot! This of course was the "gen" of the squadron for the day … she had the form, beauty, and flying know how to match any of our boys. It was only somewhat later that we learned of a number of female knowledgeable pilots who were ferrying

Groundcrew rush to assist Hurricane Mk I V6657, coded YO-D, of 401 (F) Squadron RCAF at Digby, Lincolnshire in the spring of 1941.

aircraft from maker, repair depots etc to squadrons or wherever they were needed.

'The Hurricane was an honest aircraft. Instrumentation was sound and kept to the required minimum ... These were the days previous to electronic sensors or transistorized units. The electrical circuitry was relatively simple ... The navigation instrument vacuum operated, ie, gyro, turn and bank, etc. Pressure gauges were of the Bourdon tube principle. From memory I would say that the cine-cameras, located at leading edge of the wing, gave the most trouble in so far as shorts. Also at high altitude they would jam if over lubricated. With the circuitry I would enlist the aid usually of the Wireless Section with their meters and what not.

'I must say winding up these words on the technical aspect that my all round knowledge of aero engines ... aircraft structure from rigging lectures, proved to be of great advantage. I owe a debt of

Fighter groundcrew – paint brush at the ready. Supermarine spitfire Mk IXb, coded DB-R, of No 411 (Fighter) Squadron receives hastily-applied invasion markings on 5 June 1944 at Tangmere, West Sussex. All Allied aircraft at this time, with the exception of four-engined bombers, were painted with distinctive black and white stripes for easy identification. These become known as the D-Day stripes.

gratitude to two instructors at Borden in the early days, Flight Sergeants Harry Cobb and Frank Downs, both regulars who had been appointed as our mentors. In St Hubert, to then Corporal Millar, later commissioned. Millar had been my guardian angel on engines.'

On fighter airfields each lot of groundcrew had their own fighter to work on and, as far as possible, had the same pilot. This enabled a good relationship to be built up between the groundcrew and the aircrew. At certain times however, there were many changes in the aircrew and some were better than others. Ex-Flight Rigger George Williams: 'I found that the ex-public school type were the best, it was "Old Boy this and Old Boy that", but they were a dedicated bunch and seemed to be without fear. The worst type of pilot, especially when it was an operational night scramble, was the type who invented imaginary faults with the aircraft.'

'I can honestly say', said Ron Regan, 'that the pilots you "crewed" for treated you as friends. I think the pilots of the Battle of Britain era were a different breed from some of the pilots I met later on in the war.'

Edward Curotte sums up the groundcrew: 'The sum total was that "erks" co-operated as a team ... recognizing theirs was not the total sacrifice, that it was the pilots who were laying their lives on the line at each operational take-off ... I have seen "erks" turn away and cry unashamedly when it was announced that Pilot So and So was missing ... and what joy when a call was received that he had landed or crash landed somewhere in Britain ... but sadly, this was not always the case.'

Chapter Four

Armourer's Duties

On completion of initial training and a six-month course on armaments Jack Strachan was posted to No 66 (Fighter) Squadron, at Duxford, near Cambridge, in June 1939. It was then equipped with Spitfire Is. 'It was my preference to join a fighter squadron and particularly Spitfires', said Strachan. The new arrivals were competent with all aspects of armament, but for the first week they had to familiarize themselves with the fighters and

Groundcrew working on a Hurricane aircraft. The photograph shows the 20mm cannon clearly.

U/T Armourer Jack Strachan at RAF Manby, 1939.

they soon established a rapport with the personnel, some 120–130 officers and men, of 66 Fighter Squadron. 'They proved to be an excellent team', said Strachan.

Since the September Crisis of 1938 the politicians were hailing 'peace in our time', but it was obvious that we were making preparation for war and during the interim period the armourers were practising rearming the aircraft until they were considered efficient. 'It was hard on the knees working under the wings with the loaded ammunition tanks, but we were younger fit and resilient', said Armourer Strachan. 'We made preparation and moved to our dispersal point in the south-east corner of the airfield. On Sunday 3 September 1939, at 11 am we heard the news over the radio, the declaration of war, which was no surprise. It was a beautiful sunny day and we were on stand-by, ready and waiting. I must admit that we anticipated an appearance of enemy aircraft.'

But it was to be a waiting game. From time to time fighters were 'scrambled' and in addition they were required to patrol shipping lanes off the East Anglian coast. On occasions there was a dawn patrol, which meant that the Armourers were on duty endless hours. Often when they were released to stand down at dusk many of them would jump over the hedge and nip into the 'Flower Pot' public house, the nearest in Duxford village, to get away from it all. Armourer Jack Strachan explains: 'Work continued in our hangar workshops which entailed the degreasing of Browning machine guns .303. Stripped, washed in a paraffin bath then treated in antifreeze, oil and grease after which the guns were assembled to suit left- or right-hand feed.

'Replacement aircraft were minus armament and on arrival we would fit eight Brownings, connect up to the pneumatic system, G42 cine-camera gun, 16 mm fitted nearside on the starboard wing, plug in electric, also a reflector

Armourer Ginger Dobson of No 66 (F) Squadron snatches a couple of hour's kip while on dispersal point at Duxford.

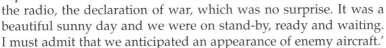

Leading Aircraftsman J. Peachell and Corporal O. Shaw clean the 20 mm cannon from a Nighthawk Mosquito.

light positioned centre screen in cockpit, plug in electric. Once the installation was completed the aircraft would be manhandled to the west side of the hangar, where we would place the machine in a flying position on to a facing wall marked with coloured spots for alignment of each gun. After we had checked to make sure that the aircraft levels were spot on, we would then proceed to harmonize the guns and gunsight with the use of a periscope inserted in the breech end of the barrel, once the colour spot for the appropriate gun was located the gun would then be fully secured. This operation was executed with each gun, locate gunsight on its respective spot and secure bracket. The aircraft would then be moved to the butts for test firing, in short bursts. When we were satisfied with the aircraft the work was recorded and Form 700 duly signed.

'When working on the flight we would prepare aircraft by arming the guns, ie "putting one round up the spout", checking all secure

Canadian Armourers of No 402 Squadron at work – note muddy boots.

for Daily Inspection and sign Form 700. When released at the end of the day, we would disarm the guns. This was the regular procedure in the early days of the war, but later we received a directive to leave the fighters armed and left in the hangar overnight. Due to an incident on a rival squadron, one of our Flight Sergeants (Fitter) did not trust the Armourers and would walk round the hangar almost bent double under the elevation of the guns just in case of a similar incident.

'I found our fighter pilots very pleasant and friendly and they could certainly handle the Spitfire. It was a fine machine in flight and the sound of the Merlin engine was fantastic in comparison to the other aero engines. We would also assist prior to take-off by pressing battery starter button, chocks away, or assisting the pilot

Armourers rearming under bitterly cold conditions.

Beaufighter being loaded with rocket projectiles, four under each wing.

with harness or ballast on tail end. Another point that always impressed me was that whenever anyone wanted assistance to move aircraft, open or shut hangar doors, or whatever, the shout of "two-six" was all that was required to bring sufficient manpower from all corners to do the job. I've no idea of the origin of this terminology.

'Generally speaking the squadron was well organized, very efficient, and the team work was tremendous. During the early part of the war we had a Fighter Blenheim Squadron, then the 264 Fighter Defiant Squadron arrived, and in those days the Air Gunners were ranked LAC upwards. Quite a number were only in their late teens/early twenties.

'We had some good sessions in the local pubs; the attitude was live for the day and let tomorrow provide for itself, and eat drink and be merry, for tomorrow you may be dead. And this, unfortunately, was the fate of most of the 264 aircrew. It was always sad when any of our colleagues were killed, whether due to flying accidents or in action. You could sense an unusual feeling, but work had to go on and you were soon back to square one again.

'On two occasions at Duxford I had confrontation with the famous A~r Ace Douglas Bader and once again here in Newcastle in December 1981. On the latter occasion he could not hold rank, as we were both retired, for all in the past I have due respect for him as he was a very courageous man, and could only assume that his approach and reaction was due to his handicap.

Ground staff fixing fuses to rockets after a Beaufighter has been revved up ready to take off.

'From time to time certain personnel would be seconded to the squadron advanced base, after a short spell at Watton we moved to Horsham St Faith near Norwich. There was very little at this point, the bare essentials being a grass field surrounded by hawthorn hedge, a wind sock, and a house called "Red Roofs". Early morning the aircraft would fly up from Duxford for the day's operations and on stand down prior to dusk, would return to base at Duxford. Our cooked meals were flown up on a Short Scion aircraft, and when the weather made flying impossible we had to make our own arrangements, perhaps beans on toast at a nearby cafe.

'After a few weeks we would change over and return to base, but we always called into the "Rising Sun" in Newmarket for refreshment. A pleasant break after being bounced in the back of a five-ton truck.

'Our accommodation at Duxford was up to standard and when certain meals did not meet with your requirements, you could always go into the NAAFI for bangers and mash. There was very little variation, but often appreciated. In the evenings if we stayed in the NAAFI with the gathering of the clans, to create our own entertainment, it was hilarious at times, but we mixed well. Different squadrons and personnel from all over the British Isles with various backgrounds. It was amazing how well this mixture blended, the banter being part of the fun, and the usual singing of the songs appropriate to the various parts of the country.'

After his period with a fighter squadron, Jack Strachan was posted into Training Command, then spent four years overseas, but his time served with No 66 Squadron was the highlight of his Service career.

Chapter Five

The Battle of Britain

The Battle of Britain was one of the most crucial conflicts of World War II and it lasted from July to October 1940. However, there has always been some disagreement over the actual period of the Battle of Britain. To meet the onslaught from an estimated 1,800 German bombers and dive bombers backed by 1,200 fighters, the Royal Air Force could provide No 11 Group in the South-east with only twelve squadrons of Hurricanes and six of Spitfires. A squadron normally held eighteen aircraft and 26 pilots on strength but operated as a fighting unit with twelve aircraft. Therefore a force of fewer than 220 aircraft could on occasion be reinforced by units from adjacent fighter groups (Nos 10 and 12), if not themselves under attack.

Hurricane GZ-V, P3522, *of 32 Squadron taxiing out from dispersal at Hawkinge on 31 July 1940. The squadron operated from here on a daily basis, flying in from their base at Biggin Hill. This fighter survived the Battle of Britain and then went to 213 Squadron. It crashed in Yorkshire on 10 January 1941.*

A Sergeant pilot sits deep in his own thoughts, waiting for battle to commence.

Many facts have wrongly been reported about the Battle of Britain. One book, written by an ex-Flight Lieutenant, described panic stricken airmen running from the camp at North Weald because of an air raid. One airman at North Weald at that period with No 25 Squadron was George Williams: 'The facts were that a lot of airmen *did* run from the camp very fast', said Williams. 'It was night-time, and the reason was that a land mine had come down by parachute and as it had not gone off, it was feared that it was a delayed action mine, with a blast radius of $\frac{1}{4}$ of a mile, so, it made sense to get your skates on.

'So much has been written which we knew to be a load of rubbish', continued Williams. '15 September was over reported. I was up for fifteen minutes that day on air test with Pilot Officer Hooper, his Blenheim was named 'Dusty Rides Again'. Our Station Commander was Group Captain V. Beamish, one of the three famous Beamish brothers who were all in the Royal Air Force. When Jerry was on his way to visit us, the Group Captain announced it over the tannoy himself. Nothing like the film *Battle of Britain*. I can remember it as though it was yesterday: "Station Commander calling – Station Commander calling, enemy aircraft are approaching the station from the south-east. All ranks not on duty take cover immediately – end of message". I liked the bit about "not on duty".'

There were many heroic battles fought in the skies over the Kent countryside in 1940 – many of which went unrecorded. During the Battle of Britain, Flying Officer Keith McKenzie ran out of ammo and took the wing of a Messerschmitt off by hitting it with his wing. He had an awful stammer, but when he was in action he didn't stammer. He finished up as a Wing Commander and is today farming in South Africa. He was one of the lucky ones, for many young fighter pilots, their first real taste of war was to be their last.

The battle was in five phases, but only four were actually fought. The scheduled fifth phase, 1 to 31 October, the daylight offensive which was to have been a prelude to invasion, was called off. The first phase was from 10 July to 7 August when the offensive was launched with probing attacks to test the Royal Air Force and with attacks on shipping. The Luftwaffe sent over massed formations of bombers escorted by similar formations of single- and twin-engined fighters. In these attacks the Luftwaffe relied greatly on dive bombers (Ju 87s), which proved no match for the Hurricanes.

The second phase, 8 to 23 August, was much more serious, with attacks on the radar chain. Fierce air fighting developed with heavy losses on both sides. Between 8 August and 18 August, Fighter Command lost 94 pilots and sixty were wounded.

The third phase, 24 August to 6 September, was the most critical for this was the period when the Luftwaffe attacked the airfields in south-east England. During this period Fighter Command had 103 pilots killed or missing and 128 seriously wounded, 295 fighters were totally destroyed and 171 badly damaged.

The fourth phase, 7 to 30 September, saw the fatal error of the Luftwaffe and this period became London versus Göring. The attack on London and its environs was the crux of the battle. Now the Royal Air Force knew exactly where the enemy was heading. Now the men, the machines and the fuel could be more carefully husbanded and directed than ever before.

During the height of the Battle of Britain Churchill asked: 'What reserves do we have?' 'None', was the reply. All Fighter Command's fighters were in the skies ... and among the pilots was twenty-year-old Sergeant Pilot David Cox with No 19 (Fighter) Squadron, the first in the Royal Air Force to be equipped with the superlative

Twin-engined Ju 88s. Dornier 17Z-2

~~Do 17~~s heading for south-east England in 1940.
Ju 88

Spitfire some eighteen months previously and destined to play a leading role in the Battle of Britain.

Sergeant Cox had joined the squadron in May but, because of his inexperience, was held back from the battles over Dunkirk. However, by August he was flying regular patrols with the squadron looking for E-boats attempting to intercept Channel convoys. 'At the time we were stationed at Eastchurch, which was a pretty old place full of wooden huts', recalled David Cox. 'The day after we arrived there I woke up as all hell was breaking loose over the airfield. The Germans had decided to give it a pasting, and I remember as I rushed out of my room meeting a rather elderly Flight Sergeant who grabbed me and pushed me into the only brick structure around – which happened to be a urinal. With all those bullets and cannon shells flying around it was the safest place to be.'

Sergeant Cox, however, got his own back on the Luftwaffe. In the next few weeks he was credited with the destruction of three German fighters and a half share in a bomber, and he finished the war with a total 'score' of eight-and-a-half enemy aircraft. He was very much the archetypal RAF Battle of Britain pilot. He had had a burning ambition to be a fighter pilot from the age of fourteen, when he would often cycle miles just to see aircraft taking off and landing again in his native Hampshire.

When he left school in Bournemouth, his first ambition was a regular commission in the Royal Air Force but he was turned down on medical grounds. Instead he went into a solicitor's office, and then spent some months working as a fish porter in Billingsgate Market to build up his strength so that he could persuade his next medical board that he really was fit enough to join the Air Force.

It was at this time that the newly-formed RAF Volunteer Reserve was beginning to grow in strength, and it proved to be the way into the cockpit of a fighter aircraft for thousands of young men like

David Cox. Cox learned to fly in the evenings and at weekends with No 19 Elementary & Reserve Flying Training School at what is now Gatwick Airport and, after being mobilized in September 1939, did his service training on the ubiquitous (and noisy) Harvards in Shropshire before finally joining No 19 Squadron.

Hurricane Mk Is of No 87 Squadron

After the Eastchurch raid the squadron was moved north to Fowlmere in Cambridgeshire, and it was here that Sergeant Cox helped to shoot down his first German – while wearing his pyjamas. The squadron was scrambled early one morning at the end of August to intercept a lone raider coming in over the East Coast and, sure enough, they found a lone Dornier near Aldeburgh. It was quickly sent spinning into the sea.

His first solo kill came a few days later when No 19 Squadron attacked a group of twenty Me 110s flying in one of their tight defensive circles over Clacton. Sergeant Cox was flying one of the few cannon-armed Spitfires which were operational during the Battle of Britain in 1940, and a burst from his 20 mm Hispano cannon sent one of the fighters down with smoke streaming from one of its two engines. But the cannon armament was looked upon with mixed feelings by Spitfire pilots and they were soon withdrawn because of continual stoppages caused by the gravity feed mechanism.

Today, we tend to think of the Battle of Britain as one of the last great chivalrous encounters. Indeed, in its early stages it involved just the armed forces of Britain and Germany with the British public nothing more than fascinated onlookers. But was it really like that? According to David Cox, 'It was like finding burglars in your own front room. I was flying and fighting over the part of England where I had grown up, and as far as I was concerned, we were doing everything we could to stop the Germans. We thought of the German fighter pilots as arrogant Nazis. They certainly gave that impression.'

He recalls one incident when a Dornier which had been bombing trawlers off the East Coast was shot down and the crew parachuted into the sea close to the fishing fleet. 'I think they expected to be picked up but, after seeing them come down, the trawlers turned and sailed off' said Cox. So much for chivalry.

And there were, of course the stories of aircraft on both sides firing on men swinging at the end of their parachutes. 'If a British pilot was coming down this side of the Channel, there was every chance he would live to fight another day, and there was nothing in the rules of war to stop the Germans firing on him,' Cox said. 'But if it was a German coming down over England, we had no right to shoot at him because once he was down he would become a prisoner of war and to shoot him would have been plain murder.' To their credit, however, most Luftwaffe fighter pilots did not fire on British pilots parachuting to safety, something David Cox himself had to be thankful for later in the Battle.

Early in September Cox claimed his second German fighter, this time a Bf 109 which he shot down after a dogfight over Maidstone. His own aircraft was so badly damaged in the fight that when he landed he got a 'rocket' from the legendary Douglas Bader, the legless fighter pilot who struck almost as much fear into young sergeant pilots as he did the Germans. 'He told me my aircraft was a bloody mess, and when I pointed out that I had got a Messerschmitt, he told me that a one-for-one ratio was not so good. I must admit my Spitfire really was a mess.'

A part of 12 Group, No 19 Squadron was often involved in the Duxford 'Big Wing' operations which Bader led, tactics which even today cause controversy. David Cox himself felt at the time, and still does, that while the 'Wing Theory' might have been good in practice it did not work. The object of the 'Big Wing' was for a number of squadrons to assemble and then attack the German bomber and fighter formations en masse. But as often as not by the time the Duxford Wing had arrived on the scene, the Luftwaffe was heading back for home. The 'Big Wing' concept was shown to be of no value whatsoever in the defensive stance. In most cases the wings would have become unmanageable.

Sergeant Cox's third, and, as it turned out, final, success in the Battle of Britain came about in most unusual circumstances on 15 September 1940, the day historians reckon was the real turning point. During one particular confused engagement Cox found himself alone, never the ideal situation for a fighter pilot in September 1940. 'The golden rule was always to attach yourself to friendly aircraft', said Cox. 'So when I saw what I took to be six Hurricanes, I made straight for them. You can imagine my surprise

Battle of Britain fighter pilots of 'A' Flight, 32 Squadron take a well-earned break at Gibraltar Road dispersal Hawkinge, September 1940. From left to right, Pilot Officers Smythe and Proctor, Flight Lieutenant Brothers and Pilot Officers Grige, Gardner and Eckford.

when, instead of Hurricanes, they turned out to be Me 109s.' What happened next was even more surprising. Four of the fighters turned away and, faced with just two adversaries, Cox fired a short burst from his Spitfire's eight Browning machine-guns and one of the Messerschmitts crashed in flames near Crowborough.

Sergeant Cox's part in the battle ended a few days later when he was shot down and wounded on his thirtieth operational sortie. It happened near Canterbury when aircraft from the Duxford Wing were 'jumped' by Me 109s as they attacked a formation of bombers. 'Two of ours went straight down, and then I found myself with one of our Hurricanes which was being attacked by four Me 109s. As I went to help him, they shot him down and turned their attentions on me. And they were really good. Finally, one got underneath me and there was a flash and a bang and I knew that was it', he said. Sergeant Cox managed to struggle clear of his stricken Spitfire – not his usual machine, with his wife's name, Pat, painted under the cockpit – and he baled out over the Kent countryside with fragments of a cannon shell in his right leg.

Cox came down in the corner of a ploughed field which cushioned the weight of his fall, and two farmhands quickly went to his assistance. 'I couldn't believe my eyes at first', he said. 'They were real yokels wearing smocks and at first I thought I had landed back in the nineteenth century.' Cox spent the next three months in hospital recovering from his injuries, and when he went back on operations flying a fighter aircraft was never the same again. 'That incident really changed my attitude to the whole business. I think that all of us had the feeling it couldn't happen to us. Well, it happened to me, and I realized that it was no longer a game of good fun anymore. During the Battle of Britain we were all scared of course. We would go dry mouthed but, at the same time, it was exciting and exhilarating. But after that it became a deadly serious business.'

Even though it was obvious to everyone that the Luftwaffe had taken a pounding, David Cox was not alone in admiring the professionalism and tactics used by the German fighter pilots. In a fighter-versus-fighter confrontation, the Messerschmitt 109s were the equal of the British Spitfires and their superior tactics, particularly the 'figure four' formations and experience of their pilots often gave them the edge. But, on the other side, the British were fighting for their very lives, and the ferocity of some of the dogfights was not equalled by some of David Cox's later experiences in North Africa.

One that didn't make it back. A Messerschmitt 109 dived at two Ansons and, in attempting a steep turn, crashed in Great Windsor Park on 30 September 1940. The pilot was taken prisoner. RAF men are seen removing the wrecked aircraft.

The German fighters were also operating virtually at the limit of their range and were often tied to the bomber formations, which gave Fighter Command an enormous advantage. Added to that was the primitive radar then in use around the coast, the excellent control structure and, by no means least, the highly-efficient Royal Observer Corps which took over where the coastal radar left off.

Back in action in 1941, David Cox took part in the first big British fighter sweeps over Northern France, the Royal Air Force using virtually the same tactics as the Germans had the year before to lure their adversaries into battle. It was in one of these engagements that Cox was brought down for a second time. After shooting down a Bf 109 in a 'hell of a scrap' over France, the glycol tank in his Spitfire – again a 'borrowed' machine – was hit over Boulogne and the aircraft caught fire. 'My first instinct was to bale out, but then quite suddenly the fire went out', he said. 'I didn't fancy becoming a PoW, so I pointed the nose out to the Channel with the idea of getting as near to England as I could before I had to jump for it.

'I nursed the engine as much as I could as the aircraft got lower and lower. Then out of the mist I spotted Dungeness and managed to put the Spitfire down on the beach. Unfortunately I had not strapped myself back in, and I bounced about like a pea in a pod when I came down.'

After a spell as an instructor, Cox was posted to No 72 Squadron at Biggin Hill and went with the unit to North Africa to support Operation Torch, the Anglo-American landing operation in French North Africa in November 1942. It was in the North Africa Campaign that Cox built up his score of German aircraft to eight-and-a-half confirmed kills during a total of 134 operational sorties in a five-month period. He was commissioned in June 1941 and by the end of 1942 was a flight commander.

Back in England Cox toured aircraft factories before becoming a flying tactics liaison officer instructing newly-arrived American fighter pilots on what to expect when they first met the Luftwaffe. It was during this period that Cox was posted to Goxhill, the most northerly of the Lincolnshire sites, and certainly one of the most isolated airfields, which was a USAAF 8th Air Force Base, Station 345 and was being used as a fighter operational training base. When Cox arrived the Americans were working up on the formidable P-47 Thunderbolts, which were destined for North Africa.

After Goxhill, Cox returned to Fighter Command as a flight commander with No 504 Squadron at Hornchurch in Essex and at the time of the D-Day landings in June 1944 David Cox was the commander of No 222 Squadron flying patrols from Selsey, an Advanced Landing Ground (ALG) in West Sussex, over the Normandy beachhead.

An injury in a car accident put paid to David Cox's operational flying for a time, but on 1 January 1945 he took command of No 1 Squadron at Manston, Kent, flying long-range escorts for bomber raids over Germany. In April 1945, Cox was posted to Burma, and finally left the Royal Air Force with the rank of Wing Commander, receiving a Distinguished Flying Cross and Bar and the Croix de Guerre.

Just how strong was the Luftwaffe at the time of the Battle of Britain? On 3 August 1940, single-engine fighter aircraft stood at 1,171 according to the records of the Quartermaster General; actual strength was 1,065 and of these 878 were ready for combat, comprising ten single-engine fighter wings with a total of 28 groups. Two of these ten wings, a total of six groups were tied to home defence duties. Therefore the number of single-engine fighter aircraft available at the beginning of the Battle of Britain was only 760. The Luftwaffe also had 310 twin-engine fighter

Mass production of the formidable Spitfire fighter.

aircraft of which 240 were combat ready. However, this was aircraft strength and there were not enough trained crews available to man these aircraft. German bomber strength at 3 August was 1,458 of which 818 were combat ready. Also at their disposal were six groups based in Norway which could have intervened effectively if called. The dive bomber strength was 446 of which 343 were combat ready. In addition, on 20 September, forty Me 109s of the II Close-Support Group, 2nd Training Wing, which was an experimental fighter-bomber group, were sent into action for the first time.

At the beginning of the battle, Fighter Command had sixty single-engine fighter squadrons, a total of 960 aircraft. Due to the fact that there were eight squadrons not prepared for immediate action, the actual strength on 7 August 1940 was 714 single-engine fighter aircraft. This figure was subject to alteration during the various phases of the struggle – for example, on 25 September, the number was down to 665. According to British data, losses during the period 11 August to 28 September 1940 amounted to 669 single-engine fighters, while a total of 936 was produced during the same period.

RAF Fighter Command lost 915 aircraft during the Battle of Britain, but inflicted fighter and bomber losses totalling 1,733 on the German Luftwaffe. Bomber Command, whose actual strength as of 8 August 1940 was 471 aircraft, played no role in the Battle of Britain. On the face of it the Luftwaffe should have won the battle but it is clear that the Luftwaffe simply did not have the means of solving this problem in the autumn of 1940. Germany did not possess the long-range, heavy bombers which might have struck a decisive blow against RAF Fighter Command's military strength. Germany failed to profit by her lesson.

The German attackers were handicapped in many ways:

1 The German fighters were tied to the bombers they escorted, therefore they were unable to manoeuvre with complete freedom and were thus more vulnerable to Fighter Command's fighters than they otherwise would have been.

2 The Luftwaffe had no ground control system for the ground-to-air guidance of fighter aircraft, whereas the British had a well-functioning one at their disposal. In some ways this was compensated by the efficiency of the German radio monitoring system.

3 The British also had a tremendous advantage in their radar equipment, which had been under development since 1936. As Kammhuber said: 'The enemy was continually peeking at our cards – and it was our own fault!'

4 The advent of the proverbial British autumn weather on 16 September 1940. The two months which Hitler had waited, in the hope that Britain would capitulate, now took their toll.

5 Prior to the Battle of Britain, Germany rashly underestimated their enemy's military strength. Underestimating enemy strength is clearly one of the most frequent causes of military failure.

Was the Battle of Britain a turning point? It is difficult to answer this question. It is important to remember that the Battle of Britain was broken off prematurely by order from the top, because the Luftwaffe was needed for the forthcoming war with Russia. It was not, however, the high losses inflicted by Fighter Command's undeniably efficient air defence which forced the Luftwaffe to withdraw from the battle. Hitler was still convinced that Russia would have to be subdued if Germany were to be safe. The Battle of Britain was the handwriting on the wall and neither Field Marshal Göring, Jeschonnek, nor Udet had been able to decipher it.

Order of Battle, Fighter Command, 8 August 1940

Headquarters No 10 Group (Box, Wiltshire)

Squadron numbers
92 (Spitfires), Pembrey
87 (Hurricanes), Exeter
213 (Hurricanes), Exeter
234 (Spitfires), St Eval
247 (Gladiators), Roborough (1 Flight only)
238 (Hurricanes), Middle Wallop
609 (Spitfires), Middle Wallop
604 (Blenheims), Middle Wallop
152 (Spitfires), Warmwell

Headquarters No 11 Group (Uxbridge)

Squadron numbers
17 (Hurricanes), Debden
85 (Hurricanes), Martlesham
56 (Hurricanes), Rochford
151 (Hurricanes), North Weald
25 (Blenheims), North Weald with detachment at Martlesham

54 (Spitfires), Hornchurch
65 (Spitfires), Hornchurch
74 (Spitfires), Hornchurch
41 (Spitfires), Hornchurch
43 (Hurricanes), Tangmere
145 (Hurricanes), Westhampnett
601 (Hurricanes), Tangmere
1 (Hurricanes), Northolt
257 (Hurricanes), Northolt
615 (Hurricanes), Kenley
64 (Spitfires), Kenley
111 (Hurricanes), Croydon
32 (Hurricanes), Biggin Hill
610 (Spitfires), Biggin Hill
501 (Hurricanes), Gravesend
600 (Blenheims), Manston

Headquarters No 12 Group (Watnall, Nottinghamshire)

Squadron numbers
73 (Hurricanes), Church Fenton
249 (Hurricanes), Church Fenton
616 (Spitfires), Leconfield
222 (Spitfires), Kirton-in-Lindsey
264 (Defiants), Kirton-in-Lindsey
('A' Flight at Ringway)
46 (Hurricanes), Digby
611 (Spitfires), Digby
29 (Blenheims), Digby
242 (Hurricanes), Coltishall
66 (Spitfires), Coltishall
229 (Hurricanes), Wittering
266 (Spitfires), Wittering
23 (Blenheims), Colly Weston
19 (Spitfires), Duxford

Headquarters No 13 Group (Newcastle upon Tyne)

Squadron numbers
79 (Spitfires), Acklington
607 (Hurricanes), Usworth
72 (Spitfires), Acklington
605 (Hurricanes), Drem
232 (Hurricanes), Turnhouse
253 (Hurricanes), Turnhouse
141 (Defiants), Prestwick
219 (Blenheims), Catterick
245 (Hurricanes), Aldergrove
3 (Hurricanes), Wick
504 (Hurricanes), Castletown
232 (Hurricanes), Sumburgh (1 Flight only)
603 (Spitfires), 'A' Flight at Dyce, 'B' Flight at Montrose

Chapter Six

Going Sick

To get any medical attention or even a couple of tablets, one had to go through the ritual of 'going sick'. It was the same throughout the Royal Air Force and on a wartime fighter station it was even more difficult with being moved at a moment's notice, in many cases, it really was more bother than it was worth. In normal peacetime situations the Orderly Sergeant would go round the barrack block or huts and, throwing open the door, would bawl out 'Any sick?' If any airman wanted to go sick his name was put on the sick report and he had to report to the Guard Room. When all the sick were paraded, they were marched to the Station Sick Quarters. It was a condition of going sick that you took a haversack containing your small kit with you in case you were detained in the Sick Quarters. Going sick in wartime varied from station to station but in addition to your small kit you also now had a gas mask to carry.

At Castletown, a remote fighter airfield in Scotland, Sergeant 'Herb' Curotte arrived with No 1 (Fighter) Squadron Royal Canadian Air Force, and it was so cold that a 'tot' of rum – about two ounces – was issued twice a day. 'It certainly took the chill away,' said Curotte, 'it gave one a glowing feeling of warmth and comfort … may God bless for ever the one who originated the issue!' But, even with a tot of rum twice a day 'Herb' Curotte had the misfortune of contracting pneumonia. At Castletown the Station Sick Quarters consisted of one Nissen hut, and the cots were low and close to the floor, which meant the patients felt all the drafts. 'The pneumonia virus was frozen out of my system rather than killed by whatever medical gunk I was fed,' Curotte said.

'I was foolhardy enough to go sick once when I was at North Weald,' said Dennis Williams, who at that time was an AC Flight Rigger of 'B' Flight, No 25 Squadron and had been in the Royal Air

Aircraftman Dennis Williams at St Athan School of Technical Training in July 1939 – was just turned seventeen years old. Note the old-type 'dog collar' tunic. The aircraft in the background is a Miles Magister and they were being instructed in the art of starting the aircraft by swinging the propeller by hand. It was quite a risky business – but not as risky as 'going sick'!

Force for over a year. It was late September 1940, and because of the earlier raids on the airfield, things had been dispersed around somewhat. The Station Sick Quarters were housed in an old rambling house in Epping. Pay Accounts had moved to a building in Ongar, which was just up the road. It was from Ongar that the 'erks' boarded the train to get to London on the old LNER to Liverpool Street.

The groundcrew of 'B' Flight 25 Squadron were all cramped into one wooden hut the other side of the airfield. 'We were all in there,' said Williams, 'Mechanics, Riggers, Armourers, Electricians, etc, plus equipment and tools. With the blackout curtains in position, and nearly everyone smoking, the air was really foul and it was no wonder that I had a terrible throat. I diagnosed myself as having tonsillitis.' Williams also had a boil on the back of his neck and this was to prove his downfall. He felt very much under the weather and although as an old sweat he should have known better, he reported sick. He got his small kit together, minus pyjamas, (they didn't possess them in 1940) and went and found the Orderly Sergeant. After a time he found himself with a couple more 'erks' on the back of a lorry on the way to Epping and the temporary Sick Quarters. It was always a standing joke in the Royal Air Force that the Medical Officers were doctors who could not get a job in city street – not true of course but that was the story. Eventually Williams found himself in front of an elderly Medical Officer. 'He chatted to me,' said Williams, 'asked how old I was and if I was a regular. I replied that I was just eighteen and that I was indeed a regular airman. After a bit more chat about the bombing of the airfield he asked me finally why I had come. I told him and he had a long look at my throat, and said "You had better stop in here for a couple of days and we will give you something for it". A Medical Orderly showed me to a bed, and I was later given some liquid to gargle with. They also supplied me with some pyjamas which to me was an unexpected luxury. Normally we slept in shirt and pants and when we were on call in full uniform.'

The makeshift ward was quite full although most airmen there were only in for minor ailments like Williams. All the windows were shut and a lot of smoking was going on and his throat was still sore and tender. On the second morning of his enforced stay in the Sick Quarters another Medical Orderly noticed the boil on his neck and told Williams that he needed a dressing on it. When the Orderly reappeared with the dressing he also had a couple of yellow tablets with him. 'Here you are, son', he said. 'Get these down, they are good for the blood.' 'I think they were sulphur tablets,' said Williams, 'anyhow I swallowed them. A couple of minutes later, the Sergeant Medic told everyone to put their cigarettes out as the "Old Man", meaning the MO, was coming round to check on the state of the patients. When he got to my bed he checked the temperature chart at the foot of the bed – of course my temperature had risen since I came – small wonder with all the windows shut. The heat was unbearable. He asked me how I felt, looked down my throat, in fact, he looked down my throat several times Did I feel worse than when I arrived? I said I did not feel any better or, any worse either. He wrote something on a pad and said something to the Sergeant who went into his little office and picked up the phone and spoke to someone for a couple of minutes.

'The Sergeant returned to the ward, and said something to the MO. He nodded and then they continued the round until they had seen everyone. When they had gone the smokers got the fags out and the room became full of smoke again. There was none of this "Smoking can damage your health" lark in 1940.'

What with a sore throat and a sore neck and the nasty taste from taking the yellow tablets, Williams decided it was best to try and sleep, and after a while he dozed off. After a nap he woke and was feeling much better. He began to sit up, suddenly the Sergeant Medical Orderly appeared from out of nowhere and told him to lie down. He then removed the pillow from beneath his head and started to pack all Williams' small kit into his haversack. Williams looked puzzled and he asked him what was going on. 'Don't worry son', he said. 'You are going in to a hospital, just lie still and keep quiet.' Two airmen appeared with a stretcher and they lifted Williams on to it. The last words from the Sergeant were 'Don't forget the pyjamas belong to this Sick Quarters.'

Williams was carried out and placed into a large old Thornycroft ambulance, which were referred to as either a blood wagon or meat wagon. The rear doors clanged shut and they were away. As the ambulance sped away Williams began to wonder why no one travelled in the back with him. 'I convinced myself that it was all a terrible mistake and that they had got the wrong patient', he said. 'Why would a bloke with a sore throat be lifted on to a stretcher? Why was the pillow taken away? Why was I told to lie still? At least I thought I would try and find out what direction I was going in. I got off the stretcher and peered through the dark windows of the ambulance but we were in open country by now and I hadn't a clue where we were and of course all signposts had been removed in case of invasion. I got back on the stretcher and tried to think calmly. If a mistake hadn't been made what the hell could be the matter with me and why hadn't someone told me? Lying there I lost all sense of time or direction till I felt the meat wagon slow up and then make a sharp right turn.'

Williams jumped quickly to look through the window again and saw that they were going up a long drive with high hedges on both sides and then a huge building appeared and he got back on the stretcher. The doors were opened and he was carried into the building. 'It was a hospital of some kind,' he said, 'I couldn't make up my mind whether it was military or civilian. A nurse appeared and directed the stretcher bearer to take me into a room which smelt strongly of disinfectant. I was placed on to a trolley, no pillows, and told to lie still.' The ambulance driver handed over his small kit, uniform, and gas mask, and then departed. The nurse then came and informed Williams that a doctor would be coming to see him. By now he was getting alarmed at what was happening and he asked the nurse what he was supposed to be in there for. She told him it was an isolation hospital and that he had been sent to them as a suspected diphtheria case. Then the doctor appeared and Williams was given an injection. 'What was that for?' asked Williams painfully. The doctor replied that it was an anti-diphtheria serum. He said he would take a swab later. Williams was put into a ward where there were about fifteen other patients, all civilian and mostly young. He was the only serviceman there and they made quite a fuss of him.

Dennis Williams at North Weald in 1975. The deserted barrack blocks and the square are falling into disrepair.

At night all the beds were moved to one end of the ward where it was more protected from the blast in case of an air raid. 'My throat was sore and I kept wanting to drink,' said Williams, 'whether it was the injection I had been given, or not, I do not know, but I felt quite light headed. Someone took my temperature and I remember a nurse staying by my bedside for quite a while. It turned out in the event that I had a temperature of 103°. I thought to myself what a ridiculous situation. I started off with a touch of tonsillitis and here I was becoming really ill. I wish I hadn't gone sick in the first place. Of course I was confident that I couldn't possibly have diphtheria. It was all the fault of that silly old quack doctor.'

A swab was taken and tests showed there was no trace of diphtheria germs. However the damage had been done, for with having had an anti-diphtheria injection, and with no diphtheria germs to fight against Williams started to come out in a painful rash all over his body. The staff were very considerate, in fact, too helpful, for they sent his pyjamas that he had arrived in, to the laundry, only to find they had no others to fit him and he ended up wearing an extra large woman's long flannelette nightdress. 'I felt a right berk wearing that,' said Williams, 'and was pleased when the pyjamas came back. My treatment for the rash consisted of being dabbed all over with calamine lotion.'

After ten days the hospital telephoned the RAF Sick Quarters for an ambulance to take Williams back to his camp. Unknown to Williams his uniform had been fumigated and when a nurse produced it it looked a right mess. A button was missing, probably removed as a souvenir. Williams dressed and could not believe his eyes, for apart from the crumpled uniform he still had red spots on his face.

The blood wagon duly arrived and this time Williams was invited to sit up front with the driver. He gave him a curious look and said 'Christ, whatever happened to you?' Williams gave him a rundown of events of the previous fortnight and told him how glad he would be to get hold of his kit again. When he told him what squadron he was on his reply shook him. 'They have gone,' said the ambulance driver, 'down to Debden'. When Williams arrived at North Weald he had to see the Orderly Sergeant who contacted the squadron at Debden who in turn confirmed his kit was safe. One of the lads had taken charge of it for him. Williams was given a railway warrant and eventually arrived at Debden. He was lucky that he managed to get there without being picked up by the RAF Provost Police or the Military Police. Some of the public did give him a curious glance and perhaps they thought he had been in a crash somewhere and was making his way back to camp.

'I never did report sick again,' said Williams, 'and the only time I went near the Sick Quarters was when I went for a compulsory visit. That being for inoculation, dental treatment and the ever popular FFI [free from infection]. On one of these compulsory attendances Williams had a chat with a Medical Orderly and asked him if he could explain how he could possibly have been suspected of having diphtheria. His theory was that when the Medical Officer first saw him, not only was his throat red, but bright yellow as well. This was due to the tablets which he had just taken a few minutes before he saw the Medical Officer. Of course that had to be it. Had Williams not had that boil he would have emerged from the Sick Quarters unscathed instead of which he had undergone a rather uncomfortable ten days.

Chapter Seven

'Grub Up'

Food was always uppermost in the minds of the ordinary airmen or 'erks' as they were called. Not for them the luxury of the Sergeants' Mess, or Officers' Mess. They had to queue up in the cookhouse, pick up a plate from the pile and go along a row of cooks who would dish out the grub; one would put some potato on your plate, another one the swedes, and one the stew or whatever. 'I served on seventeen different RAF stations,' said Rigger George Williams, 'and also lived under canvas and had food from the field kitchens. After the bombing started at North Weald, we had field kitchens and ate our food in a big marquee. As a regular airman, soon to be outnumbered by the amount of call-up men around me, I was expected to know the ropes and pass on any information which would lead to extra grub. I would stress that any system we operated would only be used at the normal cookhouse, or Airmen's Mess. When we were on duty in the crew room, and food had to be brought to us, it was fair shares for all.'

The easiest, and most often used method to get extra food was simply to queue up again after you had consumed your first meal.

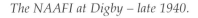

The NAAFI at Digby – late 1940.

This depended on what time you had available, sometimes if your aircraft was on a sortie, you had more time. On other occasions time was limited. If you had the time it was safer to leave the cookhouse and return after a suitable interval. If time was limited you had to take a chance and go round again almost immediately. There were Corporals on the look-out for anyone going around twice. 'We called it doing an "Oliver Twist",' said Williams, 'I was lucky, wearing glasses, because I used to go round again without them on.' Some 'erks' were spotted and when challenged admitted it. If you brazened it out and denied going round twice, you were a marked man and the Corporal would watch you like a hawk and make sure he had a witness. Of course it varied from camp to camp, on some you could get away with it. The punishment for getting caught also varied.

At Aldergrove in Northern Ireland, the food was really good. The Warrant Officer I/C really knew his stuff. There always seemed to be a shortage of seats in the dining hall because of the number of men doing justice a second time to the Warrant Officer's excellent menu. 'I think Aldergrove was the only camp I have been in where you actually had biscuits and cheese with your Sunday lunch', said George Williams. However, when they realized that the number of meals being served far exceeded the estimated number they took drastic action. Anyone caught going round twice was not only put on a charge but had to walk through the main camp to the Guard Room carrying the second dinner. It was hoped that the humiliation would deter further attempts to get a second meal.

In many peacetime RAF camps it would have been impossible to get extra food, because you were detailed to sit at a certain numbered table and two men collected the food for the whole table. Two men did this on a daily basis and then another two, until everyone had had a turn. But things were different on a wartime fighter station. Take for example butter, this was rationed and airmen were only allowed one small pat of butter at breakfast time and tea time. These pats of butter were usually stamped out in a shape of a circle with serrated edges. They were in a large bowl of water and you fished out one circle with your knife, under the watchful eye of one of the cooks or sometimes the orderly Corporal. It was possible however, to increase your butter ration by means of your mug of tea. Tea was always in a big urn somewhere handy in the dining-room. Some men filled their mugs from the urn after they had collected their meal. The best idea was to fill your mug with tea first, and when you were collecting your piece of butter with your knife you passed your mug of hot tea over the bowl. This way you could have two or three pieces sticking to the bottom of your mug of tea.

Most of these dodges were carried out by the groundcrew, these were the men who actually started up the aircraft and serviced them. Working out in all weather to keep the fighters airborne was hungry work, and the groundcrew 'erks' were always ready for a bite to eat. On some fighter airfields this proved a bit of a problem for it was often necessary to man the fighters at all times and many were dispersed quite a way from the dining hall. Therefore, at lunch time, only one man at a time was allowed away. As lunch was only served at a fixed time, say 12:30–13:30, special arrangements had to be made for groundcrews like Riggers and Fitters and also other trades who performed duties where someone must always be on duty, Wireless Operators, flying control assistants, etc. These special arrangements were that if you required a meal before the normal time you had to produce what was known as an 'early chit'. This was an instruction to the cookhouse staff to supply the bearer with an early dinner of whatever meal was required. There was also a 'late chit'.

For example, Williams' groundcrew worked out a roster, one early, one late, and one normal time. The snag with the late chit was that the NAAFI would have been closed so there was no cup of char. They rotated the meal times between themselves. The early chit was by far the best, because if the dinner was still being cooked and was not ready, they provided you with a scratch meal such as bacon and egg or corned beef. With a late chit you usually found there was plenty of food left from the main meal. If however, it had all gone then they provided you with a meal similar to what those received with the early chit. Having bacon and egg was indeed a luxury for the groundcrews.

During the periods when the groundcrews were out on the dispersal with their aircraft they were missing out on the double stakes so one time Williams and his crew decided to get that extra meal. They figured that if the man with the early chit came back straight away without visiting the NAAFI, then the second man who was on normal dinner break could go in again just before the end of the normal serving times. The man with the late chit would go as normal. It worked out at the end of the week that two of the three men had two extra dinners.

Another ruse was when there was large scale night flying, for the cookhouse would then serve a meal between 23:00 and midnight. Those airmen on night flying would simply go to the cookhouse and queue for their meal. Those who had not been on duty would simply put on a pair of overalls and queue up with the rest. Some airmen who had been out for the evening would also do this. Whatever station you were on you could get a little extra.

At Debden in Essex, an important fighter station within 11 Group, the groundcrews had a bonus in the form of an additional canteen. There was the usual NAAFI which, despite all the jokes, really did a first class job, and in addition there was a little hut which sold tea and 'wads' (cakes). After a very hectic time at North Weald, No 25 Squadron moved to Debden in October 1940 and Williams and his groundcrew were quick to sniff out the little hut with its little old ladies. In addition to the tea and 'wads', the little old ladies also sold those fruit pies which were made by the famous firm of J. Lyons. They cost 2½d each. They were packed in a small cardboard box and were of various flavours, the most popular being apple. They were known as Lyons Individual Fruit Pies and to the 'erks' on low income they were in fact a luxury. The fruit pies were the first thing that Williams and his groundcrew noticed when they visited the little canteen. 'A huge pile of fruit pies were stacked along one side of the counter,' said Williams, 'the canteen staff consisted of an assortment of little old ladies, there were usually two on duty at a time, and I would imagine they did one evening a week each, because you didn't see the same face twice in one week. I think they were an organization similar to the Church Army.

'We found out that as soon as the air raid siren sounded the lights in this little canteen went out immediately, everything was in utter darkness. The black-out curtains were in position, and we never really understood why they went out without warning. However, we decided if by any chance we should be in the hut again when the lights went out, we would quietly help ourselves to one or two of Mr Lyons' fruit pies all readily available on the side of the counter. On the future occasions when we visited this little canteen we chose to sit near the counter. There were usually four or five at

Unbelievable as it may seem, this is the Mess and cookhouse at Castletown, winter 1941. The Nissen hut is the Mess and the two smaller units the cookhouse.

a table, and we told our fellow groundcrews sitting at other tables of our intended plans, they of course, wanted to be in on the act.

'About a week later, we were in there when the sirens went off, followed by the canteen being plunged into darkness. Immediately "Operation Fruit Pie" was put into operation. There was the sound of scraping chairs, movement of many feet, and the pies were moving fast. Of course at this stage no one knew how many pies had in fact "taken off" so we were all keen for the "all clear" to sound, and the lights to go on again so that we could weigh the situation up.

'After what seemed a lifetime, the "all clear" sounded and the lights came on. What a sight met our eyes for what had formerly been a huge pile of fruit pies was now a small heap, and several "erks" had developed "busts". We had only planned on each man having one pie each. The funny part was that the two old ladies seemed totally unaware of the fact that a lot of pies had gone. We decided to test their reaction by going up and purchasing a single pie. Between us we scraped up the $2\frac{1}{2}$d and "Ginger" Bentley said he would volunteer to go and get it. The little lady asked him what flavour he wanted, and he said "apple". She turned to the now small heap of pies, and after rummaging about a bit, produced the required flavour. To our astonishment she never batted an eyelid, but we overheard her saying to the other lady "The pies seem to have gone well tonight dear, we must get some more ordered".'

The 'erks' were very puzzled by the nonchalant attitude of the little old ladies and they never did find out if they were not aware of what they had done or just turned a blind eye to it all. On 23 October 1940 the squadron moved up to Wittering in order to become operational as soon as possible. The groundcrew were flown up in an old Handley Page Harrow, still licking their lips from those fruit pies.

After disembarking from the *Duchess of Athol* on which they had crossed the Atlantic after leaving Halifax, Canada

Another view of the Mess facility at Castletown. With the mug and plates is Sergeant Herb Vurotte. His friend, debating whether to eat or throw up, is Bill McLean who was later commissioned.

in convoy, the Canadians were moved to Middle Wallop in Hampshire. One of those first ashore was 'Herb' Curotte from Campbellton in New Brunswick and he recalls: 'On entering the mess hall at Middle Wallop, which was "manned" if one can say in paradox by female personnel ... I can still hear a surprised female voice – "they're Canadians and they speak English". Possibly she had anticipated some native Indian tongue, having seen too many Hollywood westerns.'

Their stay at Wallop was brief and the Canadians soon moved to Croydon where their sleeping quarters were arranged inside a hangar. The messing arrangements were unable to cope with the sudden influx of men and field kitchens were hastily set up. Herb Curotte recalls: 'It was the most distasteful messing ever encountered in my Service life. One could taste sand and grit in all the greens served which to top it all were boiled to a "glop" soup in a large open kettle from which the contents were ladled by an enormous cook who refused to wear anything but a singlet. The weather was warm and at each bend of his bountiful body sweat droplets would fall in the soup making ringlets on the greasy surface. Finally this exceeded all proportion of decency and I therefore contacted our Medical Officer, one Dr Rankin, who applied his authority. Conditions improved but not totally.'

After seeing out the Battle of Britain at Northolt, No 1 (Fighter) Squadron, RCAF were transferred to Castletown in Scotland and Sergeant Curotte found himself stationed on Sir Archibald Sinclair's grounds. The countryside was very bleak and the messing facilities were in a 'shack'-type building. Inside the so-called Mess were plain wooden tables and forms. 'A sight and smell I will never forget' said Curotte. 'One person would sit at each end of a form, with mostly jaundiced kippers staring at you! One had to be careful to warn his companion when rising as otherwise one end of the form would end up as in playing see-saw. Not exactly dinner at the Savoy.'

From Castletown the Canadians moved to Digby in Lincolnshire, via a brief stay at Driffield. With the arrival of No 1 (Canadian) Squadron at Digby the Canadian units were allocated new numbers in the 400 series and No 1 became 401 Squadron. Digby was an operational fighter station which became officially Canadian and for Curotte and the many others far from home the mess hall was one of the best. As Curotte said: 'Digby was my all-time favourite fighter airfield. I got my Sergeant's stripe and moved into another world. The Mess was not far from our allocated barracks and messing was as good as wartime restrictions permitted. We even had our own Mess song in the Sergeants' Mess.'

CHAPTER EIGHT

Off Duty

Not unlike the Wandering Jew, fighter squadrons were posted from airfield to airfield. In many cases the off-duty hours were nil and when they did manage a few hours a number of pubs and hotels were posted 'out of bounds' on DROs. The reason they were told was owing to fifth columnist and spy activity. This was a very touchy matter at the time. No one would defy the orders, which of course restricted the number of oases, and they were always a factor with serving personnel.

The cast of the musical evening given by the Canadians in Ayr. In the centre is Sir Harry Lauder who raised £1,000,000 for ex-servicemen after his own son was killed. His song Keep right on to the end of the road *became an inspiration to many people.*

The groundcrews were allowed out after duty until 23:59 hours every other night. If they didn't go out, they either read, played cards, or went to the NAAFI. Their activities were very much controlled by the cash flow – most people were always short and awaiting the weekly pay parade. If one was short of money one could remain in the Mess, borrow a pound or so, enjoying Mild and Bitter whilst playing billiards or simply 'hangar flying', just hanging around.

Off-duty pursuits included going to dances in villages or towns near the station, also going to the cinema then the usual call in the various pubs which were the ideal meeting place, the popular pubs often bursting at the seams. 'They were happy times,' said Jack Strachan 'making the best of the situation I suppose, in an endeavour to forget the pressures of the war, however to maintain a sense of discipline was also essential.' Just about everyone stationed on the fighter airfields around London usually made it into the capital and ended up being photographed feeding the pigeons in Trafalgar Square.

The men lost no time in finding a favourite pub: 'What memories,' said Herb Curotte, 'with uncanny ability, if you wished, they would assign a "mug" to you. I always wondered how in such a short space of time the barmaid would reach for your "own" mug the moment you walked in. Miracles of the English barmaids, their humour unequalled – their usual imposing fronts a joy to behold!'

The Canadians were very lucky for they had ample free time, disposition of personnel was so arranged that duty rosters could be made in order that whilst sufficient personnel were available others

Canadian fighter pilots in London. The traditional pose for feeding the pigeons in Trafalgar Square. From left to right, McClusky, Robbie, Kilver and Brad.

could relax on or off station. Many enjoyed the countryside and a chance to meet the locals, never failing to enjoy interesting conversation about Canada or Britain. The Royal Air Force at that time was at its height of popularity so the hospitality was present everywhere. The young airmen would be invited to share tea at private homes.

The many antics of both aircrew and groundcrew on a fighter station made Service life humorous and it helped to relieve the boredom and tension. The most famous personality of the period was Group Captain Douglas Bader, CBE, DSO, DFC, who flew with Nos 19 and 222 Squadrons RAF; commanded 242 Squadron RAF

Doodles and caricatures were a favourite pastime for many wartime fighter pilots. This one depicts officers of No 13 (Army Co-operation) Squadron at Speke in the summer of 1940, after coming out of France. Note No 9 Simpson and No 10 Porteous, both mentioned in Chapter 14.

Here we see Bob Corbett (minus his white horse) just setting out on 'Circus' op into France.

in 1940–41 and was Wing Leader at RAF Tangmere in 1941. He was a great prankster. On 14 December 1931, as a result of a flying accident, Bader lost both legs, and was discharged from the Royal Air Force on 30 April 1933. On 26 November 1939 he rejoined with the rank of Flying Officer.

The Canadians were a likeable bunch of young men and the fighter pilots were a very wild bunch who liked to let off steam. While at Coleby Grange in Lincolnshire the pilots were housed at Coleby Lodge, a fine old country house near the airfield. One pilot, Bob Corbett, of No 402 Squadron RCAF somehow managed to keep, and ride, a beautiful white horse while at Coleby. It was quite a sight to see a young fighter pilot in flying gear, helmet and goggles, on horse back, racing across the airfield to dispersal. It was 'scramble' in Canadian Wild West style.

The fighter pilots of No 402 Squadron at Digby taught the station Dental Officer to fly during their free time and one day he turned up at Coleby Grange, a satellite airfield of Digby, in a Tiger Moth. He told one of the pilots, Flying Officer Robert (Bob) Morrow, that Group Captain Murlis-Green, the Digby Commanding Officer, had given him the aircraft in exchange for a new set of dentures. The teeth stayed but the Tiger Moth was returned.

Just about all the fighter pilots loved to own a little open sports car. Others owned motor cycles and they all enjoyed driving around the wartime countryside. Travelling the black-out on unknown roads with the small light permitted was a challenge to them. One pilot was arrested by the village constable for driving a motor cycle without lights. He was warned by a magistrate of the dangers of such practices and fined ten shillings. The pilot was an operational

Relaxing on the lawn at Coleby Grange in 1941.

fighter pilot and had indeed had many experiences with danger and seen many of his best friends die in a ball of flame in the skies above the English countryside.

The MT Section at RAF Digby had a certain NCO who was greatly disliked by the men, being quite authoritarian. He had reached the rank of Sergeant very quickly and would flaunt his authority at the least occasion. The 'erks' decided to take him down a peg or two. While at Digby he would frequent the local village pub which was in walking distance of the camp. However, the Sergeant preferred to cycle. On one particular evening some of his 'erks' found out that he was going to visit the pub that evening, and they decided to teach him a lesson. The route the sergeant cycled took him over a small bridge, and as he approached it in the dark, he did not see the rope strung across it. He hit the rope, and over and over he went. . .the cycle went east and he went west … neatly pressed uniform and all, into the brook. The following day in the MT Section he showed a few bruises from his experience of the night before. There were many sly questions as to his bruises, needless to say, with just as sly answers.

The Australians were also a very wild bunch and in July 1940 a number of Aussies assembled at Middle Wallop before being posted to fighter squadrons. One night the Aussies decided to visit their favourite watering hole in Andover. After a night of it they decided to commandeer a double decker bus – giving the driver short leave.

Coleby Grange 1941 – 402 RCAF Squadron relaxing.

Somewhere in the area was a civic pond which housed a few ducks – some of the Aussies without hesitation waded in, retrieving some ducks, who became passengers, until the whole lot arrived at the guard gate at Wallop. The bus was stopped at a fair distance from the guard house. The occupants disembarked faster than at the command 'dismissed'. In the confusion the ducks were not noticed until the culprits had safely passed the guard house building.

No 1 (Fighter) Squadron, Royal Canadian Air Force, was blessed with many types of musical talent. After they had been at Prestwick for a short while someone organized a musical evening by the 'Canadians' to be given in a large hall in Ayr, both for the Service personnel and invited civilians. The Commanding Officer and the Adjutant of No 1 (Fighter) Squadron RCAF both persuaded Sir Harry Lauder to give the soirée some éclat. The event was a huge success and, to everyone, Sir Harry was the 'tops'.

Whilst at Castletown the Canadians, the complete squadron, received an invitation by the caretakers of John O'Groats Hotel, which of course was closed for the duration. It was still amply stocked and they received hospitality that was to remain with them ever. It was a Sunday, and the best of everything was brought out and lavishly dispensed.

Many Canadians did not forget in a hurry the night at the Marine Bar in Troon, which was a submarine base. The Canadians had proceeded there one evening for the usual refreshment. They had named a certain drink the 'Hurricane' – it was a mixture of rum and cider. They asked the bartender to mix a number of them,

Canadian fighter pilot with his sports car.

flaunting their high octane quality. As it turned out, the bartender had worked many years in New York before returning to his beloved Scotland. The canny Scot asked the young Canadian airmen, all innocent like, if they had ever tasted a drink called 'Submarine', which he felt was superior to their 'Hurricanes'. On their negative answer he pleasantly mixed and supplied their group with a few – 'whatever it contained over the "Hurricanes" that we had already consumed, soon submerged the lot of us,' said Herb Curotte, 'I recall trying to exit through a revolving type door from the somewhat fashionable club. The best I

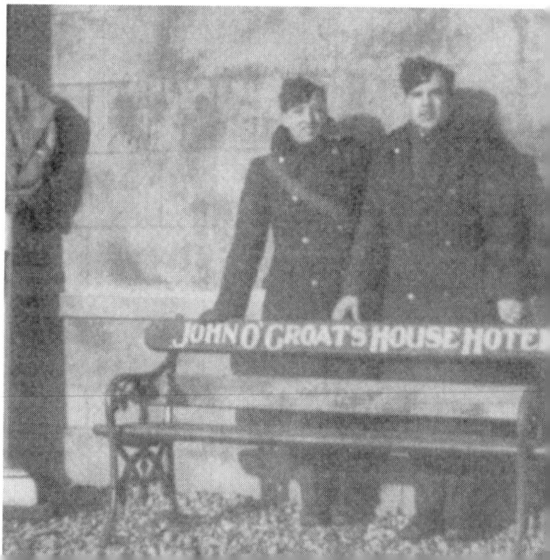

Sergeant Herb Curotte (right) and a fellow Sergeant during their visit to John O'Groats Hotel – November 1940. The party was for all squadron personnel of No 1 (F) Squadron, RCAF.

During a rare visit into town, Curotte snaps the wee laddies who were willing to pose after he bought them all some sweets. Note the VIM sign on left.

could do was a continued spin missing the exit at each turn until I was rescued by someone stopping the diabolical door.' They returned some nights later to be greeted: 'What do you think of the "Submarine" noo?'

Submarines were also a sore subject for one young Hurricane pilot. During January 1940 the Hurricanes of No 72 Squadron were at Church Fenton, a fighter airfield in Yorkshire, and while over the North Sea on gunnery practice, a young pilot spotted what he thought was a submarine just below the surface. He was very green and without thinking reported his sighting over the R/T which sparked off an air and sea search of the area to find that the sighting was only a whale. For weeks the young pilot had to stand the jokes from his fellow pilots and one morning for breakfast he was served a herring with a cardboard conning tower on top!

CHAPTER NINE

A Fighter Squadron is Born

On 22 November 1941, No 416 (City of Oshawa) Squadron, Royal Canadian Air Force, formed at Peterhead, Scotland. Its first Commander was Squadron Leader P. C. Webb, RAF, with one RAF flight commander, Flight Lieutenant K. C. Jackman. The remainder of the roster comprised newly operational-trained Canadian pilots; Pilot Officers Moffet, Marshall, Blades, Wozniak, Johnstone and Bird; Sergeants Aitken, Buckham, Harttung, Kelly, Learmouth, MacDonald, MacPherson, McNamara, Messum, Moul, Murphy, Paradis, Parlee, Ross, Scollan and Tomlinson.

The new squadron were told that the weather didn't get too cold at Peterhead but that winter was an exception and they moved heavy falls of snow on two occasions, all pilots manned a shovel and assisted in clearing the runways.

For most of the new squadron, this was to be their first Christmas spent overseas and they all received well-stocked food parcels full of Canadian goodies. By this time many of the young Canadian pilots had met civvy folk in Peterhead as George Aitken recalls: 'Many of us shared our Canadian products of Christmas cake, chocolate bars and various tin stuff with those who befriended us on our visits to Peterhead to see a show or to have a dance. I can remember that my parents had sent me a tin of Borden's condensed milk (sweetened)

No 416 (Fighter) Squadron RCAF at Peterhead, Scotland in winter 1941.

which had always been a favourite of mine and I punched a couple of holes in the tin and would forego the morning trip in the Bedford to the Mess for breakfast so that I could enjoy my parcel of goodies.'

The airfield was four miles west of Peterhead, and it had opened in July 1941, before the third' runway was completed. The living sites were also unfinished and all personnel had to be billeted in Peterhead. By the time No 416 Squadron formed, things had improved slightly with barrack blocks being available. One of the dispersed barrack blocks that the Sergeant NCOs of No 416 had was several miles from the airfield. 'I was one of the first to arrive,' said Sergeant George Aitken, 'and noticed that there was a small room with a door in the block and it had its own pot-belly stove. The block and this room was fitted with brown battleship lino which in my eyes needed a wash. I washed my room and thought how nice that lino would come up if it had some wax. When the station 'Bedford' went into Peterhead one day, when I was excused duty, I went into Peterhead and found a hardware, as Canadians call ironmongers, and was able to get the last small tin of wax that the shop had. I returned to the barrack and of course that lino really shined. When the Orderly Officer and Orderly Sergeant came through on a visit they were quick to notice my room and a few of my pals who were in the larger block were told, why didn't they do the same thing to their area. Let me tell you, I wasn't popular for a while, but when I offered help to wash the floor and gave them the wax and we got down to it, and it came up so clean and shiny, I was forgiven, as the whole block were given excused duty for the rest of the day.

'The winter was very cold and one very cold night I packed up the potbelly stove until it was red hot. I was over comfortable for most of the night but when morning came my room was back to its cold old condition. Coke doesn't keep the heat although it can be intense.'

When No 416 Squadron formed there was only a Magister aeroplane available for their use. They were told the new squadron would be equipped with Spitfires, which seemed strange since most of the pilots had come from a Hurricane Operational Training Unit, but it appears that this was the normal procedure. The pilots did not mind as George Aitken remarked: 'Behind everyone's dream I'm quite sure it was the eternal hope that we would fly Spitfires.'

However, when the Spitfires finally made their appearance they were old Mark II as that had been flown by a Polish squadron. They looked as if they had seen many battles and some had seen service in the Battle of Britain. It took the 416 Squadron groundcrew Mechanics and Engineering Officer several weeks to get the Spitfires into a serviceable condition, even then they seemed to have lots of little problems. The squadron then got a few Spitfire IIbs, which had also been flown by a Polish squadron but these were not much better than the Mark II as. Many of the Spitfires sprang glycol leaks, also undercarriage problems along with not being able to open the hood with ease. These problems were very frustrating for both the pilots and the Engineering Officer. However, they were Spitfires and the squadron was glad to have them – no matter what problems.

During the period that the Spitfires were being made airworthy, the pilots of 416 Squadron were given ground instruction relative to the handling and flying of Spitfires. Part of their training at Peterhead included work at the control tower. On 30 November it was the turn of Sergeant George Aitken and another Sergeant Pilot. They were in the control tower when suddenly the RAF instructor noticed an aircraft flying toward the airfield at a low altitude so he told Sergeant George Aitken to give it a red flare from the Very pistol. 'Just about the same time someone said: "It's a Jerry" and I had already pulled the trigger on the Very pistol', said George Aitken. 'Someone said: "Hit the floor" which we did but not before I saw the Ju 88 drop its bombs into the entrance of an air raid shelter. I saw the red flare trail at the tail of the Junkers. By this time the station sirens – were on and of course the exploding bombs brought home to us that we were at war.

'The Junkers of course was also spraying along its route machine-gun fire. Fortunately no one was in the air raid shelter which was completely demolished but one of our new flight commanders, a Flight Lieutenant Jackman, RAF, was ben~g fitted with a new flying jacket in the stores barrack and was hit by some of the machine-gun fire and killed. None of the NCO pilots had met Jackman. The story we heard was that Jackman was being fitted with a new leather flying jacket and stood between two WAAF store personnel when he was killed. The girls were not injured. This was my first introduction with "fate" and from this experience I would always refrain from the use of the open type of air raid shelter that I had seen completely destroyed this date.'

At long last the Spitfires reached flying condition and the Engineering Officer of 416 Squadron declared the Spitfires airworthy. The squadron all made their first flights without incident and the pilots were thrilled with their new mounts. George Aitken reports: 'Some of the kites however had seen better days and although some of the faults could be "pilot error", Sergeant Buckham ran off the runway, tipping the kite up on its nose and did damage to the propellor. Pilot Officers Bird and Marshall, within a few hours of one another, flipped a Spitfire on its back and another landed with wheels retracted. By this time some of the pilots including myself were told we would be posted to the Middle East or Far East. None of these postings took place. The squadron had been made operational about the middle of January but there were few 'scrambles' and the weather with the unprecedented snowfalls kept flying to a minimum.

'By 23 February 1942, the squadron had changed flight commanders and a Flight Lieutenant Chadburn became the Acting CO of the squadron as Squadron Leader Webb was on leave. On this very heavy, dull, threatening day, we were to fly north to a place called Skeabrae in the Orkneys to assist in providing naval cover to various ships proceeding to Scapa Flow. As I recall from the time we left Peterhead to Skeabrae, we never saw the ground, and as for the ships we protected, I never had a chance to see during the patrol that I was on. According to "the Commander in Chief of the Home Fleet" we had done a thoroughly efficient escort and we were all happy to return to Peterhead the next day in the same kind of weather that we had left the day previous. The groundcrew had been taken by Harrow and returned the same way.

'For the next few weeks we undertook practising formation, dogfighting, battle climbs, aerobatics and night flying under Chadburn's direction. Chadburn made us all keen and by the middle of March the squadron was split into two flights, 'A' and 'B'. 'A' Flight went to Dyce whilst 'B' Flight of which I was a member went to Montrose to carry out duties. On 19 March 1942 I was promoted to Flight Sergeant Pilot and by the end of the month found myself posted to No 403 Squadron, RCAF, at North Weald. I later discovered that the Adjutant, a Flight Lieutenant Sinclair, had been responsible for my promotion at Peterhead.'

An interesting fact about Peterhead was that Pilot Officer Wozniak later followed Sergeant Pilot Aitken to No 403 Squadron. Wozniak met his wife-to-be in Peterhead, she was the Assistant Adjutant to No 416 in those formative months.

Sergeant Pilot Buckham became an ace winning both the British and American Distinguished Flying Cross. He led Canadian fighter

No 403 (F) Squadron RCAF at North Weald – spring 1942.

wings in the last years of the war. He remained in service but was killed in a flying accident at Whitehorse, Yukon Territories where he had been posted after the war as Commanding Officer.

Those early days at Peterhead are still fresh in the mind of George Aitken: 'I will never forget the trip to Skaebrae and the patrol. I don't remember ever flying again under such bad weather conditions and with the inexperience that we had at the time it still remains a mystery to me that any of us were able to survive that trip. Chadburn who led us also became an ace and led squadrons and wings until he was killed in action.

On 2 June 1942, Flight Sergeant George Aitken ended up in the English Channel after an encounter with Fw 190s and Me 109s at Le Touquet. He lived to tell the tale and today lives in Edmonton, Canada where he still thinks of those days at Peterhead – 'Wouldn't it have been nice if my Very pistol flare had hit the Ju 88 at Peterhead,' he said, 'and I'd have been able to have claimed it as "destroyed" – a fighter squadron born without fighters downs German aircraft – what a headline it would have been!'

CHAPTER TEN

Four Months' Operational Service

After a short spell with 'Treble One' Squadron at Croydon and Debden, Sergeant Ray Sellers 'bought it' on 26 August 1940 and ended up in hospital at Debden. He was on patrol in his Hurricane at about 15,000 ft over Essex when the squadron engaged the enemy. Each Hurricane pilot singled out an enemy bomber, at the same time attacking and breaking away in a dive at maximum speed. By the time one recovered from the dive the sky was usually empty of aircraft and it was folly to attempt to climb back up for a search and possible second go. Sergeant Sellers learnt this on his second engagement when he made the fatal mistake of climbing back into the sky for a second go. His single Hurricane was climbing laboriously when suddenly two Me 110s made a head-on attack. They closed with their cannons spitting death and despite evasive action the Hurricane

Hurricanes of 'Blue Section' 111 Squadron, 19 August 1940. Sergeant Sellers is flying the aircraft coded JU-N from Debden after the squadron moved from Croydon to reform. The photograph is a bit tatty because it was in Ray Seller's tunic pocket when he was shot down and after the Sick Bay suffered a direct hit his belongings were temporarily buried in rubble.

Sergeant Pilot Ray Sellers – 1940.

was badly damaged. However, it remained airworthy long enough for Sellers to start a gliding approach on Martlesham Heath airfield, but having lost glycol, oil and fuel in the attack the Hurricane began to shudder and it finally went out of control from a hundred feet or so over a stretch of wooded heath and seconds later crash landed. The fighter broke its back on impact yet miraculously Sellers was able to walk away from the crash. Sergeant Pilot Sellers then spent a short period in hospital at Debden during which time the hospital was hit by a stick of bombs and partially destroyed. It was as if the Luftwaffe came to finish the job.

However, they did not succeed and after being hospitalized, a short spell of leave ensued, followed by a few rehabilitation flights at Drem near Edinburgh in Scotland. Then came a posting to No 46 Squadron at Stapleford Tawney, near Chigwell in Essex. This fighter airfield was a satellite for North Weald and came under No 11 Group. Sergeant Pilot Sellers arrived at Stapleford Tawney on 18 September 1940 as a replacement pilot and on the day he arrived Sergeant G. W. Jeffreys was shot down

Course No 18 at No 8 Advanced Flying Training School at Montrose, May 1940. Ray Sellers is top left. He was at Montrose from 9 April to 25 July 1940, followed by three weeks at No 6 OTU, Sutton Bridge, converting to Hurricanes. He joined 111 Squadron on 17 August 1940 with 228 hours flying in his log-book, 34 hours on Hurricanes'

so he was badly needed. Contrary to popular opinion, much of the patrol work was pretty routine although the possibility of action was always there. Out of 82 operational sorties only seventeen of them resulted in enemy contact and probably less than half-a-dozen would have involved anything in the nature of a dogfight. The Hurricane squadron was acting as a decoy at 20,000 to 25,000 ft to tempt high-flying Messerschmitt 109s to attack them so that they, in turn, could be attacked by even higher-flying Spitfires whilst their attention was distracted. On most of these patrols Sergeant Sellers was employed as a 'weaver' flying to the rear of the rest of the squadron and slightly above keeping a constant watch for enemy aircraft and alerting the squadron leader of any sightings – a much more interesting job than being a wing man. Sergeant Pilot Ray Sellers recalls those hectic wartime fighter days:

'My earliest recollections are of two Sergeant pilot veterans of the brief Norway campaign, who had, I believe, flown off HMS *Glorious* before she was sunk in the North Sea whilst bringing aircraft and personnel home to UK. These were Sergeant "Tubby" Earp and his friend Sergeant Gooderham, but who was grounded because his eyes had been temporarily damaged by the heat of an incendiary bullet which had passed through his cockpit and had narrowly missed his head.

'Action stemmed mainly from standing patrols – mostly over Essex and Kent – at heights between 15,000 and 25,000 ft, although log-book entries indicate that on the majority of patrols no engagements were reported and one can only assume that the squadron was acting as a deterrent in helping to keep enemy bombers and fighters at a considerable height rather than allowing them to dive unchallenged on targets in and around London. In most instances Me 109s had the advantage of height over the Hurricane and of speed in a dive, so that it was mostly when combat was joined that it was possible to exploit the manoeuvrability and robustness of the Hurricane. Two occasions are recorded – on 27 October and 1 November – when patrols were flown at 29,000 ft and 31,000 ft respectively and the aircraft were wallowing through the air, about as effectively as flying elephants. On the second occasion the squadron was attacked over Dover from above and behind by a flight of Me 109s and at least one Hurricane was damaged – mine!

'At that time reports were circulating that British pilots taking to their parachutes were being attacked by the enemy on their way earthwards. Consequently, wherever possible, protection was given by Hurricanes and Spitfires. On 27 September 1940, I was able to perform this role after an engagement with Me 109s near Rochford at about 15,000 ft. It was later a pleasure to meet the pilot concerned who had been badly burned in the process of baling out, but lived to tell the tale.

'An abiding memory is the familiar one of a sky full of aircraft one minute and completely empty seconds later after an evasive turn or dive. Conversely, it was possible to feel completely alone and yet be within seconds of being attacked. Constant vigilance particularly above and behind was essential for survival which entailed much screwing of the neck and weaving of the aeroplane. The mirror above the cockpit was too small and subject to too much vibration to be reliable.

'Another feature which comes to mind was the intense cold which gradually penetrated fur-lined boots, flying suits and gloves during a one-and-a-half-hour patrol at 20,000 ft in the autumn of 1940. My logbook records that on 28 November over Maidstone even the constant speed unit froze solid at 2,200 rpm which was disconcerting with numerous enemy fighters in sight overhead.

'Officially, I believe, the Battle of Britain ended on 31 October but logbook entries give no such indication and an entry on 30 November records an engagement over Dungeness at 21,000 ft with nine Me 109s which attacked the squadron from above and behind, during the course of which two of our pilots were obliged to bale out – a Sergeant Walker and Pilot Officer Ambrose.

'The squadron commander during this latter period was Squadron Leader A. C. Rabagliati, DFC (later Wing Commander DFC and Bar) who was killed in action in 1943. I took my leave of him and No 46 Squadron when posted to Flying Training Command in January 1941.'

Sergeant Pilot Ray Sellers logged 122 flying hours during the Battle of Britain and eventually managed to clock up over 3,000 flying hours by the end of the war. As he says: 'I was one of the lucky ones!'

Flight Lieutenant Sellers in 1944. The ribbons are the Air Force Cross (left) and the 1939–45 Star (right).

CHAPTER ELEVEN

A Canadian on a Fighter Station

Many Canadians wanted to get in and fight right from the start. One Canadian who did was Herbert Curotte from Campbellton, New Brunswick. He disembarked at Liverpool from the *Duchess of Athol*, a former CPR liner on which the Canadians had crossed the Atlantic after leaving Halifax, Canada, in convoy. Their first destination was Middle Wallop in Hampshire. No 1 RCAF assembled here upon their arrival on 20 June, they were duly herded together like cattle, photographed and Identity Cards issued.

Following this procedure they were assigned various duties pending further move. One duty was laying false flare paths, using metal cans with long spouts which incorporated a wick, holding about a half a gallon of paraffin oil (kerosene to the Canadians and coal oil to the Yanks). The false flare path crews were taken by lorry away from the main airfield, to a remote field, usually occupied by sheep or haystacks and the flare path party would lay the cans in two parallel lines similar to the underground lights illuminating today's modern runways. The quantity of cans varied according to the length of the runway required – it could be fifty or more.

The procedure was the same for the actual runway flare path for dealing with their own aircraft but in this case there was also a mobile

Hurricanes of No 1 (F) Squadron, RCAF at Prestwick.

The Canadians arrive at Middle Wallop and are interviewed by the Press.

generator and floodlight at the touchdown end. The equipment also included a wireless set tuned to the frequency of their own fighters. This set was set up anywhere, sometimes in the lorry that brought the mobile generator and floodlight equipment. The required number of 'erks' would be spaced out so that when their own fighters returned, and after firing the required colour of the day by Very pistol for identification, the detailed airmen would run from can to can lighting same. At the final approach the floodlight would be momentarily switched on lighting the path for the oncoming fighter.

However, occasionally the Luftwaffe would join the circling fighters, noting the colour identification. The German intruder would slip in last, dropping whatever bomb load he had. His tail gunner would 'dust' the airfield and the light would go out in one hell of a hurry. The flare path personnel would run in all directions.

The personnel for these flare path duties were preferably one control officer – you could compare his ancient duties to the present ground control approach officer; two Sergeants or Corporals, floodlight operator, generator attendant, usually two electrician 'erks' and a number of airmen ('erks') for the running and lighting of the cans. The 'erks' always did the running … but everyone ran if any bombs fell. At the false flare paths the personnel remained at a very safe distance from the cans which, from the air in the dark of night, indicated to the German intruders an outlined runway and on a few occasions they bombed the false flare paths. 'One would feel quite heroic at our deception leading to his senseless efforts', said Herb Curotte.

Most personnel liked flare path duty because they felt they were part of the action. In the RAF stores at Middle Wallop someone had put up the following notice: 'Cans complete with wicks, Mark 1 flare path for the use of: Ref No 000. CARE TO BE TAKEN WHEN ISSUING TO CANADIANS who have been known to use them as MILD & BITTER containers!'

During July 1940 the Canadians of No 1 (Fighter) Squadron, Royal Canadian Air Force, began to arrive at RAF Croydon in Surrey. At first they were housed in a hangar with their sleeping quarters arranged over the hangar space, but after a week their sleeping quarters were changed to a large building that at one time had been a school house. This was a lovely old building which the Canadians could reach by walking across Purley green. The old school house had been designed with French windows to many of the rooms. In the same sleeping quarters as 'Herb' Curotte and his section was their Pay Corps Sergeant. He was attached to their unit from the Canadian Pay Corps. It was much later before the Royal Canadian Air Force developed their own account section. In the early days it was no small task looking after the pay records of a squadron. Canadian funds had to be converted into pounds, shillings and pence. Furthermore married allowances had to be computed, and if any mistake, the Pay Corps Sergeant would get letters from the authorities. Leave pay and paybooks had to be arranged. In short, his life was one continuous misery.

As a result of it all, the Pay Corps Sergeant had developed stomach ulcers. Occasionally to relieve the stress he would take a night on the town. On one particular night he had done it too well. After duly retiring, fully dressed, he awoke when nature called. It was a warm July evening and the Sergeant proceeded, as if by radar, towards the French windows which were open … forgot he was on the second floor, started the watering process as he was going in

The dispersal area at Prestwick.

mid air. Landing in the flower beds below he soon came to reality in no uncertain terms or language. 'On hearing his shouts some of us woke up,' said Curotte, 'and we dashed to his rescue. Fortunately, no fractures, but needless to say, morning mess was "pride goeth before his fall" and the poor Sergeant was continually asked: "Did he injure the most important part of the male anatomy?"'

After seeing out the Battle of Britain at Northolt No 1 (Fighter) Squadron RCAF was transferred to Prestwick, in Ayrshire. Upon arrival the Canadians found that the station had no accommodation for them, and they were lodged in private billets. Edward Curotte had the good fortune to be assigned to a family by the name of Henderson. As a senior NCO, that had maybe something to do with it: 'My stay was very pleasant,' he said, 'real porridge in the morning. Mr Henderson was a devotee of the famous poet Robbie Burns and he would recite Burns poetry from memory, with his broad Scots accent, it took sometime before I could decipher what it was all about. To me it was the best secret cipher we could have used, no Jerry in his right mind could have understood any operational order.

'A rather funny incident occurred the very first night. It was rather cool, not having central heating, with the usual fireplaces for most rooms. In any event Mrs Henderson, in her kindness, had placed a stone jug filled with boiling water at the foot of the bed. She presumed we knew such items existed. However, once ensconced in bed, and starting the usual stretch towards the end of the bed, my feet met with the jug. Recoiling in terror, with a shout,

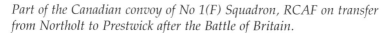

Part of the Canadian convoy of No 1(F) Squadron, RCAF on transfer from Northolt to Prestwick after the Battle of Britain.

Sergeant Curotte stops for a shave – one must keep up one's appearance – whilst in transit to Prestwick, Scotland.

I jumped out of bed. It flashed through my mind my feet had encountered some hidden rat or viper. Some members of the family came running, once the matter came to light we all shared a good laugh.'

During his stay at Prestwick Curotte had the good fortune to meet an older person by the name of Matthew Brown, who was a building contractor. He had an Austin Seven and additional rations of petrol. This good Samaritan would take Curotte through the Ayrshire countryside and they even had a visit to the Robbie Burns' cottage.

From Prestwick the Canadians of No 1 (F) Squadron RCAF were transferred to Castletown, near Thurso in Scotland, where they spent a harsh winter. They were very much exposed to the elements and the Nissen huts in which they were billeted were cold and hard to heat with only a small coal furnace using bituminous coal which was delivered in great lumps. Some unfortunate 'erk' was detailed – mostly as a minor punishment – to make the rounds of the huts to see that the furnaces were replenished. With a large coal hammer the 'erk' would break the large lumps of coal down to furnace-door size. The 'erk' would do this inside the Nissen hut, and pieces of

The Armament Warrant Officer of No 1 (F) Squadron RCAF performs another very necessary function!

Sergeant Curotte poses outside his Nissen hut at Castletown. (Note the small chimney in the centre of the roof.)

coal would fly in all directions. At 04:00 hours those who had managed to drop off to sleep were rudely awakened by the sound of flying debris hitting the metal sides of the Nissen hut.

No 1 Canadian Squadron personnel were trucked daily from their Nissen huts adjacent to Sir Archibald's Castle to the airfield at Castletown, which was about two miles south-east of the town. It was a very remote airfield with icy winter gales blowing in from the north. The squadrons at Castletown were for the defence of Scapa Flow and Northern Scotland, but the Canadians heard other stories: 'Service rumours had it that we were there to patrol the ships or fleet at Thurso against a presumed gas attack', said Curotte. By the time No 1 Canadian Squadron was taken off operations in October it had thirty kills and 43 damaged to its credit. The squadron had lost ten Hurricanes and three pilots in action. At Castletown their luck was frozen out and all they could claim were near misses. They could not catch the Germans but Sergeant Herb Curotte did manage to catch pneumonia.

It was always cold in the morning. To start the day there were no parades, only a rudimentary roll call. There was no place to go in any event. Servicing the fighters was done outside, the reason for the so-called tents. Sleeves were put on aircraft wings to prevent night accumulation of either ice or snow and therefore accelerate possible take-offs without too much delay. The Hurricanes had no deicing equipment. The cookhouse, a so-called Aladdin stove-operated van, did not give the cook much chance. The men only had portable showers and lack of entertainment and facilities finally got to them.

For some unknown reason, RAF Driffield, a bomber airfield in Yorkshire, suddenly had a change of role and when it reopened in January 1941, No 13 Group, Fighter Command, had taken over. In February 1941, No 1 (Fighter) Squadron RCAF arrived from Castletown. The Canadians were not 'over the moon' with the new

The Canadians of No 1 (F) Squadron were trucked daily from their Nissen huts to the airfield at Castletown. This one didn;t make it.

posting for their quarters were in a filthy condition. Sergeant Herb Curotte was out of his sickbed and had travelled with the squadron down to Driffield. They were never told what their role was at the former bomber airfield: 'This was obviously in the secrets of the "gods",' said Curotte, 'quite rightly so, but doubt plays havoc with troop morale.'

On 1 March 1941, No 1 (Fighter) Squadron RCAF moved to Digby, a fighter airfield in Lincolnshire, where the unit was renumbered No 401 (Fighter) Squadron. The Royal Air Force had allocated a special block of numbers to the dominion air forces, the Royal Canadian Air Force squadrons 'overseas' were assigned the No 400 series.

As the Canadians began to get themselves organized at Digby the Luftwaffe paid them a sneak visit and caught them with their trousers down, literally in the case of one Flight Sergeant. The Flight Sergeant had developed the habit of taking his shower at noon to avoid morning and evening crowds. On this particular day Flight Sergeant Herbert Curotte had returned to his barracks after Mess for the usual noon rest, and was reading a *Reader's Digest*, when

A cold start to the morning – Hurricanes of No 1 (F) Squadron at Castletown in December 1940.

suddenly all hell broke loose: 'Our friend Jerry had sneaked in under cloud cover', said Curotte. 'Our barracks were not far from the main entrance, where he let off his load, of what I think were 250s. In any event it blew out the windows in my barrack, also lifted much debris in large chunks, a piece of which, fell on, and through the somewhat flimsy wartime barrack roof of the unit in which the Flight Sergeant was showering.

'We of course were all assigned particular shelters by numbers … my compatriot, in the excitement as well as the "buff" ran out of the shower block towards the first bomb shelter already occupied by mixed personnel, namely WDs. He arrived as God had created him – out of breath and out of clothes, to the great merriment of all concerned. It was usual to have a few service blankets in shelters, and someone with the usual presence of mind wrapped one of them around the naked Flight Sergeant. No warning of an attack had been given but the "all clear" was sounded. The Chiefy was taken back to barracks surrounded by male friends, complete with blanket serving as a Roman toga. Needless to say he took a lot of ribbing in the Mess for many days, being introduced as the "naked angel" etc.'

However, not everyone was as lucky as the Flight Sergeant for the enemy aircraft had scored a direct hit on a small Austin lorry, killing the driver and one airman from 402 Squadron, Royal Canadian Air Force. Fate has strange ways in one's life. The young Canadian airman had been waiting for the bus into Lincoln but had been offered a ride in the service lorry just a minute before the attack. The bus was a few minutes late and was not harmed. A full military funeral was held for those killed in the raid.

The war brought heartaches for many, and Sergeant Herbert Curotte was no exception. 'However, regardless of the amenities, hospitality, pleasures of service life, for me newly married, having left a small wonderful baby girl back home in Canada, I cannot deny the constant apprehension in one's mind. How would it all end, would one see one's little family again … how long would the separation be … one would wake up from a dream having seen his little girl … letters from home would detail her new ventures, walking etc. If a sacrifice was made for one's country … this was it … the loneliness of personal feelings that cannot be shared. Fortunately for me a few months later I was promoted to Flight Sergeant became supernumerary to the Squadron Establishment and together with others of the same category was repatriated to home establishment.

The winter dress was used at Castletown during the winter of 1941. It kept ice and snow off the aircraft to eliminate time loss in removing ice etc in the event of hurried requirement. Kerosene heaters were used to provide relative comfort for servicing. Obviously they were not placed on Sections which were at readiness, however at the time readiness was minimal.

The Battle of Britain had been won – it would be nice to say that all was at peace with the world, but to the contrary war was just starting in earnest. Squadrons were being reorganized and new ones formed, intruder and night squadrons and 'Rhubarbs' initiated. Royal Canadian Air Force personnel were being reassigned to various squadrons and there was an air of uncertain feeling only a service person can appreciate. There was all sorts of 'gen', some true and some 'duff'. But, it was true that Curotte was to be repatriated and he continues the story: 'So, on a beautiful July day, around noon to be exact, and after messing, we, the Canadians, were assembled for roll call, rather unusual for that time of day. Once duly formed, the officer detailed, placed, or called the men at ease, stated briefly that a certain number of personnel were assigned for repatriation. A list was read and the ones involved advised they had two hours to obtain clearances from various sections, pack their gear, to be ready for entrainment for about three in the afternoon. We were provided with a packed lunch by the Mess which obviously indicated the journey would be of some duration. Destination of course was not identified ... so on board we loaded and away we went ...

'Personally I had mixed feelings, I had enjoyed and still enjoyed Digby ... on the other hand one always has a certain longing for home. Food in the UK had become a problem. I therefore with others dreamt of steaks, cakes, and ice cream, cold beer, not being

Rehearsal of Firing Party for the funeral of the young airman from 402 Squadron who was killed by the bomb dropped at the entrance of Digby aerodrome in 1941. There was no siren warning and the bomb demolished a small Austin truck, in which the airman was travelling.

the least. So it was likened to the chap who sees his mother in law going over the cliff with his new Buick that I took the new situation!

'During the train journey we were then advised that owing to the great Empire Training Scheme, starting in earnest back in Canada, the service was in need of experienced personnel. We noted that each branch of the technical sections were represented by senior men. So away we went into the night. With daylight we duly arrived in Manchester! I forgot frankly the name or number of the Repatriation Depot, but I do recall the hospitality of the Mess and its well stocked bar with every conceivable brand for the welfare of *homo sapiens* in uniform. The Repatriation Depot personnel were, we were soon to find out, in frequent contact with ships of various registry and would replenish their bar stocks in various schemes and ways!

'The barracks were very rudimentary indeed ... wooden frame two-tier bunks with some sort of wire mesh as bottoms for the proverbial RAF, so-called "biscuits". However the hospitality of the Mess made up for the rather stark accommodations! The latter led to a rather personal humorous episode which I will describe shortly.

'Manchester had been extensively bombed ... a group of us decided to view the City in style. As usual in a group there is always one type who rises above the others as well as the occasion. Somehow Slim Burgess (his real name) managed to hire no less than a Rolls-Royce, somewhat vintaged but still a Rolls. With adequate fortification we started our tour of Manchester! The damage inflicted now can be said was extensive. I recall the side of one hospital which had been sliced from roof to basement as though with a knife by a Jerry bomb, only to explode at basement level. The damage was so extensive that we no longer could enjoy high spirits with appreciation, for we could not help thinking what the population must have gone through, so back to the Mess we went to try and forget what we had observed.

'It was during the day or two we were at the depot; that one night having had one over the eight as the Scottish so well describe, that I went back to barracks on instruments. I had been assigned a top bunk ... being rather heavy this had been a mistake! In any event during the night nature called. Somehow, being accustomed to lower accommodation I forgot the top bunk position, rolling out about 2 am. Obviously I fell to the wooden floor. The barracks on flimsy bottoms shook with a vengeance once I hit the floor. All other occupants of course had had their share of experience with bombings from the various places they came from. Thinking a bomb had hit the unit ... most wakened, and without further ado, made one hell of a rush for the exterior! I did not dare explain what had occurred as one would not live it down for some time! So after many enquiries most believed a delayed bomb had gone off somewhere in the vicinity ... it was back to the chicken wire bunks!

'After what I remember was a day or two of good food and good refreshments we entrained once more for a journey in the night ... destination of course unknown. There is a somewhat morbid feeling, at least with me, to leave for destination unknown ... in any event we wound up in Gourock or Greenock to board the SS *Volendam*, a ship of Dutch registry ... ha my friend once more luxury! The ship had not been through the cruel conversion to a troop carrier. There was even a souvenir shop aboard and I duly purchased various small souvenirs to take back to Canada. The food was excellent, we were four to a cabin and we looked forward to a pleasant journey back home! My boy come to your senses ... this is the military. As we sailed on we noted the weather getting colder, until one fine morning we awoke to see a city perched on some hills or mountains. Through the usual fast shipboard guff we found ourselves in Reykjavick; but without permission to go ashore. We were told it was a transfer point. We would board a larger ship via

The same Firing Party under Warrant Officer Syd Collins for the funeral.

lighters. With us was a Flight Sergeant Alec Laxstall, and he was of either Norwegian or Swedish descent. In Canada he was from the West. A more powerful chap I have yet to meet … he had joined the permanent RCAF from a farm on the prairies … so in some fashion or bribery or brute strength, he managed to join the landing party of officers, who obviously went ashore for official purposes. He returned to entertain us with his sightseeing tour.

'We remained at anchor for one night … then suddenly we had to pack up, and I was horror-struck as we were ordered down a rope mesh on the leeside of the ship on to lighters … a short trip to a large ship fitted with large guns etc etc … once more the fear of the landlubber airman as we climbed, with pack, up this time, on similar rope meshing, to board the SS *Ausonia*. Quickly we learned we were part of a large convoy … the *Ausonia* was an armed merchant cruiser and the main defence of the convoy! How many aboard I forget or maybe never knew … there was RAF of all types proceeding to Canada for training etc … We were escorted by sailor personnel to what I can only describe as the bowels of the ship. She was a troop transport … hammock on steel hooks side by side, so close, that when the ship rolled the least bit, your bottom struck the other fellow's bottom. Rolling in and out of a strung hammock is an art practised by sailors … to an air force type it proved an exercise in balance, semi-judo with the usual landing on your arse on the steel deck!

'In any event I was assigned a location near some steel box marked in large red letters "DANGER". My immediate enquiry was that this was one of the ammunition storage boxes, feeding the gun on the upper deck … Not being a naval type I said, like many others, to hell with this and would quietly climb to the upper deck and sleep in more security until we were told this was against rules and orders! We were further advised that in the event of hostility developing in the convoy we were to remain well below … I shall never forget the feeling … somewhat akin to the bomb shelters which I always detested and avoided if at all possible … this was the only time I envied the infantry ie, if you are about to get it, let it be in the open.

'After a few days at sea most began the usual sickness. Fortunately I am not subject to sea sickness, but I am not slip proof and, with the decks awash from both the fog and you know what … plus the odour of the steaming mess we were served, I certainly did not cost the liner much in the way of food.

'Whether it was for practice or the real thing, we were of course never told, *Ausonia* which up to now had maintained the speed of the slowest ship, put on a burst of speed … we were told to proceed "below" in naval jargon and one of the bloody guns was fired. I know now how a trapped animal feels ... well below decks, close to the now identified powder magazine, I looked forward to a speedy trip to glory! In any event nothing further developed and possibly it was all part of a sea practice, I still shudder however, when I recall the episode. Water was rationed, so many times per day for both drinking and personal hygiene. After the odours (various) from the troops, crew, and the ship itself, I did not care what I gave off in the way of odour. Obviously there was no "liquid" messing which could make one forget ... it was temperance all the way.

'Oh blessed be the good living airmen ... for some day they shall see Halifax ... and so it was after six or seven days in convoy when I identified the Canadian coast! Blessed be the meek ... so after much procedural landing officialdom yours truly finally "kissed" the pavement of the Halifax Harbor! We were home! Thence on to a complete train all to ourselves travelling in daylight...with serving waiters, etc, etc. The journey between Halifax and Ottawa, our destination, is a day and a night. At the end, the dining car conductor made the diner available to us with "eat up boys", we are about to reach Montreal ... so into celery, cold beer, etc, all courtesy of the railway line, or kindhearted conductor ... when you are well off never enquire too close!

'At Ottawa, specifically Rockcliffe RCAF Station, we were advised to ask for our preferred posting ... I wanted to get to the West Coast, ie, British Columbia, with the usual perverse sense of humour the service posted yours truly to a flying boat squadron at Dartmouth, Nova Scotia, across from Halifax where I had just disembarked!

'The last humorous episode at Rockcliffe ... we were duly lined-up in a hangar ... for so-called medical examination ... a young Doctor, may God rest his soul, was standing at a table with a Medical Orderly ... as we advanced we were told to lower our trousers for rectal examination. Experience had taught the Service from World War I days that haemorrhoids were prevalent and many pensions had been paid for the condition ... this time the great father was making sure ... in any event, air service is not trench warfare but the usual bureaucracy prevailed. I can still see our young Doc with the Orderly handing him the proverbial rubber glove ... (finger) he would duly stick the index into a large petroleum jar ... for ease of entry and smartly rammed ... you would reflex at attention ... some with a shout ... depending on the sphincter fit! Now I knew I was back home! To this day I think this Doctor must hold the record for keel cruising!'

CHAPTER TWELVE

The Hurri-bomber

In late March 1941 the battle cruisers *Scharnhorst* and *Gneisenau* reached Brest. Immediately a round-the-clock watch was put on the two battle cruisers to prevent a breakout. It was not practicable with heavy fleet units so it was aircraft. A nightly line patrol by one radar-equipped Wellington from dusk to dawn; a daily crossover patrol by one ASV Sunderland or Hudson from one hour after dawn to two hours after dusk; one daily pre-dusk visual reconnaissance off the Rade de Brest and one nightly patrol by a torpedo Beaufort.

Despite the laborious air patrols the battle cruisers *Scharnhorst* and *Gneisenau* and the cruiser *Prinz Eugen* made a break for it on 12 February 1942. Hitherto one or all of them had been in dry dock since April 1941. The German ships went down the English Channel from Brest and got back to Germany more or less intact. The Germans had blacked out the United Kingdom radar and picked a period of very bad weather to do the operation.

Air and naval attack had failed utterly to arrest the progress of the enemy ships and this caused quite a flap in high places and many changes. After the *Scharnhorst* and *Gneisenau* incident in February 1942, Coastal Command made a new attempt to organize anti-shipping activities on a sound basis: Fighter Command operated Hurricane-bombers in the Strait of Dover.

At the time of the breakout from Brest by the German ships, Squadron Leader Robert (Bob) Morrow was at Warmwell in Dorset to pioneer the use of the Hurricane as a fighter-bomber on selected targets. Morrow was Commanding Officer of No 402 Squadron, Royal Canadian Air Force. They had arrived at Warmwell on 5 November 1941 from Southend, where they had test flown the Hurricane armed with two 250 lb bombs.

When the bombs had arrived at Southend on 13 October 1941, the pilots of No 402 Squadron RCAF were sitting at dispersal on readiness and they could not believe their eyes when the three tractors, each towing two bomb trailers loaded with four 250 lb bombs pulled up in front of them. 'Whose cocked this one up', shouted one of the pilots. They all broke out laughing at the stupidity of the top brass for sending a load of bombs to a Hurricane fighter squadron. But, their laughter died away when Squadron Leader 'Bob' Morrow appeared and informed them that there had been no mistake, and that the bombs were indeed for them. 'From now on,' he said, 'we will be known as Hurri-bombers'.

The following day Morrow's Hurricane was armed with two 250 lb bombs and it was manoeuvred to the far end of the airfield to give him maximum length of take-off run. Chocks were then put under the wheels and four groundcrew held the tail down. Four more held on to the wings and two stood by to pull the chocks away. Morrow put the flaps half-way down and opened up the throttle, and then, at almost maximum rpm he gave the 'all clear' and everyone jumped out of the way. The Hurri-bomber roared down the runway and was soon airborne. It was a successful trial flight and the pilots soon discovered that the bombs had no appreciable effect on the flying characteristics of the Hurricane.

On the morning of 4 November 1941, Bob Morrow briefed his pilots for a low-level raid on a German airfield at Berck-sur-Mer in France. 'Our job is to get the hangars,' said Morrow, 'and we will come into the target area at 100 ft.' This was the first Hurri-bomber raid and it was successfully carried out.

On 16 February 1942, a few days after the *Scharnhorst* and *Gneisenau* broke out from Brest, a recce Spitfire spotted, again in bad weather, five of the German escorting destroyers returning to Brest. They were not seen until they were in the Cherbourg area. Immediately the German ships were sighted Squadron Leader Morrow was contacted at Warmwell and asked to take as many aircraft as possible to Perranporth in Cornwall, which was only a few miles from Land's End. 'At that time we were very low on aircraft,' said Morrow, 'we were about to convert to Spitfires – which we did on 4 March – and only had eight serviceable aircraft and only GP bombs with eleven-second delay fuzes.'

Squadron Leader Bob Morrow's Hurricane while with No 402 Squadron RCAF at Digby in 1940.

The pilot watches his Hurri-bomber being loaded up by the groundcrew.

Previous experience in attacking the battle cruisers *Scharnhorst* and *Gneisenau* at Brest suggested that the chances of doing serious damage with existing bombs was remote. Nevertheless, Bob Morrow flew to Perranporth with his eight Hurri-bombers where he was told to try and intercept the German ships. He hurriedly briefed his pilots and he was given an excellent course to fly by the Ops Room. As it was bound to be a night return in bad weather Morrow left two Hurricanes behind.

Bob Morrow takes up the story: 'We headed out at about 1,500 ft, which was the ceiling, and in bad visibility. We were escorted by a squadron of Spitfires. About ten miles off the Isle de Batz, which is just off the French coast near Roscoff, we made a perfect interception. The five destroyers were in line astern and going flat out. We split into three groups and flew straight ahead at sea level. I think the destroyer crews were relaxing after a hard trip and felt safe in the poor weather, because they did not start firing until we were close in. When they did open up fire, all hell broke loose,

A Hurri-bomber Hurricane Mk IIb, BE485 *of No 402 (F) Squadron coded AE-W crossing the channel with two 250 lb bombs beneath the wings on an intruder sortie into occupied France.*

Close-up of Bob Morrow in the cockpit of his Hurricane, ready to take off on the first Hurri-bomber sortie.

especially with the 40 mm guns. Streams of red tennis balls, which, while hard on the nerves, were fairly easy to avoid by skidding and constantly dropping under their tracer.'

The Hurri-bombers attacked the German ships under a hail of shells and bullets. The Germans threw everything they could at Bob Morrow and his gallant pilots. Under Morrow's coolness they closed on their targets and the Spitfires reported that three bombs went off in two of the destroyers and they were credited with one sinking and one damaged. 'Due to the delay fuzes I did not see any bombs explode,' said Morrow, 'I was too busy getting the hell out of it and gathering up the squadron to head home. We were advised to land at Portreath in Cornwall, due to bad weather and lighting availability. My log-book shows the operation took 1 hour 40 minutes of which 40 minutes is night. Fuel was very low and one Hurri-bomber ran out and crashed on the airfield perimeter. I was given the Distinguished Flying Cross for this effort.'

Bob Morrow modestly says he was awarded the DFC for his effort. It was his cool leadership that got his squadron of Hurri-bombers in, and out, of the target area, which resulted in a very successful operation, carried out in very poor weather conditions and under very heavy fire. Bob Morrow pioneered bombing with the Hurricane and the technique of low-level bombing where a short fall would likely bounce it into the target became known as 'skip' bombing in the Pacific and this is probably as good an example of the use of the technique as could then be found.

CHAPTER THIRTEEN

They Shot Down the First Mistel

The two world wars were the proving grounds in promoting all kinds of innovations. The rapid evolution of the aeroplane is a classic example. By the outbreak of World War II, metal-framed-and-skinned aircraft had become general, and the monoplane had replaced the biplane for most purposes. Other novel features of the war years included the helicopter and the German V1 flying bomb, a pilotless aircraft. One of the strangest weapons developed during World War 2 was the Mistel (Mistletoe) composite aircraft. The whole combination was unofficially referred to as Vater and Sohn (father and son). The concept for the Mistel was for one unmanned aircraft to be loaded with explosives while a guiding fighter pilot flew in a separate aircraft attached above it. Once his target was in view the pilot detached his aircraft from the pilotless explosive-laden aircraft.

The seeds for these strange weapons were planted in Sweden, about the turn of the century, when Wilhelm Unge invented a device described as an 'aerial torpedo'. About 1909 the Krupp

Church Parade at Castle Camps for 410 Squadron RCAF.

armament firm of Germany purchased the patents. In 1931–32 gasoline/oxygen-powered rockets were made by the German Rocket Society. Wernher von Braun became the technical leader of a small group developing liquid-propellant rockets for the German Army. By 1937 the Dornberger-Braun team expanded to hundreds of scientists, engineers and technicians, and moved its operations from Kummersdorf to Peenemünde on the island of Usedom in the Baltic. Here the technology for a long-range ballistic missile was developed and tested. Technology had a tremendous social impact in the period 1900–45.

During World War 2 Germany made efforts to produce effective surface-to-air missiles. The Schmetterling, Enzian and Rheintochter were three under development but these were subsonic. Among the first air-to-surface guided missiles developed by the Germans were the radio-controlled, armour-piercing Fritz-X glide bombs launched from Dornier Do 217K-2 bombers which sank the Italian battleship *Roma* after its surrender to the Allies in 1944.

In early 1944 the Operations Staff of the Luftwaffe had decided that the Mistletoe project should continue. Tests had been carried out with the Ju 88A4/Me 109F-4 in late 1943 and these were successful enough to go a stage further. Warhead tests were then made at Peenemünde and a training base under the command of Hauptmann Horst Rudat was set up with five Mistels at Kilberg on the Baltic.

But the wind of change was blowing and the planned targets for the Mistels had to be changed when the Allies landed in Normandy in June 1944. The Mistels of KG101's unit were hurriedly ordered to St Dizier in France with orders to attack the invasion shipping. The Mistels were now at a great disadvantage and because of their lack of defence they were to operate at night.

The Allies had air supremacy at this period and many night fighter units were released from their defensive duties over Britain to fly protective patrols over the convoys and beachheads and keep a weather eye open for the approach of hostile aircraft which might interfere with the invasion bomber forces' operations in that area. One such night-fighter squadron on protective patrol duties in support of the invasion forces was No 410 (Cougar) Squadron, of the Royal Canadian Air Force. They were then operating from Hunsdon in Hertfordshire as part of No 85 Group.

At 22:35 hours on the evening of 14 June 1944, Flight Lieutenant Walter Dinsdale and his Radio Operator Jack Dunn, took off in their Mosquito XIII, *HK476* 'O' Orange, and set course for Fighter Pool

Mistel (Vater und Sohn), made up of an Fw 190 and a Ju 88. After parting the Fw 190 guided the bomb-laden Ju 88 on to its target by radio.

No 1, at the beachhead area. The weather was good, with a few broken clouds, and for some time no enemy action was reported. They were under control from a seaborne GCI unit and when they arrived over the beachhead they began to orbit. Vectored south, then on 100°, they followed the River Seine where bandits were reported about. Pilot Officer Dunn was busy watching for any sign of activity in his radar scope while Flight Lieutenant Dinsdale scanned the sky for any sign of visual contact. Vectored 280° they experienced heavy window on the screen of the aircraft's radar. Several contacts were obtained simultaneously. Suddenly Dinsdale's Radio Operator calmly announced: 'Bandits in your immediate area' and from the particular blip on his radar screen he vectored Dinsdale on to it, closing quite rapidly on the target. By now Dunn had got a fix on his radar screen: 'Bandit dead ahead and closing fast.' In fact, the target was moving so slowly that when Dinsdale saw it he had to put down wheels and flaps to avoid overshooting. When he got visual contact, he was at a range of 2,000 ft from the unidentified aircraft, flying at 11,000 ft. It was 23:35 hours then, exactly one hour after take-off.

Closing to 1,000 ft Flight Lieutenant Dinsdale positioned the Mosquito behind and under the target and identified it, with the aid of Ross night glasses, as a Junkers 88 with a glider bomb attached to the top of the fuselage. They speculated that the target must be an airborne launching platform for V1 buzz bombs.

While this strange flying monster of Hauptmann Rudat's unit was lumbering slowly in the direction of the Normandy beachhead, the Mossie closed in further to 750 ft, astern, and slightly below. Dinsdale could now see the superstructure of the combination but not very clearly. In fact, it consisted of two steel-tube struts attached to the Ju 88 wing main spars on each side of the fuselage, the forward strut being vertical and the aft strut being inclined forward, these attaching at their tips to the arms of a V strut connected to a fuselage mainframe, thus forming two inclined tripods. The apexes of the tripods were intended to marry up with connections on the mainspar of the above forming the upper component. A single strut supported the tail of the Messerschmitt 109 (which the Canadians did not recognize, thinking it was a glider bomb instead). They also failed to notice that the Ju 88 had not its usual nose section. When prepared for operations the nose section was replaced by a warhead using the same attachment points.

Dinsdale calmly took up a firing position and, speculating that the 'bomb' would be located on top of the Ju 88, he aimed at the starboard wing. A short burst of 32 rounds from his cannon caused a terrific explosion as the cockpit and port wing root of the Ju 88 burst into flames. The enemy aircraft banked slowly to port, then went down suddenly in a steep dive burning fiercely and leaving a trail of sparks all the way down. A lot of debris flew back in the direction of the Mosquito but they were fortunate in not having any of it strike their aircraft. All this had happened in the space of only a few minutes.

At 23:40 hours the Mistel hit the ground with a terrific explosion some 25 miles to the south-east of Caen, lighting up the whole countryside. It was not surprising when we consider that the warhead of the Ju 88 was of the hollow-charge type containing 3,800 lb of high explosive. The 2,200 lb steel core of this warhead had a theoretical armour penetration of 24 ft; in actual tests this core burst through some 60 ft of concrete! By way of comparison the V1 flying bomb was capable of delivering a 2,200 lb warhead.

Being satisfied with the destruction of the enemy aircraft, Mosquito 'O' Orange continued patrolling, but the rest of their sortie was uneventful and finally they landed back at base at 02:00 hours. During the debriefing period, Dinsdale and Dunn stuck to their story that they had shot down a Junkers operating as an airborne launching pad for a V1 and Dinsdale filled out the following official Form 'F' Personal Combat Report:

> '*Pilot*: Flight Lieutenant Dinsdale RCAF
> *Navigator*: Pilot Officer Dunn RCAF
> *We took off from base at 22:35 hours and set course for Fighter Pool No 1, at the beachhead area. Arrived at 23:20 and started to orbit, vectored south, then 100°, following Seine River. Told bandits were about, vectored 280°, and experienced heavy window. Several contacts were obtained simultaneously. Pilot obtained a visual immediately, at a range of 2,000 ft, height 11,000 ft, time 23:35 hrs. Closed to 1,000 ft, and identified, with the aid of Ross night glasses, as a Ju 88B; with a glider bomb attached to the top of the fuselage. Closed in further to 750 ft, astern and slightly below. Opened fire with a short burst. The cockpit and port wing root burst into flames immediately. Enemy aircraft banked slowly to port, then went down suddenly in a steep dive burning fiercely leaving a trail of sparks all the way down. It hit the ground with a terrific explosion, lighting up the whole countryside. Enemy burned on the ground. Combat took place at approx 11,000 ft, 25 miles south-east of Caen, at 23:40 hours. Enemy aircraft did no evasive manoeuvres during combat. I was controlled by FDT 217 Mobile GCI. Landed at base at 02:00 hours. I claim this enemy aircraft as destroyed.*'

The next day Flight Lieutenant Dinsdale and Pilot Officer Dunn were called to London for further debriefing. Obviously there was great interest in this first report of another possible Hitler secret weapon. It was only a few days later that a Mistel was observed flying in the day time and the true nature of this weapon was revealed to the Canadians. So was the story of this historical event during which Flight Lieutenant Dinsdale and Pilot Officer Dunn were the first fighters of World War II to shoot down one of these flying monsters, the Mistel. They had shot down the first German 'piggyback' flying bomb – incorporating an Me 109 mounted on an explosive-laden Junkers Ju 88. Dinsdale described the piggyback as: 'An awkward thing which lumbered along at about 150 mph. I recognized it as a Ju 88 but couldn't figure out what the thing was on the top.' During the same night 14–15 June 1944 another Mistel was brought down by a night crew of 264 Squadron, but this was later on.

Ten days after Dinsdale and Dunn's encounter with the Mistel, the other remaining Mistels attacked Allied shipping in the Seine Bay. They hit their targets but no ships were sunk. After this attack orders were issued to adapt 75 combinations, this time Focke Wulf 190A-6 or F8 were to be used with the Ju 88G-1. These Mistels were later used in small attacks against bridges and although many bridges were destroyed the Mistel units suffered severe losses.

The story of Walter 'Dinny' Dinsdale began at No 13 Elementary Flying Training School at St Eugene, Ontario, Canada in June 1942 where he trained on fleet before transferring on Harvard in August at No 2 SFI at Uplands, Ontario. When he was posted overseas at the end of his training in Canada, Dinsdale's log-book showed he had already 272 hours 25 minutes of flying to his credit.

In March 1943, Dinsdale commenced training at Spitalgate, near Grantham in Lincolnshire, England with No 12 (Pilot) Advanced Flying Unit, flying Blenheims until 17 May, when posted to No 54 Operational Training Unit where he trained on Beauforts and Beaufighters. It was at Charter Hall where he began flying with Sergeant Jack Dunn who became his Navigator/Radio Operator for the remainder of the war.

Now working as a team, Dinsdale and Dunn went training at Winfield, a satellite airfield to Charter Hall and at the end of August was posted to No 410 (RCAF) Squadron which was an operational night-fighter unit. The squadron was actually engaged in offensive operations into enemy-held territory by day and night to disrupt Nazi rail, road, canal and air traffic. In November, it was back again to the night defence of Britain. During the period November 1943–May 1944, known as the 'little blitz on Britain', the Cougars were able to come to grips with the Luftwaffe. On 19 October 1943, No 410 Squadron moved from Coleby Grange to West Malling, a few miles west of Maidstone in Kent. During the Battle of Britain, this area had become known as 'Hell's Corner'. The move brought the Cougars into No 11 (Fighter) Group, with which it was to remain until the spring of 1944. At the beginning of November 1943, No 410 moved again, from West Malling to Hunsdon in Hertfordshire, about 20 miles north of London. From there the Cougars moved again to Castle Camps in Cambridgeshire, and it was from this airfield that the Canadian crew Dinsdale/Dunn drew first blood. The night-fighter crew had made their first patrol on 31 October 1943 on Mosquito IIs and up to 3 February 1944 had made thirteen more patrols and scrambles on Mossie IIs and XIIIs (having transferred to the latter model in the middle of December 1943). During that period Jack Dunn had been promoted to Flight Sergeant and both Canadian flyers were now eager to come face to face with the Luftwaffe. Their chance came on the night 3–4 February 1944.

On that night, after quite a dull period, the enemy activity increased, and no less than 135 raiders came over. The squadron made fifteen sorties between 20:00 and 07:00, several crews going up twice during the night. Flying Officer Dinsdale and Flight Sergeant Dunn scrambled for the second time at 04:00 hours from Castle Camps.

They were under North Weald searchlight control when they were ordered to orbit at 23,000 ft. They went chasing about, investigating ack-ack fire and searchlight 'blobs' on the clouds when a contact was picked up. Dunn guided the Mossie to the target and Dinsdale closed in rapidly after visual contact. The aircraft was flying straight and level, scattering some 'window' and Dinsdale had to draw to port to prevent overshooting. The Mosquito was quite close to the target now and the Canadian flyers immediately identified it as a Ju 88. He was flying at 19,000 ft and was doing 220 mph. Dinsdale turned to attack when suddenly the Ju 88 turned straight at the Mossie. As the German aircraft grazed by them Dinsdale fought to regain control of the Mossie and they had a few desperate moments. After regaining control, Dinsdale returned to base. Dinsdale examined Mosquito *HK476* 'O' Orange and he remarked to Jack Dunn how lucky they had been. The following is his Personal Combat Report for that sortie:

'*Pilot*: Flying Officer W. G. Dinsdale RCAF

Observer: Flight Sergeant J. E. Dunn RCAF

We were scrambled at 04:00 hours from Castle Camps and landed at 06:30 hours. While under North Weald searchlight control, we were ordered by "Offside" to orbit "U" for Uncle, height 23,000 ft; told to go over to Maynard on Button "F". Gave Springler "D" for Dog. Instructed to go back to "Offside", where we received orders to proceed to "G" for George. From "G" for George, gauntleted 045° in direction of searchlight blobs on the clouds. No joy received. Investigated many

Pilots and crew of No 410 Squadron at Castle Camps. From left to right, Squadron Leader Red Sommerville (the Flight Commander) his navigator Robbie Robinson who was later killed, Flying Officer Mac MacKenzie and Deputy Flight Commander Flight Lieutenant Walter Dinsdale.

searchlight blobs on clouds and ack-ack fire. "Offside" gave information trade south, height 14–18,000 ft. Turned south-westerly, losing height to 19,000 ft. Contact obtained well below range 3 miles, proceeding in southerly direction. Reported to "Offside" and received permission to investigate. Closed in rapidly, interrogated and received no response. Visual obtained at 2,000 ft slightly below. No resins seen. Target flying straight and was identified as a Ju 88. Indicated air speed 220 mph at 15,000 ft. Experiencing mild window. I had just commenced to turn to starboard to get into position for attack, when enemy aircraft peeled off violently to port and headed directly for our aircraft. Enemy aircraft passed underneath grazing my starboard prop as he did so. Our aircraft went temporarily out of control. Regained control and dived to port. Many contacts obtained due to presence of window. Nothing further seen of enemy aircraft. Reported enemy aircraft probably damaged to "Offside". Time of interception was approx 05:15 hours. I claim this aircraft as damaged. I experienced no flak whatsoever during the engagement.

'Intelligence Officer's Report

An examination of Flying Officer Dinsdale's aircraft "O" by the Engineering Officer reveals that two blades of the starboard propeller have paint scraped from the tip, lateral scorings across the blade up to the widest section, zig-zag scorings up to the boss. There are also traces on the prop as of having rubbed against olive green or grey paint. The opinion of the Engineer Officer is that the marks have been caused by the blades of the propeller striking something which clung to them through one revolution, being drawn into the boss, and then thrown clear. It is suggested that some part of the Ju 88 such as the fin or tail plane was partly or completely severed on impact with the Mosquito's starboard propeller.

'In view of the above it is requested that on receipt of the report by the Technical Intelligence Officer, consideration be given to stepping this claim up to destroyed.'

During February 1944, Flying Officer Dinsdale flew on fourteen operational sorties but nothing more was seen of the enemy except for a sortie he flew on the 20th, teaming up with Pilot Officer Christie that time, and during which they came head on with a Ju 88 but Warrant Officer Miller, also of 410 Squadron, flew in his path preventing an attack. During that period Jack Dunn was promoted again, from Flight Sergeant to Pilot Officer, and during the spring and early summer many missions were executed though uneventful. Then came the invasion in June 1944 and with it a lot of activity.

On the first two nights of the invasion, Dinsdale and Dunn patrolled over the beachhead and did see much evidence of activity on the ground, numerous fires, and the flashes of guns and bombs that flickered like sheet lightning in the night sky, but the only AI contacts obtained were on Lancasters that filled the skies in great numbers. One hawk-eyed Lancaster gunner even put a few holes in Dinsdale's Mossie. After two more uneventful patrols on the 10th and 12th, they came to grips again with the Luftwaffe bringing down the first Mistel of World War 2, an historical event. This kill was the first confirmed one for the crew Dinsdale/Dunn and the 26th by the Cougars.

'O' Orange with its nose shot-off – Dinsdale's Mosquito which was hit while flying over Dunkirk. The Germans were by-passed at Dunkirk during the invasion and Dinsdale happened to stooge too close for comfort. Fortunately the shell exploded just in front of the armour plate or his careers would have ended abruptly.

Another nine uneventful patrols followed for Dinsdale and Dunn during June and July, and in August they met the Luftwaffe again. The newly-promoted Flight Lieutenant and his friend Jack Dunn were working as usual with Pool 2 in the western area that night when they were informed of 'trade' approaching from the east and given a course to intercept. Through some 'window' interference Dunn got a contact approaching head on. Dinsdale swung about, came in behind, and closing rapidly, soon identified an Me 110. It was carrying bombs externally but, unlike the Ju 88 they were suspended outboard of the engines. Dinsdale let off a longish burst at the enemy aircraft. It apparently missed. From dead astern he fired again. This time the starboard engine caught fire. With a start the Messerschmitt crew

Flight Lieutenant Walter 'Dinny' Dinsdale operating from Lille/Vendeville, France – November 1944.

woke up and the rear gunner fired a wild burst, while his pilot took violent evasive action. Dinsdale went down after him until his navigator cautioned him that they were approaching the ground rapidly. Yardley control also broke in with a warning that the Mosquito was getting very low. At 800 ft Dinsdale pulled the Mossie out of its dive, leaving the Me 110 still going down with its engine ablaze. After pulling out, the Cougar crew searched the ground for signs of a crash, but there were so many fires burning in the area around Avranches that no particular explosion could be distinguished. Yardley control, however, reported that while it could still plot the Mosquito it had no further contact on the enemy aircraft. Back at base Dinsdale claimed a probable with the request that, in view of the circumstances, consideration be given to upgrading.

In October, the Commanding Officer received the following letter from No 85 Group's Headquarters: 'Reference your letter 410/S.79/Air dated 9 October 1944, information has been received from Headquarters Fighter Command that Flight Lieutenant Dinsdale is credited with one Me 110 destroyed, his claim having been upgraded from "probably destroyed".' Also, as reference to this night of 3–4 August 1944, many important sources inexplicably credited the crew Dinsdale/Dunn with the downing of an Hs 126 though they never met such an aircraft!

In the middle of August Walter Dinsdale and Jack Dunn began training on the powerful Mosquito XXXs and flew their patrols with their new mounts at the end of the month. At the beginning of September the sojourn of 410 Squadron at Colerne ended. After weeks of hard fighting in Normandy the Allied forces had broken out of the beachhead and, wheeling eastward, were now driving ahead rapidly in pursuit of the Nazi Wehrmacht as they fell back on their Rhine defences. It was time for the night fighters to cross to the Continent and hunt in more distant skies. In preparation for the move, the Cougars returned to Hunsdon on 9 September. Here the squadron remained for a fortnight, shifting its patrols from the familiar areas of Normandy to Paris, Bruxelles, Antwerp, Liege, Maastricht, Arnhem, Nijmegen, etc. Dinsdale and Dunn flew a further 25 uneventful patrols to such areas during September, October, November and December of 1944. The only thing seen was a V2, and they could do nothing about it. Since 22 September, the Cougars were stationed in France (Amiens/Clisy), at B.48, moving to Lille/Vendeville (B.51) in November.

At 20:30 hours on the evening of 27 December, 'Dinny' Dinsdale (as he was nicknamed by his squadron pals) and Jack Dunn took off from the latter aerodrome to meet the Luftwaffe for the last time during their World War 2 careers. Patrolling for a short time over Sittard they were soon informed of a trade, heading south, and vectored after it. The Flight Lieutenant continues the story:

'A contact was obtained at a range of 3 miles ahead, target slightly above and descending. Our height at the time was 4,000 ft. We followed the target down, closing to 2,500 ft range, with target still ahead, 20° above – our height 1,500 ft above. No visual was obtained. GCI informed me that the target was 2,500 ft above. Jack informed me that "weapon" was partially bent and that he was unable to verify the target's elevation. The target entered the IAZ (ack-ack zone) and the chase was abandoned. We continued our patrol at a height of 4,000 ft and shortly afterwards were informed that FO Camaron "weapon" had bent and a vector of 240° was given. I asked the GCI to watch the heights closely on account of our "weapon" trouble. The target's height was given as 7,000 ft. I climbed up to 7,000 ft where a contact was obtained at a range of 3 miles, dead ahead, the elevation of which we were unable to determine. We continued the chase at angels 7, obtaining a visual of 2,000 ft range, 15° above, ahead, weaving gently. I closed to 300 ft range, directly below and identified as a Ju 88 night fighter. The enemy aircraft was carrying what appeared to be long range tanks outboard of the motors. The tank was very streamlined and faired into the wing. Identification was confirmed by Jack with the aid of night glasses. I fell back directly behind and opened fire from a range of 400 ft. Strikes were seen on the port side and the port engine burst into flames. The enemy aircraft then went into a slow turn to port and dived into the ground – exploding on contact. Position was approximately K.3878 (Helchteren area). GCI confirmed the kill stating they saw the enemy aircraft crash. No return fire was experienced. I claimed a Ju 88 destroyed. We were put on another chase immediately and obtained contact. Unfortunately, however, my port engine packed up due to debris in the radiator and I was forced to abandon the chase and return to base.'

This kill, the third confirmed for the crew Dinsdale-Dunn was a fine example of the perfect cooperation that often existed between ground controllers and the night-fighter teams. However for this Canadian night-fighting crew their World War 2 operational days were almost over and after doing another four uneventful patrols during December 1944, and January 1945, they were rested from operations. With Jack Dunn his Navigator, Walter Dinsdale saw his World War 2 flying career crowned by the award of the Distinguished Flying Cross which they received on 8 May 1945. The crew Dinsdale/Dunn was the eighth and last Cougar crew to be decorated simultaneously. The citation on which this award was made reads as follows:

'Flight Lieutenant Dinsdale as pilot and Flying Officer Dunn as navigator have taken part in a large number of operational sorties during which they have destroyed three enemy aircraft and damaged another. At all times they have displayed exceptional keenness for operational flying and a high degree of skill, courage and devotion to duty.'

During March 1945, Flight Lieutenant Dinsdale was transferred to No 1 Ferry Unit at Pershore in Worcestershire and he retired from the Air Force on 25 September 1945. He had enlisted on 21 November 1941 to serve his beloved Canada and the cause of the Allies. During seventeen months of operational service (September 1943 to January 1945), Walter Dinsdale had flown on 89 sorties against the enemy, meeting the Luftwaffe on only about a half dozen occasions, gaining four successes; quite a good percentage!

Enemy aircraft claimed by the crew Walter Dinsdale and Jack Dunn

Date	**Type**	**Area**
3–4 February 1944	1 Ju 88 damaged Ju88 A-4	Stapleford Tawney
14–15 June 1944	1 MiStel Me109F-4 confirmed	25 miles south-east of Caen
3–4 August 1944	1 Me 110 confirmed	North-east of Avranches
27–28 December 1944	1 Ju 88G confirmed	Helchteren area

CHAPTER FOURTEEN

Hurricane IId 'Tankbuster'

The land warfare of World War II was radically different from that of World War I. In the first great war the infantry predominated and were used as cannon fodder in ways which we now deplore. Against them were artillery, machine-guns, poison gas, minefields and mud. But during the war the tank was invented by the British.

When World War II began, many of our generals were still arguing about whether tanks were cavalry or artillery. However, while they argued a French Officer, named Charles de Gaulle, made the remarkable discovery that they were tanks! He wrote a textbook on how they could best be utilized in warfare. Neither the French nor the British took it seriously. But the Germans did, and the most

Firing Range Ground Party, Shandur, Egypt, No 6 Squadron RAF.

effective tank force proved to be the German, composed in 1939 of 3,195 vehicles, including 211 PzKpfw IVs. What made the German tanks so formidable was that instead of being divided between various infantry and cavlary tank units they were all concentrated in the Panzer divisions. With their tanks the Germans developed the Blitzkrieg – the lightning war. Combining it with the Schlieffen plan for invading France through the Low Countries, the Germans made short work of things in 1940. From then on tanks were tanks and the name of the game was Blitzkrieg.

Having invented the tank the next major problem was how to blow it up. A lot of time, money and effort was spent on finding ways of countering the tanks. Tank traps, ditches, minefields, and concrete obstacles were developed. 'Sticky' napalm bombs were dropped from ground-strafing aircraft. As the war developed, rockets came on the scene. But, before more powerful and longer-ranged and recoil-less rockets, came the 40 mm Simeon or Vickers 'S' Gun. These guns had been adapted from an earlier weapon system with a quite different application and they could well have been used for installation on motor torpedo boats.

In 1942 No 6 (Army Co-operation) Squadron was awaiting re-equipment. By early 1942, Middle East Command was over supplied with army cooperation squadrons, which in any case were becoming redundant with the emergence of No 239 Wing, as a pattern for reconnaissance-strike spearheads to give effective air support to armies. The Commanding Officer of No 6 Squadron was Wing Commander Roger Porteous and the Flight Commander was Squadron Leader Allan J. Simpson. Wing Commander Dru-Drury and an Armament Officer named Jeffries came out from England to Shandur on the Suez Canal where No 6 Squadron were located at that time. Their purpose was to teach the squadron how to use the Hurricane IId with which they had just re-equipped.

The Hurricane IId 'Tankbuster' was a Mark II with a different type of wing, one designed to carry a 40 mm cannon for tankbusting. It was armed with two

Spring 1942 – No 6 Squadron, awaiting Hurricane IId aircraft, practised airfield defence. This airman shows how close he came with a rifle-launched hand grenade. The rock was the target from about 100 yds.

A Hurricane IId.

.303 in Browning machine-guns in the wings, firing a sequence of armour-piercing, incendiary, tracer and high-explosive bullets. No ordinary ball ammunition. The main punch was the pair of Vickers Simeon guns, with fifteen rounds per gun, firing a 40 mm $2\frac{1}{2}$ lb armour-piercing projectile. It had a slug of soft metal in the base which plunged forward on impact into the conical hollow core, to force a sort of mechanical, rather than chemical, explosion or to give it another thump to make good its entry into the target. These guns were slung partly exposed on the underside of the wings, with a streamlined fairing to prevent too much interference with the airflow.

The projectile was able to penetrate the 20 mm armour plating on a German Mark III tank and to weld itself into the metal on the far side. The Hurricane IId 'Tankbuster' had a still air range of 480 miles and at 19,000 ft its maximum speed was 316 mph. Its service ceiling was 34,500 ft. Apart from the first few production machines, all Hurricane IIds had additional armour to protect the pilot, radiator and engine from small-arms fire.

Squadron Leader Simpson, the Flight Commander of No 6 Squadron, takes up the story: 'We didn't have long to train and we were desperately short of aircraft. But we set up two rails from a railroad, painted a life-sized tank on a piece of canvas, and secured it to the two vertical rails. That was our target practice.

'Then we listened to lectures on our new aircraft and its weapons system; tanks and their vital spots – tracks, bogey wheels, drive wheels, engine, fuel tanks, ammunition, crew; the tactics tank formations used; and the tactics we should use. Then we sent out a range safety party in a truck about ten miles into the desert, from our base at Shandur on the Suez Canal, and day after day we would fire at the target.

'We wangled some old captured Jerry tanks from the Army and put a can of gasoline inside one of them. Then we attacked it and the results were quite dramatic. Later we inspected the damage and

The captured German Mark III tank. Standing left is Wing Commander Roger Porteous and centre, with arms folded is Flying Officer Tony Morrison-Bell who later commanded the Squadron.

agreed that we had an effective weapon. Our skill level was also high; we had an average of more than seventy per cent hits, firing six to ten shots per attack, not counting the machine-guns.'

The aircraft were worth their weight in gold. One day at breakfast Flying Officer Fairbairn-McPhee, a white hunter and safari leader from Kenya, said to the Commanding Officer: 'You know, Sir, I think anyone who "bends" one of these new toys of ours should be dealt with severely.' Up to that time, the few that they had had not even been scratched. The CO told Mac to make sure that he wasn't the first to 'bend' one.

Later that day Mac was coming in to land when he suddenly had a funny feeling that something was wrong. He therefore decided to get down as quickly as possible and in his hurry to do so he forgot to let down the undercarriage. He made a perfect belly landing. His punishment was the laundry run. This entailed flying, in true Biggles style, their old patched up Audax biplane into Cairo or Alexandria while the rest of the squadron flew the Hurricane IIds.

The Hurricane IId 'Tankbuster' made its operational début with No 6 Squadron in the Western Desert on 6 June 1942. By 16 June they had made 37 sorties, immobilized 31 tanks and destroyed or severely damaged 28 large vehicles, some of them troop carriers. Throughout the retreat to El Alamein, the squadron still only had one flight of Hurricane IIds. Replacements were only keeping up with the losses. 'We had lost only one pilot killed,' said Squadron Leader Simpson, 'but later on it got worse. For every three Tankbusters that went out on a sortie, one was being shot down, one was being damaged, and one was coming back unscathed. The worst hazard we had to face was the 88 mm guns, mounted on truck platforms at the end of each flank of the tank V formations. Thankfully, many pilots who were shot down made it back to base, either by foot or other means, thus qualifying for the Winged Boot insignia.'

On one important operational sortie, Squadron Leader Billy Drake and his 'flying sharks' of No 33 Squadron, flew top cover for the Hurricane 'Tankbusters'. The three Hurricane IIds, piloted by Allan Simpson, Tony Morrison-Bell, and Mike Besly took off in formation from the sand strip at Gambut East and headed towards their targets in the Bir Hacheim area, where the Free French under General Koenig were surrounded. 'Our mission,' said Squadron Leader Simpson, 'was to relieve the pressure on them from tanks, which were lobbing shells at them from a few thousand yards away. A few days later those gallant Foreign Legionnaires made a desperate break for it by night, and escaped.

'As we neared the target, we dived to pick up speed and attacked level from about 1,000 yd at 10 ft off the deck. The book said 25, but that was based on a flying speed of 250 kt, which our aircraft couldn't quite attain and maintain in the desert. A lower altitude seemed to compensate, although some of the boys took off their tail-wheels by hitting tank turrets.'

One pilot got back with his props bent. It was also on this raid when Squadron Leader Simpson 'bought it'. 'I remember the bullet that hit me', he said. 'I saw it coming, the way you see a snowflake coming at your windshield. Flak normally breaks away from an aircraft like snowflakes, too, as I had seen it in France and Belgium in 1940 from a Lysander. But this one out of all the others kept coming. An explosive bullet, it detonated as it entered the hull of the aircraft by my left hand. It burst a few inches in front of my chest. My goggles were cracked, and my right arm still has the blue marks to this day. I picked pieces out of my chest for weeks

Inspecting the damage to a captured German Mark III tank, near Shandur, after firing 40 mm live ammunition at it. Left, with hands on hips, is Morgan from Kenya; second left, in battledress, Fairbairn-McPhee from Kenya; walking right is an Army Liaison Officer.

afterwards. Some of the pieces went through my right lung and had to be extracted from my back, and my chest X-rays still show bits and pieces. I have a "tented diaphragm" from adhesions.

'They say your whole past life flashes before you at a time like that. Maybe it does when you're older, but I felt too young to die and my mind reflected on the things I had hoped to accomplish and hadn't.'

Squadron Leader Simpson made it back to no man's land and bailed out at 500 ft. His luck held for he was picked up and taken to Tobruk hospital by a British Army ambulance. By sheer good luck he was flown out of Egypt, on a stretcher, five days later, just hours before the town was captured with 25,000 South Africans in it.

Another 'Tankbuster' who was hit on that same sortie was Tony Morrison-Bell, who later commanded the Squadron, but he fared much better than Simpson. After Morrison-Bell was hit, he crash landed then hitch-hiked rides on tanks and armoured cars to get back to the squadron the next day.

Mike Besly, who was on his first 'tankbusting' sortie wondered what had happened to Simpson and Morrison-Bell and he flew north to the coast, to navigate more easily to Tobruk, from where he could easily find the Squadron landing ground at Gambut East. However, he should have flown north-east, but he flew north-west, and followed the Mediterranean coast line to Tobruk where he landed to refuel. All unsuspecting, Mike Besly had flown over several German fighter bases on the way! While he was being refuelled at Tobruk, Besly phoned to let the Squadron know where he was and not to worry about him. 'That's good,' they said, 'but what about the other two?' At that stage Besly had visualized they were back at base worrying about him.

It was not long before Wing Commander Roger Porteous, the Commanding Officer, and Flying Officer 'Mac' Fairbairn-McPhee were tying with nine tanks each to their credit. Flight Lieutenant 'Pip' Hillier had $14\frac{1}{2}$ when he was wounded in the leg. When he got out of hospital they sent him back to Shandur to train new pilots and while doing a demonstration run he flew into the old canvas target, took both wings off on the steel rails which supported it, and ploughed into the ground at 200 mph. 'With the tragic death of Flight Lieutenant "Pip" Hillier they called me down from the Lebanon where I

Squadron Leader Allan Simpson and a Hurricane IId at Shandur, Egypt.

Pilot Officer Mike Besley with No 6 Squadron, training detachment at Shandur.

was recuperating from my gunshot wounds', said Allan Simpson. 'We trained new pilots, including some from India, and all of No 7 Squadron South African Air Force. We also retrained our own pilots whose accuracy had dropped off to about half of what it had been.

'This points out the fact that although there is absolutely no substitute for operational experience, the smartest soldier is a recruit newly trained. By 27 October the squadron score was 76 tanks, twelve armoured cars, 46 trucks eleven troop carriers, two fuel bowsers, one tracked vehicle, one gun and two tracked vehicles with guns.'

The squadrons, No 6 RAF and No 7 SAAF, had done their job by the time Africa was cleared of the enemy. The sturdy Hurricane IId 'Tankbusters' nicknamed the 'tin openers', which soon became the scourge of Rommel's armoured units, were not useful elsewhere. Only one squadron of Hurricane IIds was employed in Europe. They were soon recognized as a thing of the past and superseded by rocket-firing aircraft.

The aircraft in which Flight Lieutenant 'Pip' Hillier was killed in 1942 doing a demonstration for new pilots.

Chapter Fifteen

The Doodlebugs

In 1944 a new threat was posed by the V1 pilotless aircraft, also called flying bomb, buzz bomb or doodlebug. It carried a 2,000 lb (900 kg) warhead at about 360 mph (580 km/h) and proved a most effective weapon against south-east England. The first flying-bomb operations opened on the night of 12–13 June 1944, six days after the beginning of the Allied invasion they had been designed to prevent. The threat was countered partly by defensive measures – involving fighters, anti-aircraft guns and barrage balloons – and partly by bombing the launching sites.

To abate the flying-bomb menace, fighters were to be the first line of defence and were to patrol at 12,000 ft along three lines, 20 miles to sea between Beachy Head and Dover, over the coastline between Newhaven and Dover and inland between Haywards Heath and Ashford. The gun defences (363 heavy and 522 light anti-aircraft guns by 28 June) were sited along the southern slopes of the North Downs, while a barrage of nearly 500 captive balloons between Cobham and Limpsfield formed the third line of defence.

A Tempest V. This aircraft was very successful against the Doodlebug. Nos 3, 56 and 486 Squadrons were equipped with Tempest Vs.

Thus the fighters of ADGB (Air Defence of Great Britain) now found themselves facing an urgent and difficult task. The diversion of the Mosquito night-fighter squadrons to this new duty was directly at the expense of Operation Overlord commitments. It was soon found necessary to strengthen the day patrols with Mustangs withdrawn from Second Tactical Air Force because only they and the Spitfire XIV and Tempest V were really fast enough to intercept the flying bombs at the speed and height at which they operated.

After the ten V1s launched on 12–13 June, when only four actually fell on southern England, there was a lull for three days while the Germans ironed out some minor difficulties. On 15–16 June nearly 250 flying bombs were dispatched of which 144 crossed the English coast and 73 reached Greater London.

Three Royal Canadian Air Force Squadrons, Nos 406, 409 and 418 formed part of the air defence against the V1 offensive. On 16 June Wing Commander Russ Bannock of No 418 Squadron made what was probably the first night spotting from a fighter of a V1 flying bomb. While on patrol, he and his navigator sighted what they thought was a burning aircraft. As it crossed the English coast they saw anti-aircraft guns open up on it. Later on they learned it was a V1 they had seen. The next night 418 Squadron downed three V1s.

In the early stages of the V1 bombardment which began on 16 June and was to continue day and night until the end of September a lot of confusion developed among the defenders. Fighters pursued flying bombs into the gun belt and were themselves attacked by gunfire. A general nervous state developed among pilots and anti-aircraft gunners alike so that, to avoid errors, many chances of attacking flying bombs were lost. It was soon necessary for ADGB to define three separate lines of action according to the prevailing weather. One gave complete freedom to the fighters and forbade guns to fire; another gave freedom for the guns and restricted aircraft patrols in the channel areas only; the third laid down strict guidelines for weather when both fighters and guns could harmonize in the landward area.

During the first week of the campaign anti-aircraft guns claimed the highest number of successes against flying bombs, destroying 43 as against fifteen destroyed by fighters and none by balloons. However, the next two weeks gave the fighter pilots the opportunity of studying the characteristics and performance of the flying bombs. It was then a different story and by the end of June the fighters had destroyed 410 flying bombs, guns had destroyed 169 and the balloon barrage, thirteen.

Before the end of June, Flak Regiment 155 (W) succeeded in launching 1,579 flying bombs which cleared the French coast en route to London. Of these 1,421 reached England and 724 fell in the Greater London area. The buzz bombs which flamed menacingly across the sky and then plunged earthwards as the engine was cut-off by predetermined setting or remote control had a psychological effect much greater than the purely military one. If you could hear the engine you were safe; if it cut out, dive for shelter.

Night intruder crews soon devised techniques for attacking the V1. It was observed that after launch, they rose to about 500 ft then proceeded across the channel at 350–400 mph depending on atmospheric conditions. At that level the Mosquito could manage 360–370 mph, not enough to cope with their prey. This considered, the Mosquitoes would stooge along the French coast at about 10,000 ft, watching for the launch of a V1. The target could easily be observed thereafter by the glow from its engine exhaust, but this did not immediately enable a pilot to estimate range or the appropriate cutting-off vector. Ground control and searchlight aids were of some help in estimating range and bearing but any slight misjudgment inevitably resulted in an opportunity lost. Also, the Mosquitoes were not fast enough to overtake the flying bombs in straight and level flight, so it was necessary to gather speed, reaching about 440 mph, by diving from a height well above the target. Only the most skilful pilots were able to co-ordinate accurately the essential loss in height and the turn-in for a perfect interception.

What also had to be taken into account was the lethal nature of the target which meant it had to be detonated at a sufficiently safe distance from the pilot. Generally, the idea was to fire from about 300 yd, for it was dangerous getting much closer because of the chance of explosion. One Canadian crew had a V1 explode just 50

This was painted on 'Buck' Feldman's Typhoon QO-E whilst at Manston.

Flight Lieutenant 'Buck' Feldman's Hurricane IIc of No 3 Squadron at RAF Hunsdon, 1942. The Squadron mascot 'Patsy' poses on the wing.

yd away. They lived to tell the tale, but their aircraft had most of its paint scorched off!

Another hazard for the pilots of 'Divers', as the V1 interceptions were called, was that the explosion of a flying bomb ruined a pilot's night vision. To counter this, crews used the standard practice of closing one eye as they fired, thus preserving partial night vision if a bright explosion occurred. When the cloud base was low the work of the night fighters was almost entirely frustrated. The exceptionally bad weather during June gave very little chance for successful night attacks, and although on several nights many pilots attempted to make interceptions they failed to do so. Many pilots were very disappointed by their lack of success during June, but crews rapidly learned to improve their technique; for the moment the problems posed by the flying bombs became almost a personal challenge.

Over fourteen weeks No 418 Squadron RCAF flew 402 sorties against the V1, destroying 83 of them. Wing Commander Bannock and Flying Officer Bruce topped the list for individual effort, downing $18\frac{1}{2}$. On one $1\frac{1}{4}$-hour sortie they destroyed four! On another occasion Bannock assumes he damaged a V1's auto-pilot, for it turned around after he fired on it, and flew back to France.

Among the RAF squadrons of ADGB committed to daytime defence against the flying bombs was No 3 (F) Fighter Squadron.

Their Tempests, like the Typhoons and Spitfires also enrolled for attacking the V1s, had the extra speed and manoeuvrability to make interception relatively easy and daytime operations also helped range estimation so that their task was far less onerous than was that of the night fighters.

In late 1942 Flight Lieutenant 'Buck' Feldman was posted to No 3 Fighter Squadron at which time the squadron Hurricanes were being phased out and replaced with Typhoons. Upon becoming operational with their new mounts, No 3 (F) Squadron was engaged mainly as a fighter-bomber unit, in operations against enemy shipping, airfields, canal traffic, railroads and motor transport. On other occasions the squadron replaced bombs with long range tanks and became active in fighter escort duties, fighter sweeps and night intruders. During the latter part of 1943 and early 1944, No 3 (F) Squadron was engaged in dive bombing V1 launch sites which were known as 'Noball' targets. 'Noball' was the code name given to the campaign against V-weapon targets such as ski sites and supply depots. Bomber Command was also employed against these targets.

During the month of February 1944, No 3 (F) Squadron re-equipped with the Tempest V and eventually became part of the Tempest Wing under Wing Commander Roland Beamont at Newchurch in Kent; Nos 56 (F) and 486 (F) New Zealand Squadrons were the other two units that comprised the Wing. The Wing was to be part of the 2nd TAF and once the beachhead had been established after D-Day, were eventually to occupy fighter airstrips and act as close support for the invading armies. However, the V-weapons changed all that and the squadron found themselves chasing doodlebugs. 'Anti-diver' patrols were often very dull for the fighters, which were forced to remain in the air at all times of the day. This was admittedly a prodigal use of aircraft but was the only feasible way of having fighters in position to meet fleeting attacks which might come at any time. Once a salvo of flying bombs was launched there followed an exceedingly dramatic few minutes which partly

'Buck' Feldman and his Tempest V in Holland with No 274 (Fighter) Squadron – 1945.

'Buck' Feldman whilst with 3 Squadron at RAF Newchurch – July 1944.

offset the monotony of inaction. Very often, in spite of very capable ground control distributing targets, some pilots would find themselves 'queueing' up on the same flying bomb. Some of the doodlebugs (145 in June 1944) might be shot down over the sea; those that got through ran into intense concentration of anti-aircraft fire (169 destroyed by guns in June) and the remainder would pass into the landward fighter zone, where again ground control greatly aided pilots and they claimed 265 in June. The flying bombs that escaped the inner fighter patrol still had to get through the barrage balloons.

'I had personally shot down eleven flying bombs,' said Flight Lieutenant 'Buck' Feldman of No 3 (F) Squadron, 'my first success being during the initial launchings on 16 June. Being over ambitious, I opened up fire with four 20 mm cannon from about 50 yd. The blast blackened the aircraft and burned off a part of the rudder. This was my first success.' Flight Lieutenant Feldman served with the Royal Air Force as an American volunteer from 1941–48, flying Hurricanes, Spitfires, Typhoons and Tempests. He was stationed with No 3 (F) Fighter Squadron (which is the oldest aeroplane unit, having formed on 13 April 1912 from the Air Battalion of the Royal Engineers) at Hunsdon, West Malling, Manston, Swanton Morley, Bradwell Bay, Ayr and Newchurch. In July of 1944 he was decorated with the Distinguished Flying Cross. He did a second tour of ops with No 274 (F) Squadron 2nd Tactical Air Force, flying the Tempest V from various airfields on the continent. This most versatile aircraft achieved utmost success right until the very end of the conflict.

Tempest fighters from 150 Wing at RAF Newchurch, destroyed 638 V1s during the height of the doodlebug campaign which lasted from mid June to mid August 1944. The Tempest aircraft were outstanding and while flying Tempests with No 3 (F) Squadron, Flight Sergeant Bailey and Flight Sergeant Mackerras each accounted for eleven doodlebugs. These successes were not gained, however, without risk. Sadly Mackerras was killed on 6 August

'Buck' Feldman receiving the Distinguished Flying Cross from King Geroge VI – July 1944.

during a patrol near Box Hill. Although the doodlebugs had no defensive armament, attacks on them made from too close a range, and any approach to a missile already damaged by fire from another aircraft were dangerous.

The V2 (Vergeltungswaffe 2) followed the V1 flying bomb and the first of these fell on Britain on 8 September 1944. Because of its supersonic speed there was no direct defence against it. The V2 was a long-range fin-stabilized rocket weighing 13.6 tons on launching and carrying a warhead of one ton of amatol and ammonium nitrate HE. Some 10,000 were produced and between September 1944 and 29 March 1945, 1,115 V2 rockets fell in England. A further 1,341 were aimed against Antwerp and several others against Brussels, Paris and Liège.

Guided weapons, despite their great potential, had failed to achieve any notable military success. They were used only once in a tactical role, when eighteen V2 rockets were fired against the Ludendorff Bridge at Remagen. Total casualties in England from the total of 8,246 flying bombs actually launched amounted to 6,139 people killed and 17,239 seriously injured. From the 1,115 V2 rockets 2,855 were killed and 6,268 seriously injured. There was considerable damage to property and they were very unnerving. The V2 rocket missiles presented a very serious threat, but it was quickly eliminated by the bombing of launching sites and the Allied advance into Europe.

Chapter Sixteen

Typhoon Pilot

As the Allied armies set foot in Normandy in June 1944 they were fortunate to have the direct support from fighters and fighter-bombers, limited only by lack of airfields in France and control machinery rather than availability of aircraft. The first airfield engineers went ashore on 6 June and quickly made three Emergency Landing Strips (ELS) for aircraft in distress; they then concentrated on Refuelling and Rearming Strips (R&RS), four of which were ready by 10 June and which were progressively enlarged to Advanced Landing Grounds (ALG). Finally, as the Allied armies pushed further inland, they were turned into completely equipped airfields. The air plan called for eighteen airfields in France by 10 June and 27 by the end of the month, but delay in securing some of the sites chosen in advance, coupled with

Hawker Typhoon Mk Ib MP149, *coded 18-P, of No 440 (FB) Squadron taxys cautiously through the maze of Jerrycans at Eindhoven, Holland on 22 December 1944. On 1 January 1945 the Luftwaffe conducted mass air strikes on Allied targets. An hour-long raid upon 143 (RCAF) Wing at Eindhoven resulted in 45 aircraft hit, including four typhoons in readiness,prepared to take off in case of just such an attack.*

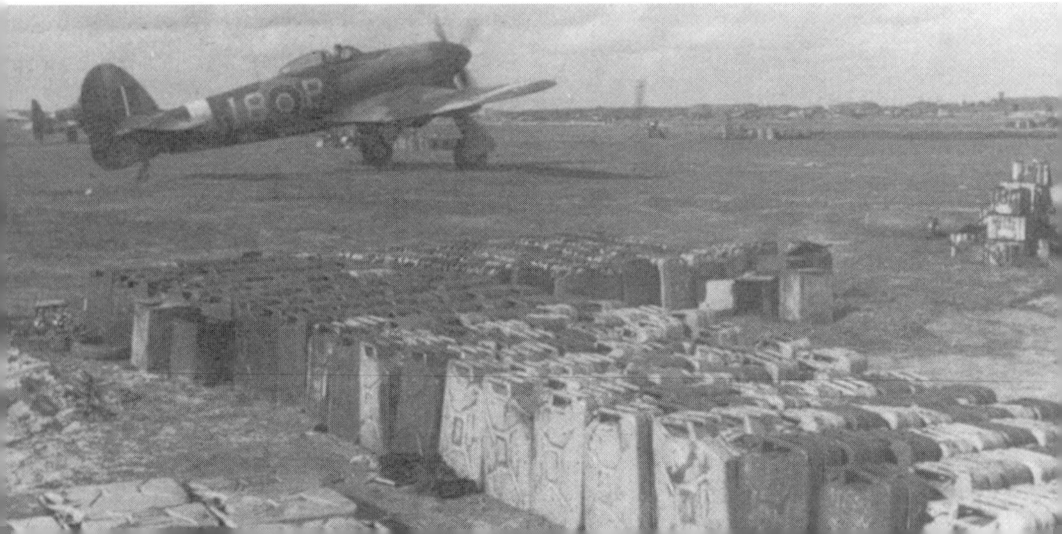

the fact that metal runway material was not available, meant that in fact only seventeen airfields were ready in that period. By 20 June eight Spitfire, three Typhoon and three Auster squadrons were established in the beachhead and, although several of the airfields were subject to enemy shell fire which at times caused temporary withdrawals, there were nineteen British and twelve American squadrons in France by the 30th. The Luftwaffe could put up little resistance, for at that time they had under 500 fighters. By 13 June all German fighter resources in France had been amalgamated under Jagdkorps II and the policy of turning fighters into fighter-bombers had been reversed.

The Army commanders were satisfied with the situation, but not so Air Chief Marshal Leigh-Mallory and Air Marshal Coningham who continually stressed the need for airfields in Normandy so that they could put into full operation the highly integrated system of reconnaissance, group control centres, fighter direction posts, forward control posts, and air support signals units, specially developed to bring fighters into action immediately by operating either in a 'Cab rank' or on demand.

After 6 June the six Mustang squadrons of the planned pool of readiness were released to assist the eighteen Typhoon squadrons over the British sector. The general aim was still to disrupt the enemy tactical control system by attacks on Headquarters, radio units and telephone exchanges, and to delay the arrival of German armour moving into the Caen area. Each Mustang was armed with two 500 lb bombs and the Typhoons with rocket projectiles.

As implied in the air plan, almost all the operations of the Typhoon squadrons were in close and direct support of the ground

This photograph clearly shows the need for the Advanced Learning Grounds in France after the Allied armies set foot in Normandy in June 1944. A Ju 88 lies in front of a bomb-damaged hangar in a German airfield in France which was captured by American Forces. The Royal Air Force had done a very good job.

forces. Typical early targets were of the static variety such as oil and storage dumps but as the Germans began to retreat their targets became of the fleeting type – tanks, self-propelled guns and temporary strongpoints in villages, the exact position at the time of the aircraft's arrival frequently being indicated by smoke shells fired by Allied artillery.

The Typhoons attacked elements of the 21st Panzer Division south-east of Caen but deteriorating weather reduced the number of sorties. The sorties dispatched by AEAF during the first week of the invasion were: 6 June – 6,643; 7 June – 7,465; 8 June – 5,073; 9 June – 662; 10 June – 5,528; 11 June – 3,078; 12 June – 5,157. During this period the highlight for the Typhoons was on 10 June when they attacked a battery of guns at Tanquerolle, northeast of Evrecy, and a late-evening attack against a château at La Caine, south of Caen, thought to be the headquarters of Panzer Group West. With their rockets the Typhoons almost completely eliminated this headquarters and its staff who were there planning a major German counter attack. The Typhoons also operated under command of the visual control posts and were called upon many times when enemy tanks dug in and needed to be prised out into the open. Their rockets screamed mercilessly down on the enemy.

However ground surveys made at a later date showed that the 60 lb HE rocket was not the lethal weapon against enemy armour that it was believed to be, an assumption which permitted inflated claims from these patrols. Enemy sources admitted that it had at times a shattering and unnerving effect on morale so that vehicles were temporarily abandoned, but the number actually destroyed was relatively small in relation to the effort expended.

Not all targets were land based and during the Allied landings on 6 June, No 137 Squadron, armed with Typhoons carrying rocket projectiles, had the special task of attacking enemy vessels attempting to enter the eastern approaches to the assault area. They maintained a strike force of six aircraft at continuous readiness throughout the day, but made no sorties except a dawn patrol from Cap Gris Nez to Flushing, which saw no enemy shipping.

The pilots loved the rocket-carrying Typhoons. One such pilot was Squadron Leader John David ('Jake') Coupland. He explains how he came to be flying Typhoons: 'Wing Commander W. Dring, DSO, DFC, was Wing Leader of 123 Typhoon Wing in France. I met him at 84 GSU; he had me posted to his old Tyffie squadron, 183. I arrived there on 1 September 1944. We flew "Cab ranks" supporting the Canadian Army as it cleaned up the coastal ports of France. The

'Jerries' feared being rocketed. Sheltered in the large concrete cross-channel gun pits, the German garrison at Boulogne surrendered when threatened with attack by the rocket Tyffies of 123 Wing orbiting over their heads.

'On my last flight but one I was leading a section of four on "Cab rank". Troops of the Canadian First Army were trying to cross a narrow canal but were held up by gun fire directed at them by a German spotter from his position in a church steeple. The Air Contact Team in its Jeep located with the stymied troops called on R/T, "Boswell Yellow leader 'winkle' that bastard please." In line-astern we went in at 50 ft just above the small hay stacks behind each of which Canadian troops were trying to keep out of sight from the German spotter. They were about 200 yd from the Germans and normally we fired rockets at about 700 yd short of the target. Our rockets would roar just over a bunch of very scared Canadian heads!

'Firing my four 20 mm cannon to keep the Jerries' heads down, I got to within 400 yd of the church before letting all eight rockets go in one salvo, breaking away sharply to avoid my own rocket explosion and flying debris. I had been concentrating so hard on the target that I failed to heed the trees between me and the target! My Tyffie flew through the tree tops scattering leaves and branches everywhere. When I gained altitude to reform with my section, I found that I couldn't throttle back so pushed it forward hoping it might loosen. It made the matter worse. I called my No 3 and told him to lead the section home as I was obliged to go on ahead!

'Reaching my aerodrome I called up the controller explaining my situation. After a short delay during which I was tearing full-bore around the aerodrome, Wing Commander Dring came on the R/T.

A GI examines the remains of a German Mark V at Le Desert, France, that was knocked-out by a rocket projectile from a Typhoon. On the rear of the tank is the charred body of one of the tank crew members who was caught in an attempt to escape. The Typhoons played a large part in the Battle of Normandy, and near Avranches they disposed of no fewer than 137 tanks.

This picture shows destruction wrought by air support of the 2nd and 9th Tactical Air Force and the Typhoon Wing during battle activities in the Falaise Gap on 20 August 1944 when Argentan was taken by the British, Falaise, by the Canadians and Trun by the Poles.

He told me to climb to 2,000 ft and bale out! I got to 2,000 ft very quickly, but on looking over the side decided to attempt a landing. I dropped to deck level, and on the downwind leg pulled the nose up to lose speed, downed the undercarriage. On the landing approach, the speed was climbing fast so once again I pulled the nose up and when the speed dropped, I lowered my flaps. The speed was increasing rapidly as I descended but I was nearly at the runway so I switched off! Immediately seven tons of Typhoon began falling like

Port du Graviere railway bridge across the Seine River, south of Rouen, France after bombing the US 9th Air Force and British 2nd Tactical Air Force. The stranded trains made easy pickings for the Typhoons and their rocket projectiles.

a brick. I was going to hit the fence at the end of the runway. I flicked the switches on and 24 cylinders generating 2,200 horsepower snapped into life. Before my psyche and my anatomy could suffer a second twitch, I switched off. Happily the sudden burst was enough to get me over the fence to make a perfect three pointer.

'Winco Dring was across the field in his Jeep before I had pulled off the runway. He pulled a large stick protruding from my air scoop and we just missed being doused in glycol. "Close call Coup but nice flying", said Dring as we climbed into his Jeep for the drive to dispersal. A few days later I was sent to No 8 RAF General Hospital in Brussels with stuffed and inflamed sinuses and while there, applied for transfer to the Royal Canadian Air Force. I returned to London on 22 December for documentation and became a member of the RCAF on 24 December 1944. With three operational tours completed the RCAF grounded me.'

So ended Squadron Leader John David Coupland's career with the Royal Air Force. It had all started with the *Boy's Own Annual* that his uncle gave him for Christmas 1934. His career had begun in 1935 at the lowest level possible, an RAF Boy Entrant. Young David Coupland had dreams of becoming another 'Micky' Mannock wearing pilot's wings and a chest full of medals but that quickly faded as the training got harder. But Coupland continued with grit and determination to be a fighter pilot – it was a long hard road as Coupland explains: 'Shortly after I got my A/G Wings, my uncle asked me to accompany him to his Queen's University reunion dinner, hoping no doubt that I would absorb a little wisdom, through some sort of osmosis.

'It was my first experience in the world of stiff (and stuffed!) shirts and black ties. Surrounded by intellectuals many years my senior, I was completely out of my own milieu, ignored and lonely. My uncle was at the bar with a man of his own white-haired years. He wiggled his finger for me to join them. "A/C Coupland meet A/C Tyrell." The handshake was firm, the smile friendly. I read the miniature medals on his dinner jacket starting with a DSO & Bar. He was Air Commodore Billy Tyrell, Principal Medical Officer, Royal Air Force. "Your uncle tells me that you want to be a pilot!

Mistake my boy! Navigation is the thing of the future. Who is your CO?". "Group Captain Coningham, Sir", I replied. "Oh! Mary and I are old friends. I'll speak to him about you and see what can be done." "Thank you, Sir". I was dismissed wondering how my CO with his DSO, MC, DFC, AFC could ever be called "Mary". The explanation was simple; Group Captain Coningham was a New

A locomotive that had been at the receiving end of a salvo of rocket projectiles from a Typhoon. The American soldiers cannot believe what they see.

Zealander, and in his early Air Force days was nicknamed "Maori"; it became "Mary". Anyway, a couple of weeks later, I and six other airmen were called before "Mary" Coningham for interviews for selection as Air Observers. Waiting outside the CO's office my six companions were sure I would be the winner, not because of A/C Tyrell about whom they knew nothing, but because I was an "ex-brat". The Boy's Own Annual was shaping up! By September 1939 I got my second aircrew Wing, the Air Observer's "Flying Doughnut" (which enjoyed other appellations as well) and was posted to No 229 Fighter Squadron at RAF Digby.

'We were equipped with short-nosed Blenheims. I was the Squadron Navigator and NCO i/c Air Gunners who at that time were A/Cs, not Sergeants. My flight commander, Flight Lieutenant Fred Rosier, was to become Air Chief Marshal Sir Frederick Rosier, Commander-in-Chief of Fighter Command,

'War was declared at 11:00 hours on 3 September 1939. 229 Squadron flew "Kipper patrols" providing cover for convoys sailing up and down the east coast and at night were targets for searchlight crew training. Pilot Officer Lomax and his gunner were our first casualties. Blinded by a searchlight they crashed and were killed. Bad weather and boredom was our operational lot. One moonlit night "Rosie" relieved the boredom by looping our Blenheim at 4,000 ft over Lincoln Cathedral. "Still awake back there Coupland?" My reply was both prompt and breathless. March 1940 the squadron converted to Hurricanes. "Rosie" asked me which I would prefer, recommendation for a commission, or pilot training? I chose pilot training, took the medical and thought I was on my way when France fell. All deals were off. I was posted to Andover and met my new pilot, Flying Officer Bill Wigmore, an RAF Canadian from Niagara Falls, and my Air Gunner, LAC Joe Burrows from Liverpool. After a few familiarization flights we joined 53 Squadron at Detling in Kent in time to participate in the Battle of Britain.

'With a top speed of 260 mph and modest armament, the Blenheim was a fair bomber, but a mockery as a day fighter. Casualties were very high and shortly after the Germans pulverized Detling with a devastating bombing on 2 September, the Squadron was moved to Thorney Island. For the next several months we bombed shipping and "invasion ports" with loads of three 250 lb GPs and a 250 lb cannister of 4 lb incendiaries.'

The Blenheim was in fact classed as a bomber. It had twin engines and a crew of either two or three. It had a still air range of 1,475

An American tank moves through Saveur Le Compte, a small French village caught up in fighting. The buildings have been blasted by rocket-carrying Typhoons to drive out the Germans.

miles with 1,000 lb bomb load. The maximum speed was 270 mph at 13,000 ft and it had a service ceiling of 24,000 ft. Its gun armament was either five or seven .303 in. It could also carry torpedoes.

Coupland continues: 'In July 1941, I was sent on "ops rest" to No 1 Air Armament School for specialized training as a Bomb Aimer earning my third aircrew Wing. I sewed it under the lapel of my 5A "Best Blues" with my A/G Wing for a quick and ready line-shoot!

"My ops rest was to be the senior bombing and gunnery instructor at OTU Chivenor, North Devon. Now a Flight Sergeant, I always flew as navigator for Squadron Leader Peter Rolt, the Chief Flying Instructor, who was also on an ops rest. He was a pre-war Permanent Commission Officer, RAF Cranwell College trained, the son of Sir Peter Rolt, Bt. He walked around the hangars with hands in his overall pockets and no cap and always disappointed because no one picked him up for his sloppy dress. "Gutless young pups! No bloody sense of discipline, letting me run around dressed like this! Disgraceful!" It was largely tongue-in-cheek stuff, but I often wondered what he would have said to any sprog Pilot Officer who had dared to pull him up for his dress. Bought him a drink in the Mess I suspect.

'At the end of this rest I was detailed to join one of the crews about to complete training. I howled to Peter Rolt that it was unfair that after all my operational flying with 229 and 53 Squadrons, I should have to go back on ops with an inexperienced crew and that I had earned a crack at becoming a pilot. Peter had known nothing of my posting; he was incensed and immediately stomped off to see the newly promoted to Group Captain Station Commander.

Blenheims of No 62 Squadron, the type of aircraft in which Coupland was the Squadron Navigator and NCO i/c Air Gunners when with No 229 Squadron at Digby.

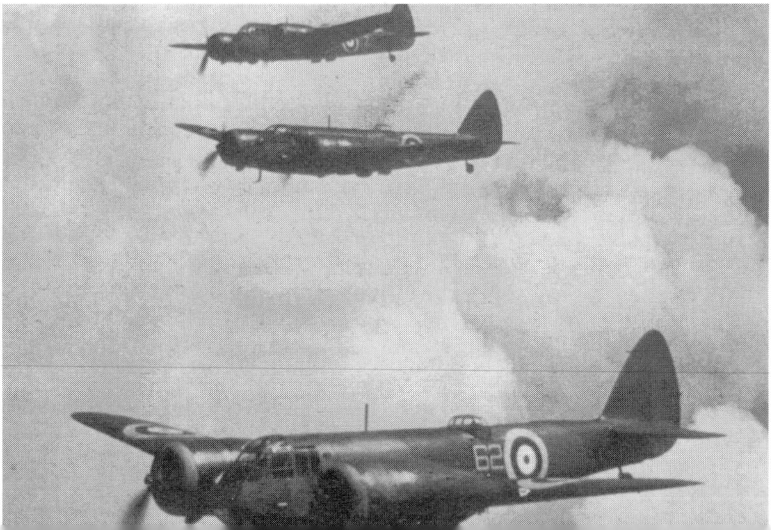

Three days later I was on my way to EFTS. Two weeks later Peter was killed in an Anson demonstrating an anti-shipping attack on an RN destroyer in the Bristol Channel.

'Having spent many hours at the controls of Blenheims and Ansons, and done everything with them but take off and land (and the novelty of flying had long passed) I was able to solo my Magister at EFTS in $1\frac{1}{2}$ hours, so this phase of my training was cut short and I was posted home to Canada and EFTS Neepawa, then SFTS Medicine Hat. In February 1943, I at last replaced my flying "O" with pilot's Wings.'

With his cherished pilot's Wings Coupland fulfilled his boyhood dream of becoming a pilot. He also got his commission and returned to England in March 1943 for advanced flying training on Hurricanes. He was then posted to No 137 (Rocket Projectile) Squadron flying Hurricane IVs. After a spell in hospital Coupland was sent to 84 GSU to await posting to another squadron, which was to be a Typhoon squadron.

It was men like Boy Coupland who saw Britain through its darkest hour. It was their determination to win that made victory possible. Squadron Leader John David 'Jake' Coupland earned four aircrew Wings, completed three operational tours, was awarded the Battle of Britain gilt rosette to the 1939–45 Star, and was a commissioned officer. His boyhood dream fulfilled Coupland had only one regret: 'My one real regret was one rooted in vanity,' he said, 'I didn't get a "gong"! Wing Commander Dring had indicated very strongly in November 1944 that he was putting me "up for a DFC". I never got it; maybe he hadn't time because on 6 January 1945, when landing at Helmond from a weather recce, he crashed and was killed.

'I never flew again as full time aircrew. I got stuck with staff work from the day I joined the RCAF until, as a Squadron Leader, I was retired at my own request on 4 February 1967. I was grateful for having had the opportunity to live, fight, party and struggle with so many knights of the air, a generation the likes of which we will never see again!'

Group Captain (Mary) Coningham, young Coupland's CO in the early days, later became Air Marshal Sir Arthur Coningham, KBE, CB, DSO, MC, DFC, AFC, AOC Desert Air Force 1941–43, North-west Africa Tactical Air Force 1943, 2nd Tactical Air Force 1944–45; AOC-in-C Flying Training Command 1945. He was a regular air force officer until he was killed in an aircraft accident on 30 January 1948.

Chapter Seventeen

'Flying Desert Rats'

When, on 27 May 1942, Rommel's Panzer Army Africa began to move forward it forestalled a British offensive already ordered to begin early in June, for which Auchinleck had tried to husband his forces. Immediately after the failure of the Axis attempt to break through to the Delta in September 1942 the British 8th Army began to prepare for a full-scale offensive, timed to take place about the middle of October. For many days a fierce battle raged at El Alamein.

By the morning of 4 November 1942 the Axis army was in full retreat and, although a rearguard action was fought at Fuka, intensive bombing attacks gave Rommel little chance to regroup his forces and the Battle of El Alamein was over. Three days of heavy rain, which hampered air operations, and two desert outflanking thrusts, enabled the Germans to draw ahead of their pursuers and by 11 November Egypt was left behind. Thereafter there was no halt until Agheila was reached twelve days later. The role assigned to the air force in the pursuit was that of causing the greatest possible congestion along the line of retreat. As early as 2 November No 239 Wing was ordered to check its mobility and on 5 November Wing Commander R. H. M. Gibbes of No 3 Squadron and Wing Commander M. C. H. Barber of No 450 Squadron dispatched westwards the advance parties of their squadrons. The first army

A painting by Wing Commander Stocky Edwards, DFC, DFM – one of Canada's top Aces. It shows a Hurricane 'Scramble' for a formation attack on Gialo. Bert Houle is flying AK-W.

units reached Daba airfield that day to find Group Captain W. J. Duncan already there selecting sites for RAF supply dumps. Duncan was temporarily in charge of supply columns, which, with the airfield reconnaissance (RAF) and construction parties (Royal Engineers), went ahead with the forward troops. In the afternoon of 5 November four Australian Kittyhawks flew over Daba and, their report being favourable, the servicing parties continued their journey to arrive at dawn the next day, followed during the afternoon by the aircraft of No 239 Wing.

A few days later the wing moved forward again to Sidi Haneish and until 19 November, when it reached Martuba, it was constantly advancing. These movements were not always easy for heavy rain and enemy mining confined traffic to the single coastal road. Air force convoys merged into an apparently endless stream of army vehicles packed nose to tail and moving westwards, fortunately immune from attack by the enemy. Progress was consequently slow and sometimes road parties took more than 24 hours to move from one airfield to the next. However, the speed the fighter force pressed forward sometimes astonished the army and on 9 November 'B' party of No 450 Squadron, en route for Mischeifa, was halted by an armoured column whose commander suggested that it might be wiser to wait until Sidi Barrani was captured.

The 8th Army reached Benghazi on 19 November, by which time No 239 Wing was at Martuba. The untiring and often dangerous leap-frogging advance of the ground parties permitted air operations to continue without a check. Squadron Leader B. M. Terry, formerly adjutant of No 3 Squadron but now attached to Headquarters No 239 Wing, was killed on 16 November when the vehicle he was driving ran over a land mine. One of the 'Flying Desert Rats' who took part in that dangerous leap-frogging advance was Group Captain Albert (Bert) Houle, DFC and Bar, CD who explains what it was like: 'On 7 November we moved our Hurricane IIcs up to Landing Ground 20, on the coast near Daba, and had a whale of a time picking up abandoned equipment. I was then a Flying Officer acting as 'B' Flight Commander of 213 Squadron. Particular care had to be taken because many articles were boobytrapped. Although many of the boys took chances, there were only a few casualties. Motor cycles, trucks, revolvers and rifles, things that Jerry knew we would be interested in, were the main items booby-trapped. The line had broken so quickly that they hadn't time to pack anything except essential equipment, and not all of that. It sounded like a miniature war with machine-guns, rifles, revolvers and even a 25 pounder shooting out to sea. Some of our boys uncapped Italian red-devil hand grenades and threw them over the cliffs. I picked up a good Mauser rifle which I kept for fifteen months. On afternoons off, I took it out to the desert for target practice.

'Our landing ground was littered with crashed and damaged enemy planes, and LG.104 had over one hundred planes left behind. Their maintenance system was not as good as our own, as our aircraft were taken to maintenance units away behind the lines for repair. On the retreat to El Alamein only two Allied aircraft were left behind. Some were towed back by tying the tailwheel to the flat bed of a lorry.

'Dead bodies lined the road. Some of them could not be removed as the retreating Hun had even boobytrapped his own dead. We lived pretty rough at LG.20 as it wasn't worth while pitching camp. The line had moved so far that we couldn't support it from our aerodrome and the landing grounds forward had not been cleared of mines. We did one patrol to prevent Fieseler Storchs (small communications aircraft used by the Jerries) from picking up some entrapped German Generals, and two trips with long-range tanks to protect mine sweepers clearing up Mersa Matruh harbour. Roads were blocked with German and Italian soldiers making their own way to some wire encampment to get fed. They even stopped our troops on the road and wanted to be taken prisoner. They were usually told to go and ask someone else. Some of them drove themselves to wire enclosures in their own trucks and buses. Roy Marples commandeered one bus and made the Italian occupants get out and walk the rest of the way. He tried to take the shoes off a high-ranking German officer because he liked them. Meeting with some resistance, he used more persuasive measures. They were a pitiful, beaten, disillusioned bunch, wandering aimlessly east for food and shelter. For our part we had tasted defeat in the summer and now we knew the elation of victory. What an uplift in morale, noticeable from the CO to the lowest "erk"!

'Fighting, like any game or contest, is a lot easier when things are going your way. It seems that once the breaks start working for you, they continue for some time. Almost everyone has sat down at the bridge table when their hands were not only good to excellent, but the missing kings and queens were situated so that they could be finessed successfully. If a suit was required to be divided a certain way it always seemed to comply. It is much easier to be a happy, contented, observant and chatty bridge player under these conditions. In a hockey match the puck bounced right. It hit the

An operational break –Bert Houle snatches a quick cuppa to wash out the sand. From left to right, Tigger Smith with his back to the camera, Bert Houle, Wing Commander Jackie Darwin and an Army Liaison Officer named Captain Field.

goal post and glanced in for your team and out for the opponents. Your team ends up playing over its head and the opponents get dejected. But as the saying goes, and is pretty true, when the going gets tough the tough get going. I claim that is what we did in the Western Desert. We had it pretty rough and the losses were heavy.

When twenty to fifty per cent don't come back on a sweep it doesn't take much of a mathematician to calculate that his number must come up. Many pilots built up their courage with a philosophy that went something like this. There is only a 25 per cent chance that I'll get shot at, and if I am there is only a 25 per cent chance that my aircraft will be hit. If the aircraft is hit there is only a 25 per cent chance that the hit will be serious. If it hits a vulnerable spot there is only a 25 per cent chance that I will be hit. If I am hit there is only a 25 per cent chance it will be fatal. With odds like that, why should I worry? However, it is better to increase all odds by preventing the enemy from getting that first shot.

'Up to this period, the Axis air forces had had it too much their own way. Their losses seemed to be much smaller than ours. A few squadrons of "Spits" made them a little more cautious. They were beginning to feel as if that extra man above had switched sides for a change. The Axis army had not enjoyed having things all its own way, but it is a good bet that by now they were beginning to think that Montgomery had done his homework, had resisted the bad, uninspired, unreliable and misguided orders from the politicians and now had a pretty invincible army. We had a feeling that the breakthrough at El Alamein was indeed the first yards on the invasion of Germany itself. We were right and history has proved it.

'On the 11th we took to the air for the LG at Sidi Haneish. That night all pilots were gathered together and "Squad" Oliver told us there was a big show coming up. We weren't to bank too much on coming back as we were to land well over 100 miles behind the enemy lines to operate, strafing enemy transport on the roads between Benghazi and El Agheila. Hudsons were to fly the groundcrew, food, equipment, gasoline, water and ammunition in. Outside of that we were to take only what we could put in our aircraft. 238 Squadron were coming with us, each squadron taking fourteen aircraft and a select group of experienced pilots to fly them. It looked like a suicide "do" to us. We went away from that meeting not knowing what to think. Most of us wrote home to say that we might not be writing again for some time. The next day everyone going on the trip was busy testing his aircraft and long range tanks to see that they were working satisfactorily. Those not going were wearing faces long with disappointment, and trying to convince someone that they should go. I was acting Flight Commander as Borneo Prince was sick with yellow jaundice. It was my job to pick out the pilots and groundcrew from my flight. At the end of the day everything was in order for a pre-dawn rise and early take-off. In the evening we visited 274 Squadron for a farewell party, as they had some drinks and Roy McKay had a brother with that outfit.

'Very early on Friday 13 November 1942, I was getting ready for another big step to buck the jinx. I had joined the Royal Canadian Air Force on a Friday the 13th. Breakfast was bolted in silence. All pilots had their orders and knew their position in the formation. We gathered our bedrolls and took them down to be stowed in the aircraft. Just after dawn the Hudsons landed to pick up the groundcrew and equipment. We were soon on our way. The fighters acted as escort to the transport aircraft and Group Captain Whiteley, DSO, DFC, led the formation. He had operated from this little-known airfield years before. We steered a straight vector from Sidi Haneish, crossed "the wire" near Fort Maddalena, and flew on, passing the odd wreck of an aircraft on the sand. Our course was too far south for the main battle and there were no eyes to mark our passing. After two hours we saw two conical sand dunes, freaks of nature in an otherwise level expanse. From the sand dunes we doubled back on vector 030° for 20 miles and found ourselves over a landing field with rough runways marked by empty gasoline barrels. The transport aircraft landed first. The fighters landed whenever they saw a clear space on the runway. There was complete R/T silence.

'One groundcrew man was assigned to each aircraft. The pilot assisted him with refuelling from four gallon tins which had been unloaded from the transport. It took a long time to put more than one hundred gallons through a funnel into an aircraft. By the time this chore was completed lunch was ready, and we hit it with gusto. Immediately after lunch Wingco Darwin gathered us around him for a briefing for the first show. He told us that sections were going out on divergent vectors to hit the road at seven points from El Agheila to Benghazi. We marked our own positions on the map, and drew vectors and distances to various points on this road. These had to be memorized as we were not allowed to carry the maps. Our R/T switch was not to be turned on and under no circumstances was it to be used, even if it was a case of life or death. After strafing we were to keep down low so that Jerry couldn't plot our line of flight and thus find the landing ground. My section included Flying Officer Roy McKay, Flight Sergeant Harry Compton from Canada and Pilot Officer Gordie Carrick from Australia. Our striking point was about 10 miles north of Agedabia. We were then to swing north until out of ammunition, and return. I had primed the boys to waste no time after the briefing so that we could get off first. It worked and we roared away to draw first blood.

'I would have thought that the operation would have been planned so that the sections with farthest to go would be ordered off first, and those with progressively shorter distances would go off in order. This would roughly have everyone hitting their target area about the same time. Possibly this tactic would have been too hard to organize, especially if some aircraft turned out to be unserviceable. Since there were no such limitations, I reasoned that those first in would stir up the hornets nest, if any, and maybe get out without getting stung.

'After an hour of flying right on the deck the country got a little greener.

Then we could see transport, bags of them in the distance, rolling for safety behind the El Agheila line. We hit the road and turned north, weaving across from side to side, taking shots at any target that presented itself. As soon as we had knocked out a few vehicles there was a pile-up behind. That gave us a field day. We attacked big six-wheelers absolutely jammed with troops, packed so tight that only a few could extricate themselves and jump clear before canon bullets started tearing into the mass. Then McKay and I spotted a Fieseler Storch stooging down the road towards us. We both went for it. I was making a 60° attack and didn't even know that Mac was attacking it. When the Storch saw one or both of us, it did a violent turn to port, stalled, spun and went straight in. It had two occupants and I don't think that either one of us had hit it. It burst into flames on hitting the deck from a height of about 200 ft. Both of us went back to shooting up the defenceless trucks and armoured cars. There was no return fire so we had little to worry about. When all our guns were empty we turned for home and found it without much trouble. As we were the first section back the groundcrew were all waiting to hear how we made out. When we told them about the pickings, they went wild with delight. There was more shooting there than we had had all summer. Things looked easy providing the Jerries didn't bring in fighters or ack-ack.

'The other sections came back one by one with exactly the same story. The venture was a howling success, although we lost Bart Campbel1 and Gordie Waite. They had hit the telegraph line stretched close to the road. Both ended up Prisoners of War, but it was later established that Gordie Waite was missing, presumed dead to this day. The CO hit the same telegraph line, but it merely tore the long range tank off and he was in the clear. 238 Squadron lost one pilot. Friday the 13th was an unlucky day for a good many of the enemy.

'A spirit of comradeship prevailed that night. Fires were hidden as well as possible, and a guard was mounted in case of a surprise attack. We put our beds up in the open and slept like children. The next morning the CO took twelve aircraft to attack the aerodrome at Agedabia. I was left out of this show. Three hours later we began to get worried as there was still no sign of them. We knew they must be lost as it was impossible to wipe out a whole squadron. One flight of six aircraft had become separated and when they got lost they headed for El Adem, which was in our hands. They got refuelled, and returned later that day. Flight Lieutenant Jock Cameron – later Air Chief Marshal, Chief of the Air Staff Sir Neil Cameron GCB, CBE, DSO, DFC, ADC, RAF – was leading this flight and Squadron Leader Oliver was leading the other one. There was no sign of the other six at noon, so Wingco Darwin and I prepared to go in search. We took off and searched the desert to Jerabub, then along "the wire" to Fort Maddalena, and back home. It is impossible to map read over that type of terrain. I had mentally noted the times on each of the first two legs and since we had made about a right angled turn at the wire I calculated the time required to fly the hypotenuse of the triangle. It was a good thing that I did. I knew Darwin was starting to get worried. Finally he broke radio silence and queried whether I thought we shouldn't be seeing the sand dunes. I gave as brief a transmission as I could and suggested fifteen more minutes. It worked. Still no sign of the lost flight and they weren't back when we landed. Shortly after that dust clouds appeared on the horizon. A ground column was approaching, and we took off to inspect them. If they were enemy, we were to put them out of commission as quickly as possible. They proved to be friendly and shortly after we landed Squadron Leader Cassano, an English Desert Rat with the Long Range Desert Group of armoured cars and mobile radio stations joined us. He had been sent in to give us protection. We sure were glad to have him with us.

'Just before dusk a single Hurricane appeared in the circuit and we rushed out to see who it was. It was Baxter from our squadron; he informed us that his flight had become lost and, when almost out of fuel, had set down in the desert. They had drained the gasoline from all the aircraft and put it into his so that he could go in search of the aerodrome. He gave an approximate pin-point. Two of the armoured cars sped off with fuel and some rations. Shortly after dawn the next morning a cold, hungry, bedraggled bunch landed. It can get pretty cold in the desert at night and they were quite willing to admit it.

'As soon as the aircraft were refuelled, Wingco Darwin led six of us off on a strafe of Gialo, sometimes spelled Jalo, an airport about 100 miles to the south-west. We had gone about 40 miles when Darwin spotted a dust cloud and went over to investigate. We were using the R/T sparingly by this time. Suddenly it came to life with "Prang them boys. They're Heinies". We went to work. There were eight armoured cars on the way from Jerabub to Gialo and after ten minutes with six two-cannon Hurricanes, each carrying 240 rounds, they were completely destroyed. One group made for a hill to set up a machine-gun, but one of the boys blew it and most of its would-be gunners up. Other dust clouds could be seen farther along the trail. We hit back for base to rearm and refuel. The Wingco laid on aircraft from both squadrons to go out in relays of six and get everything on that back trail. He also ordered me to lead a formation of six to complete our interrupted visit to Gialo.

'We took off and after about 40 miles hit the real Sahara Desert; giant cones of sand possibly 200 ft in height stretched as far as the eye could see. It was a forsaken land, a bad place to have engine trouble. We only passed over a corner of the Sahara and struck level country beyond. Finding the Gialo Oasis was not hard and I was right over the landing ground before I realized it. We certainly weren't expected. Mechanics continued to work on the aircraft as we attacked. When we were finished six burning wrecks were all that was left of a few Cant 1007s, Savoia 79s and a Ju 88. One English pilot described his attack saying; "when I fired there was a bloke still wiping the windscreen".

'The surrounding desert was literally covered with dispersed armoured cars. We did target practice until out of ammunition. McKay ran out of ammunition before I did. He was spotting my shots, calling up now and again to say, "That's good" or "That wasn't so good". There was no return fire to speak of. Literally thousands of bodies were stretched on the sand in various poses trying to make us think they were dead so we shouldn't shoot at them. Harry Compton's aeroplane was hit and he called up to ask for a vector back to base. I was reluctant to give it out over the air, but what was I to do? If he stayed with us he might have to force land and the natives would not be too friendly. He might end up with his private parts sewn into his mouth. Also, if he took a wrong vector and had to bale out over the dunes we wouldn't spot him on our way back to LG.125. I was also reluctant to call off the operation before we had done all the damage we could. I gave him the vector only once. He got back okay. I was sure glad of that. It was bad country to walk out of and almost impossible to take any type of vehicle into the dunes. When

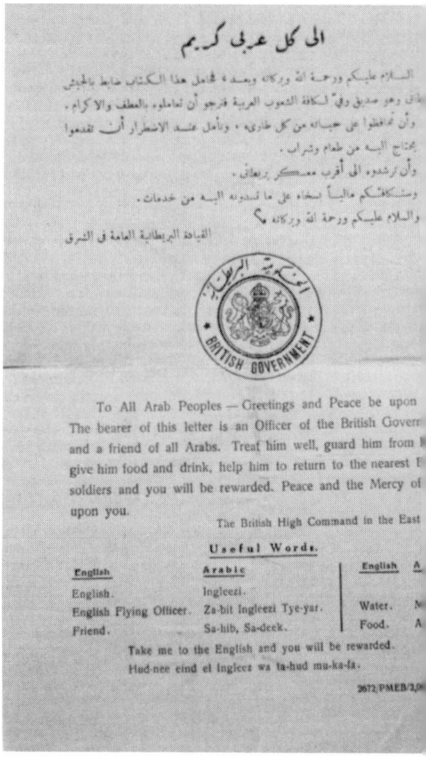

الى كل عربي كريم

السلام عليكم ورحمة الله وبركاته وبعد ، فحامل هذا الكتاب ضابط بالجيش
اني وهو صديق وفي لكافة الشعوب العربية فنرجو أن تعاملوه بالعطف والاكرام .
وأن تحافظوا على حياته من كل طارىء ، ونأمل عند الاضطرار أن تقدموا
يحتاج اليه من طعام وشراب .
وأن ترشدوه الى أقرب معسكر بريطاني .
وسنكافئكم ماليا بسخاء على ما تسدونه اليه من خدمات .
والسلام عليكم ورحمة الله وبركاته

القيادة البريطانية العامة في الشرق

BRITISH GOVERNMENT

To All Arab Peoples — Greetings and Peace be upon
The bearer of this letter is an Officer of the British Gover
and a friend of all Arabs. Treat him well, guard him from
give him food and drink, help him to return to the nearest
soldiers and you will be rewarded. Peace and the Mercy of
upon you.

The British High Command in the East

Useful Words.

English	Arabic	English	A
English.	Ingleezi.		
English Flying Officer.	Za-bit Ingleezi Tye-yar.	Water.	M
Friend.	Sa-hib, Sa-deek.	Food.	A

Take me to the English and you will be rewarded.
Hud-nee eind el Ingleez wa ta-hud mu-ka-fa.

2672/PMEB/2,0

The actual document carried by Flight Lieutenant Len Devonshire, called a 'gooley chit' by the RAF pilots. No man flew without it for if he had come down in the desert and was captured it could save his life. Without it he was in danger of having his privates cut off and sewn into his mouth – hence the name.

we landed I told Darwin about the good pickings. It was too late to go again that day. However, he did lay the plans to lead us back there the first thing in the morning.

'Flying Officer "Tigger" Smith had made a trip to Western Desert Headquarters and was in with Air Marshal Sir Arthur Coningham when pictures, taken by a PRU Spitfire, were brought in. Everyone was commenting on why the traffic was so badly jammed when Tigger jumped up and said: "That's our work. That's what we were doing." Only then did they realize what kind of show the two squadrons, Nos 213 and 238, were putting up. Tigger's mission was to get permission for us to pull out as the element of surprise was over and we feared a trap. They granted it.

'On the morning of the 16th, we gave Gialo another working over, packed up, and left immediately. Jerry had despatched a force to seek us out, but the birds had flown. Flying Officer Knapton and I left first, as we had to find a Jeep and an armoured car and drop them a message, then make our way back to LG.13. I learned later that the Jeep had picked up a German warrant officer who had been wandering in the desert for days. He had been trying to avoid capture at Fort Maddalena and was trying to walk to Agedabia. He had run out of water and was carrying a bottle of his own urine. I think this is the first time that I heard of recycling. He was delirious when found. I never did hear whether or not he survived his ordeal. During the day there was no place to hide from the hot sun and burning hot sand.

'The squadron had beaten us home and given the news to those who had been left behind in suspense instead of having the

In a blast pen at Malta, June 1943, Stan Turner takes over 417 Squadron. From left to right Pat Patterson ('A' Flight Commander), Stan Turner, Bert Houle and Jimmy Sinclair, the Squadron Adjutant.

Bert Houle's retirement dinner in 1965 when he was presented with this painting by Bob Hyndman (left). The painting depicts a Spitfire over the North African cast and Hyndman did the portrait of Bert Houle from a photograph taken the day he was promoted to Squadron Leader to take over 417 Squadron.

excitement of action. A rough estimate showed 125 lorries and armoured cars had been destroyed (flamers), over 250 had been damaged or destroyed and ten aircraft had been destroyed on the ground and two in the air. Our losses were three aircraft. It was a howling success, with the most concentrated target practice any of us had had in some time. It was just the type of mad operation Jackie Darwin would lay on. The very audacity and element of surprise were the factors which contributed most to its success. I think some of the leaders were decorated for this, but can't be sure. Medals seemed harder to come by so far away from the seat of power. In retrospect I wonder if we had been sent on this mission as expendable. The aircraft were almost in that class. They were pulled out of active service at the front a few weeks later and put into a defensive role. Experienced pilots would be harder to replace. It would have been very easy for enemy bombers to wipe us out at night. The armoured cars that we demolished on the back road could have surprised us also. I presume that the results were worth the risk. We will never know how many troops were killed during the strafing attacks on the packed transport vehicles. The German retreat was certainly delayed and their digging in behind the El Agheila line must have been disrupted also. It was a show that few of us will forget.'

Intelligence briefing for No 417 (City of Windsor) Squadron RCAF on 22 January 1944 at Marcianise near Naples, for the first patrol of Anzio Beachhead. On the back of the lorry from left to right; Jack Evans (Intelligence Officer), Bert Houle (CO of 417 Squadron) and Hendley Everard, Flight Commander. Standing are most of 417 Squadron pilots.

After the Western Desert, Bert Houle cast aside the sand and moved to Italy to take part in the Anzio Operation. However, it was still wind and sun, flies and sores, bully beef and chlorinated tea. He then saw service in Malta with No 248 Wing and served as flight commander in Nos 213 and 145 Squadrons, and as flight commander and then squadron commander of No 417 Squadron, Royal Canadian Air Force. While in Italy he was promoted to Squadron Leader to take over 417 Squadron from Stan Turner. By the end of the war Bert Houle had $12\frac{1}{2}$ kills to his credit and many near misses. Men and vehicles were too numerous to count. During the pursuit to Benghazi, the two Hurricane Squadrons, Nos 213 and 238, had destroyed or damaged some 300 vehicles, many by the guns of Bert Houle. He was a born flyer and a born leader and sadly his like are few and far between. Bert Houle was born on 24 March 1914 and he retired from the Service in 1965 with the rank of Group Captain.

CHAPTER EIGHTEEN

Desert Airfield

The part played by the Royal Air Force in the desert campaigns was truly tremendous. The Desert Air Force and the 8th Army were one big fighting family, working with a single purpose, to destroy the Axis forces in North Africa.

On 10 April 1941, Doug Mills was posted overseas and set sail on the *Dominio Monarch* for the Middle East, at a time when the situation in the Middle East was full of anxiety. His first stop was at No 103 MU at Aboukir and then at the end of September 1941 was posted to Tobruk, which was already under siege. The RAF party was made up with Armourers, Airframe Fitters, and MT Drivers. They boarded a frigate at Alexandria along with a group of soldiers. Once on the frigate they were told that as soon as they were in Tobruk Harbour, there was only twenty minutes to disembark, owing to the big German guns at Bardia. Twenty minutes was the time it took to get its range on the harbour.

Aboukir airfield, near Alexandria, Egypt in July 1941. In April 1941, No 3 Squadron RAAF and No 73 Squadron RAF were both incorporated into No 258 Wing. The latter squadron had remained static at Sidi Mahmud charged with the defence of Tobruk. No 3 fell back into Egypt to Aboukir to protect Salum and reinforce No 73 Squadron as required. The building in the background is the Watch Office.

A street in Tobruk.

The RAF unit at El Gubbi (Tobruk) that Doug Mills and the others arrived at was an RAF Liaison section. Their job was to maintain one Hurricane which was used solely for reconnsaissance. The small party also had to refuel or rearm any other RAF aircraft that might drop in and that might be Spitfires, Hurricanes, or even old Gladiators of No 3 Squadron which maintained fighter patrols over the battle area. Even in these early days, the RAF fighter squadrons were showing the effects of sustained operations under desert conditions. Fortunately they met surprisingly little enemy opposition. The numbers of Italian aircraft serviceable in Libya when Tobruk fell are now estimated at only 45 bombers and 35 fighters.

With the gradual conversion to single-seater aircraft many Gunners, Wireless Operators and Photographers were rendered superfluous. So, at the request of Headquarters RAF in the Middle East, these men, together with ground tradesmen associated with them, were attached to RAF squadrons which were under strength, in particular the two army cooperation squadrons, Nos 6 and 208.

Tobruk Harbour 13 March 1942. Petrol on fire after an attack by Ju 88 Stukas.

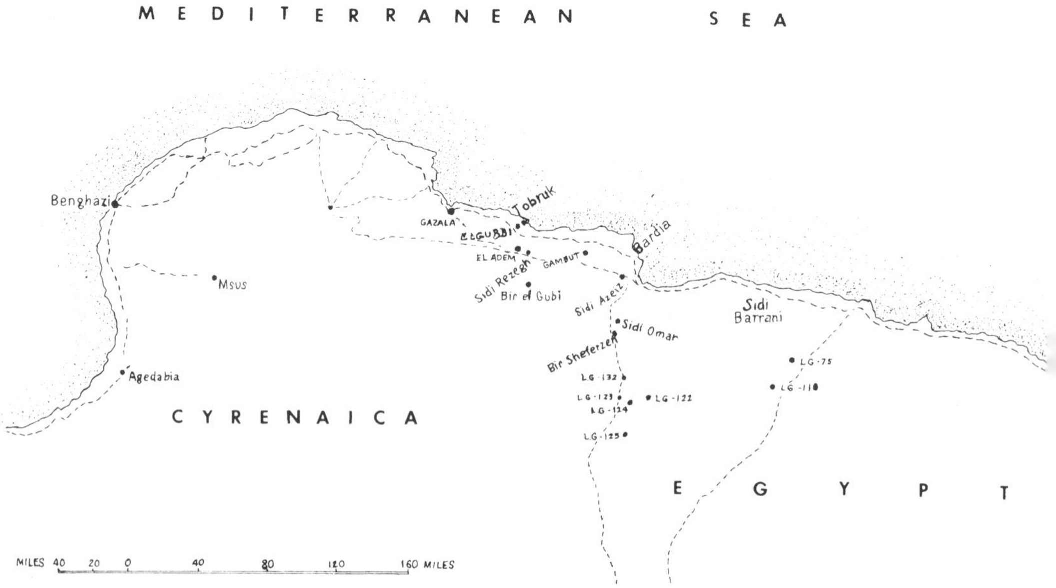

Map showing positions of landing grounds.

On 14 January 1941, Corporal V. J. Jarvis of Perth, Australia, who was a Wireless Operator from No 3 Squadron then attached to No 208 Squadron, set out with Leading Aircraftman J. G. Parr from No 3 Squadron to check wireless equipment in use with artillery units near Tobruk. Even under normal circumstances accurate navigation in the featureless desert was difficult, but during a dust storm almost impossible. On that particular day Jarvis and Parr ran into a dust storm which caused them to drive their tender almost on to the guns of the Tobruk defences, Jarvis being killed and Parr captured, although Parr was released a few days later when British forces entered the town on 22 January. Parr was the only British prisoner in Tobruk. On the morning of 22 January he took charge of the gendarmerie barracks where he was being held and when the troops entered the town Parr was virtually in control of the local police. Not surprisingly Parr was later commissioned and became a Flight Lieutenant.

Land battles still raged around Tobruk and the situation was very changeable. The single Hurricane at El Gubbi had to be kept out of sight of the enemy that was only about four or five miles away. To do this the men had to cover a small wadi with netting, but it was on a fairly steep gradient so they had to manhandle the Hurricane down and turn it round ready for day-break the following day. Weather permitting the Hurricane would be airborne. To get it airborne was quite a feat as Doug Mills explains: 'The procedure of the operation was this, Sergeant Cross – who was our Chiefy – stood at the top of the slope to make sure that the sky was clear of the

'Ave Maria' outside Tobruk Church 1941/42.

enemy. And, if it was clear we would then pull and shove the Hurricane up the slope. When at the top, start up the aircraft, and away it would go. The pilot just used to lift it enough to retract his undercarriage and keep it at that height until out at sea, which was two or three miles away. When out at sea the pilot would climb, come back and survey the perimeter and then come in as low as possible after the recce sortie.'

The area around El Gubbi was littered with many wrecks and close by their billets was an Italian aircraft a CR42 'It was u/s,' said Mills, 'and it looked as though it had the RAF markings on it at some time or another.'

The billets for the men was a cave which housed all twelve of them and it was one place where they all felt safe. 'It was where we all felt safe even while the shelling was going on all around us', said Mills. 'Our off-duty hours were nil, as we were on call 24 hours a day – so we spent much time in what was our billets. We lived pretty rough but the food wasn't too bad, we made a good stew out of dehydrated potatoes – which came to us chipped like crisps – dehydrated cabbage, soya, tinned sausage and bully beef. The highlight was the fresh-baked bread which was full of weevils (little beetles) that was baked in Tobruk. Many meals were bolted in silence.

Tobruk Cenetry – 1941.

'We were called out many times in the middle of the night to light the flare path. These were petrol tins, half full of sand soaked in petrol. The aircraft usually brought in top army brass for we were right in the thick of it.'

By trade Doug Mills was an MT Driver but during his time in the desert he was in charge of refuelling. At El Gubbi he had to turn his hand to anything. With Tobruk cemetery only about half a mile away there was a constant reminder about the horrors of war. 'It was a daily scene to see them burying the chaps that had bought it the night previous', said Mills.

Before being posted overseas Mills had seen service in Norway with No 46 Squadron and during ops his job had been refuelling the fighters, using four-gallon tins which were very flimsy and often leaked. He also helped to rearm the aircraft, so he was quite an old hand at it by the time he reached El Gubbi. 'But things were much different in the desert', recalls Mills. 'Refuelling was a long job, we had to use a funnel and a chamois leather and even topping the Hurricane up would take an hour or so. The 100 octane fuel came in 44 gallon barrels, it was much later before we got a bowser.'

During May 1941 the British military position in the Middle East had deteriorated further. However, after a few anxious days, the revolt in Iraq was suppressed and Tobruk held firm thus preventing an immediate enemy invasion of Egypt. However relations with Syria worsened and by the end of the month Crete was in German hands. The Fliegerkorps X, formerly based in Sicily, moved to Crete and Greece. This now gave the enemy a strong hand for they could now attack in strength from airfields on Crete the main British disembarkation port of Suez. Air power now replaced sea power in the eastern Mediterranean basin, for ships were subject to crippling attacks once outside the very limited range of fighters

Land and air battles ranged continuously around Tobruk. A British fighter lies with a broken back, engulfed in flames.

he Italian CR 42 ·rcraft with nglish markings. obruck, March 942.

Jack and Doug Mills in Tobruk, 1942.

'Home Sweet Home' – the cave (hole at right) where the twelve airmen lived. Doug Mills relaxes after getting his washing out on the line! El Gubbi, November 1941.

operating from Sidi Barrani. With the Germans on the doorstep, Tobruk bore the brunt of the Fliegerkorps X attacks.

In June Tedder ordered all fighters to concentrate on ground strafing. This was done, the Tomahawks of the newly-formed No 250 Squadron concentrating on the main Capuzzo-El Adem roads. Pilot Officer C. R. Caldwell (later Group Captain) soon emerged as top fighter pilot. On one sortie, while escorting a Tobruk convoy he shot down two Ju 87s and shared an Me 110 with Sergeant Whittle. Caldwell developed an uncanny gunnery sense and he assiduously practised this by low-level firing at his own aircraft's shadow when other targets were lacking. When Caldwell left the Middle East, Tedder wrote a personal assessment in Caldwell's log-book: 'An excellent leader and a first-class shot'. This was a rare and highly-valued honour from the AOC-in-C.

In mid 1941 there was a rethink about the workings of army co-operation squadrons. Marshal of the RAF Lord Tedder ruled that

The complete detachment pose over 'The Cave' at El Gubbi 1941.

The remains of an Me 110 near Gazala with Doug Mills in the cockpit.

Christmas Day, 1941 at Gazala. Proof that the unknown RAF Hurricane Unit did exist. From left to right, standing; Kaiser, Foster, Tucker, Mills, Thomas, 'Patsy' Mayor, Sparks and 'Liverpool' Moore, kneeling; 'Ginger' Corporal Healey, Jenkins, Flying Officer Wingate-Gray and Corporal Lumley. 'Lofty' Horsley took the Christmas Day snap.

Christmas Breakfast – Gazala 1941. Note the rocky surface of the desert and how everyone is well wrapped up.

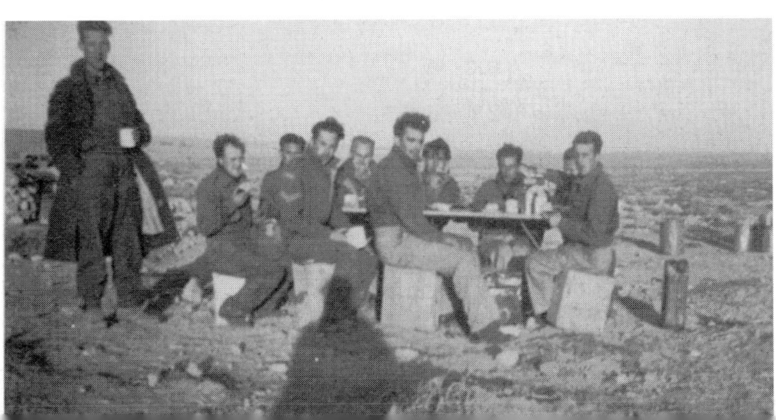

consequent on the arrival of German fighter aircraft of superior performance in the Western Desert, there must be husbanding of resources during periods when the land battle was static. Individual aircraft must no longer carry out lengthy tactical reconnaissances, and such tasks would only be done under cover of adequate fighter protection. In August, as casualties had been negligible and photographs were required of enemy dispositions around Tobruk, the Hurricanes of No 451 Squadron began to penetrate more deeply into Cyrenaica. Squadron Leader V. A. Pope (later Group Captain) inaugurated these Tobruk flights on 9 August. Pope had only recently taken over the squadron, he had previously been in command of RAF Station Haifa in Palestine. When Pope took over No 451 Squadron from Flight Lieutenant Pelly it was in a shambles. Pelly had only been with the squadron a few weeks. At the end of June he was ordered to take his ground staff, hitherto employed at No 103 Maintenance Unit, forward to Qasaba to take over the Hurricanes, transport and equipment of No 6 (Army Co-operation) Squadron RAF.

The squadron's career, therefore, began with inexperienced groundcrews; only one Warrant Officer, one Flight Sergeant on loan from No 3 Squadron; eight Sergeants, of whom six were from No 3 Squadron, and 28 Corporals, of whom four were from No 3 Squadron. The senior airman in each flight was a Corporal. Workshops were in the charge of a Sergeant; there was no Engineer Officer, nor Warrant Officer, nor even a Flight Sergeant. Poor equipment was also a problem – for one month there were insufficient parachutes for all pilots; for two months insufficient flying clothing and life-saving waistcoats; oxygen supplies were also very low.

On top of all that, a motley collection of pilots assembled from various parts of the command, many of whom proved completely unsuitable for army co-operation duties. Of 45 pilots posted to 451

'Picadilly Circus' approximately 40 miles inland of Mersa Matruh – June 1942.

'Grub-up' – piring margarine on bread during a stop over at 'Hellfire' Pass – June 1942.

Squadron before October 1941, no fewer than fourteen were reposted as quite unsuitable, another ten left the Squadron for various reasons and nine had not yet arrived. Pope himself had not flown a Hurricane before he joined the squadron.

However, it did not take Pope long to knock the squadron into shape and after a few practice tactical reconnaissance and photographic sorties, the squadron was ready. Before the end of August the Hurricanes had made an intensive reconnaissance of the eastern and western perimeter sectors. On each sortie they had a strong fighter escort. Photographs taken during these flights were immediately taken to Bagush (HQ Desforce), developed and then flown back to Tobruk by squadron aircraft to be dropped on the landing ground there after a slow approach from the sea at 1,000 ft with wheels down so that the friendly nature of the visit would be evident.

Throughout all this Mills and his little party carried on with their lonely cave-like existence, like desert rats. 'The great problems were flies and sand with everything,' said Mills, 'when you are in the

A Hurricane of No 238 Squadron lands at LG. 121, Sidi Barani.

Lofty Davis and Doug Mills take shelter under the aircraft at Sidi Barani.

desert, you are alone and you feel like the man in the moon. The fine dust clogged up everything.'

The success of Pope's Tobruk sorties led, on 13 September, to a proposal that two Hurricanes should proceed to Tobruk on attachment while the main squadron party continued to operate as before until the siege was raised. The two Hurricanes of No 451 Squadron established themselves in Tobruk and operated thence for some months. Like the Hurricane with Doug Mills and his party, the two 451 Squadron Hurricanes were hidden in underground shelters. Dummy aircraft were dispersed round the landing ground and these attracted the attention of German and Italian pilots.

The cookhouse at Sidi Barani.

After living like a desert rat for many months, Doug Mills (centre) and two pals pose after the clothing parade. Gazala, February 1942.

On 11 September aircraft on the Tobruk reconnaissance reported an unusual concentration of enemy tanks and armoured vehicles near Acroma. Rommel's supply position had eased following the arrival of a convoy at Tripoli, and the completion of a road by-passing the Tobruk perimeter, so this concentration was thought to herald some forward thrust.

The main aims of the RAF between 14 October and 12 November (D minus 6) was to weaken the enemy air strength, neutralizing enemy airfields especially those used by German fighters and dive

Jack Moore stops to look at the notice board on the Gazala road which was known as 'Straff Alley'.

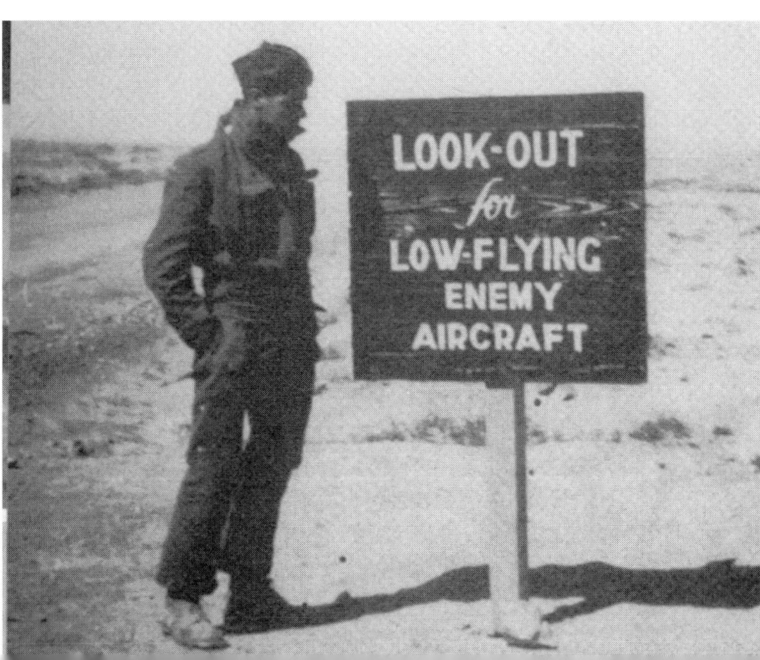
LOOK-OUT
for
LOW-FLYING
ENEMY
AIRCRAFT

A Junkers 52 shot down near Gazala in December 1941. Doug Mills standing with his overcoat on and hands in pockets which shows how cold it gets in the desert.

bombers, and winning air superiority over the triangle formed by Bardia, Tobruk and Maddalena, in which area German fighters were most likely to be encountered.

The essence of the 8th Army's plan was the destruction of German armoured vehicles. To achieve this the best British tanks were concentrated in XXX Corps, which was to open the offensive by striking towards Tobruk and seizing the ridges of Belhamed, Sidi Rezegh and Schifet El Adem, which dominate for some miles the Tobruk by-pass and the Trigh Capuzzo. In the expectation that the German armoured division could not ignore this threat, they would

By 1942 the much vaunted Luftwaffe had been completely surpassed and, indeed, made to look very amateurish in its own special field of tactical support. This Ju 87 lost its battle with RAF fighters – it came to rest in the Stocne Pass.

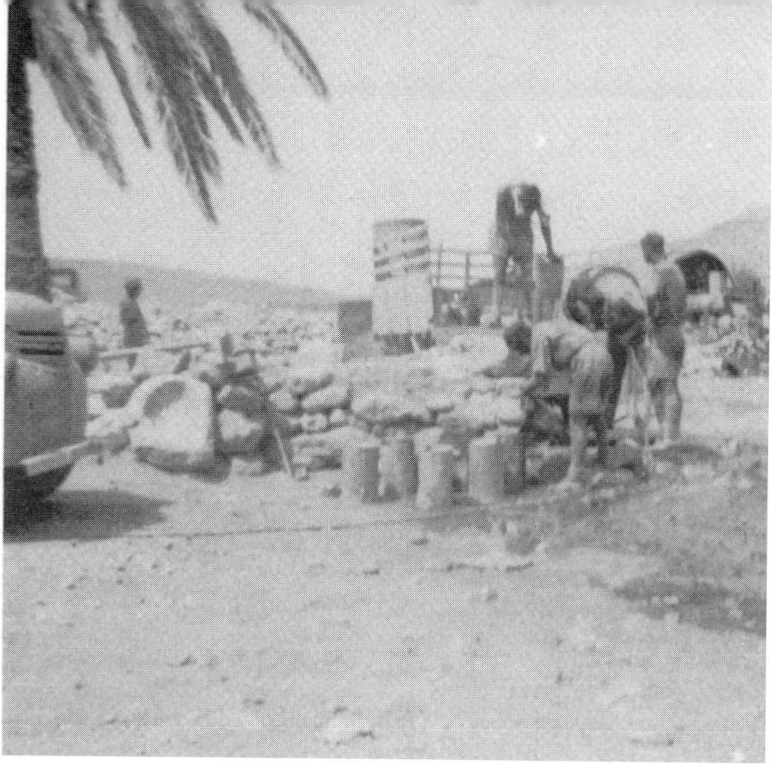

Doug Mills and his forgotten unit replenish their supplies from an oasis near Gambut.

be drawn on a battle area of the 8th Army's choosing. Then, at the appropriate moment the Tobruk garrison was to break out and attack the enemy at the rear.

Lady Luck smiled on the 8th Army at the outset, for a very heavy rainstorm swept Cyrenaica during the night of 17–18 November. This left enemy airfields waterlogged and many German tanks of the 15th Panzer Division and motorized units immobile, while XXX Corps, operating inland and on the eastern fringe of the rain-soaked area, could still carry out the original plan. They advanced throughout 18–19 November and the Royal Air Force gave full support during these two days, taking advantage of the absence of enemy air opposition to bomb the advance landing grounds and strafe the rear airfields. To enable operations to continue unchecked a flight of 237 Squadron which had been in reserve, was attached to 451 Squadron which had moved to LG.132. They had only just arrived there when they were attacked by four Messerschmitts. Three Hurricanes were damaged while on the ground.

Throughout all this Mills and his small party sat tight in their cave and after the rainstorm they felt like drowned rats. However, the Tobruk Hurricanes made three flights over the Acroma El Adem

Doug Mills acting the goat with the Italian pump that they had just found.

area to estimate possible dangers from that region which might interfere with the garrison's proposed breakout towards Bu Amud. These fighter sweeps became more vital as enemy air activity increased, because although it had been hoped to benefit from newly-installed radar facilities at Tobruk and Sidi Barrani, in practice these failed to give adequate early warning of enemy aircraft

The link-up with the Tobruk garrison seemed remote after the first two glorious days. General Rommel, the 'Desert Fox', soon took command by sending the 15th and 21st Panzer Divisions racing north to Sidi Rezegh where they found only the 7th Support Group and the 7th Armoured Brigade. The Germans attacked immediately before British armour could arrive. Once the British armour did arrive a tank battle continued for two days.

After bitter fighting the 4th and 6th New Zealand Brigades captured Belhamed and Sidi Rezegh on successive days and made contact with the Tobruk garrison which had itself advanced to Ed Duda. However Sidi Rezegh fell again on the 30th and Belhamed on 1 December, leaving the Tobruk garrison isolated once again. Tobruk, though, was a thorn in Rommel's side. This second Battle

Sergeant Sainty and Doug Mills after a trip in a sand storm.

of Sidi Rezegh entailed ceaseless operations for No 451 Squadron, first in giving continuous accurate reports of enemy progress towards the ridges, and then, when it passed with XIII Corps into Tobruk, in covering the battleground itself. The squadron then stood down until replacement pilots and machines could be obtained.

Tobruk had seen much fighting and on one occasion when No 112 Squadron engaged enemy fighters while No 250 Squadron dived to attack the vulnerable Stukas, Flight Lieutenant C. R. Caldwell shot down five Ju 87s. Extracts from his Combat Report reveal his cold determination:

'I was leading the formation of two squadrons, 112 acting as top cover to 250 Squadron to patrol a line approximately ten miles west of El Gubbi and had just reached this position at 11:40 hours when I received R/T warning that a large enemy formation was approaching from the north-west at our own height. Both squadrons climbed immediately and within a minute the enemy formation consisting of Ju 87s with fighter escort was sighted on our starboard side ... 250 Squadron went into line astern behind me and as 112 Squadron engaged the escorting enemy fighters, we attacked the Ju 87s from the rear quarter ... At 300 yd I opened fire with all my guns at the leader of one of the rear sections of three, allowing too little deflection, and hit No 2 and No 3 one of which burst into flames immediately, the other going down smoking and went into flames after losing about 1,000 ft. I then attacked the leader of the rear section ... from below and behind, opening fire with all guns at very close range. The enemy aircraft turned over and dived steeply down with the root of the starboard wing in flames ... [at another Stuka I] opened fire again at close range, the enemy caught fire and crashed in flames near some dispersed mechanized transport ... I was able to pull up under the belly of the one at the rear holding the burst until very close range. The enemy aircraft diced gently straight ahead streaming smoke, caught fire and then dived into the ground ...'

For Doug Mills and the others living in the cave, the XIII Corps made a welcome sight, but there was no time to rest as Mills explains: 'When the garrison was relieved at Tobruk we were formed into an Advanced Landing Ground Party, our Commanding Officer was Flying Officer Wingate-Gray, an RFC pilot, who used to father us more than command us. We would have done anything for him – he was the greatest.

'Our duties took us up to Gazala and all the Forward Landing Grounds to Benghazi. During this period I was driving back to Gazala Landing Ground after picking up the rations from Tobruk, and I had just reached the section of road known to everyone as "Straff Alley," when suddenly I heard an aircraft and the sound of gunfire. I was only driving slow for the tarmac road was full of pot-holes and there was often a diversion owing to bomb-holes. As soon as I heard the gunfire I stopped the truck and was out in a flash looking for somewhere to hide. But there was nowhere, I instinctively dived under the truck and lay spread eagled on the road underneath the truck with my eyes closed and hands over my head. After a second or two I felt as if the road was slipping backwards. Later I opened my eyes when the Me 109 had gone only to find that the truck had slowly passed over me leaving me exposed on the road. I had been in such a hurry to get out that I hadn't applied the handbrake.

'During the retreat we came back to Gazala, and just got settled in our cave, about 23:59 hours, when a voice from the mouth of the cave, told us to get out quickly. It happened to be a Kiwi Sergeant and he told us that German tanks were about 5 miles away. So we hopped it and joined the convoy on the retreat.'

After leaving Gazala on 16 December Rommel had retreated swiftly to Agedabia, keeping ahead of the pursuing XIII Corps until the 23rd. The RAF made great efforts to keep up with the advance, one maintenance party arriving at Mechili airfield as the last Germans were leaving, stores and petrol arriving the next day, so that within 24 hours four squadrons were based there. Two days before Benghazi fell, Msus was cleared of obstructions and No 258 Wing of fighters brought forward immediately.

Mills continues: 'We arrived at El Adem the following night and had just got settled in an old transport workshop when Jerry started bombing. We got down into the pit after the first bombs fell and it was lucky we did for one HE hit the far end of the workshops. It was the start of my grey hairs.

'When daylight came you could see why the Germans had been so persistent for there were three or four fighter squadrons with Kittyhawks and Hurricanes. The Kittyhawks had a shark mouth painted on them and I believe they were with No 112 Squadron.

'We stayed at El Adem for two or three days and then went on to Gambut doing the usual refuelling and rearming. Things were fairly quiet with only the odd strafing – until a couple of squadrons came in and then it was bombing and strafing nearly every night. The army came with their Bofors later, which improved our situation.

'I was returning to Gambut one morning with rations and water, along the bottom of the escarpment, when a Hurricane, flying just above the ground – about ten feet, shot past me about a hundred yards to my right with bullets hitting the deck under him, and then, about a hundred yards or so behind him was an Me 109 still firing at him. A short distance past us the Hurricane climbed and banked to the right, with the Me 109 still behind him, bringing both of them almost over the Gambut Landing Ground.

'I had just said to my mate that one of them was going to get it when the Me 109 just turned into a fireball and crashed on the other side of the Landing Ground. We learned later that the Bofors had got it.

'We moved on to several Landing Grounds during the retreat, still organizing petrol dumps. On one occasion we came across an Italian pump. Dead bodies lined the road and many could not be removed as they had been booby-trapped.

During the siege of Tobruk the Aussies published a daily news sheet called the 'Tobruk Truth' and this was a great morale booster to all the men. Doug Mills looked forward to his daily copy and read and reread it many times. The following is an extract from the issue dated Tuesday 23 December 1941:

'Pressure on Benghazi is increasing, and our mobile columns are striking further and further westwards. News comes tonight of the attack on yet another advanced aerodrome at Jedabya, when 37 planes on the ground were destroyed. This raid follows close on the heels of an attack by our advanced columns on an aerodrome 150 miles into Tripolitania, when 24 planes were destroyed. Other advanced columns

Tobruk Cemetry 1954.

have reached the coastal plain of the gulf of Cirte, South of Benghazi. Other forces are still pressing the enemy back towards Benghazi and it is stated in London that it is practically certain that Barce is in our hands. 74 enemy planes in various stages of disrepair came into our hands when Derna was taken, and 23 enemy planes have been destroyed in raids during the last few days. Extremely bad weather has continued to hamper air operations, but nevertheless, the Air Force continued its raids on enemy transport and concentrations of retreating enemy. At one point a long line of over a hundred lorries was successfully bombed. Attacks on enemy bases included Casto Benito and Tripoli, which is the only remaining port for Axis supplies brought across the Mediterranean. Three of our planes are missing from operations.'

In July 1942, Doug Mills was posted to No 106 Maintenance Unit at El Khanka and three months later to No 51 MTC driving a 'Mack' lorry and trailer carrying stores and spares up to Beirut in the Lebanon and then later petrol, etc, up to Benghazi and Tripoli. After four years in the desert, Mills found himself on the way home to Blighty and on 20 February 1946 he was demobbed.

The two Hurricanes of No 451 Squadron that established themselves in Tobruk and operated thence for some months, were hidden in underground shelters and, like the Hurricane looked after by Doug Mills and party, were never discovered by the enemy, despite the fact that air raids and reconnaissance were carried out almost daily. One of the Australian pilots concerned was Flying Officer R. M. Achilles, but efforts to ascertain the name of the other one have not succeeded. Indeed there is no record at squadron, group or command level or in the records of the Ailo Tobruk or in the fortnightly operational summaries that the detachment took place.

Like the Hurricane with the small RAF Liaison Section at El Gubbi (Tobruk) there is no record, and sadly Doug Mills cannot remember the pilot's name. Fortunately he did take many photographs, some of which are unique, and published here for the first time.

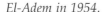

El-Adem in 1954.

Chapter Nineteen

Mohawk Fighter Squadrons

The Mohawk fighter squadrons served in India and Burma under South-East Asia Command. There were three Mohawk fighter squadrons, Nos 5,146 and 155, but No 146 (F) Squadron hardly rated as a Mohawk squadron The approximate dates that the three squadrons had Mohawks on strength were as follows:

No 5 Squadron – 29 December 1941 to 12 June 1943, a total of 530 days.

No 155 Squadron – 24 August 1942 to 6 January 1944, a total of 501 days.

No 146 Squadron – 21 March 1942 to 8 April 1942, a total of 19 days.

No 5 Squadron received its first Mohawks at Dum Dum, Calcutta in December 1941. The Squadron had moved by rail and air to Dum Dum, to take over the defence of Calcutta, the need for which was brought about by the entry of Japan into the war. It was to be many months before the first Jap was downed over India. This honour went to Sergeant W. S. Garnett. The American pilots of the P-40s received the equivalent of £125 sterling for every Japanese aircraft they shot down when fighting over the soil of China. No such luck

Mohawks of No 5 Squadron over the Arakan Coast (near Chittagong).

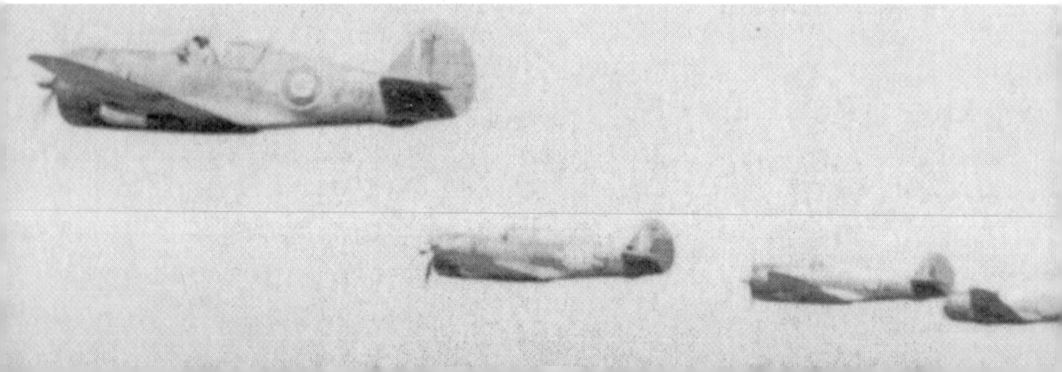

for Sergeant Garnett, but he did have the satisfaction of knowing it was one Jap less to torture his comrades.

No 5 Squadron is one of the original squadrons of the Royal Flying Corps. It was formed on 26 July 1913 at South Farnborough, from a flight of No 3 Squadron, the first aeroplane squadron ever formed. With the run-down of squadrons at the end of World War 1, No 5 Squadron moved to India when it was reformed at Quetta, from No 48 Squadron on 1 February 1920, and was designated No 5 (Army Co-operation) Squadron in May 1924. It was to remain there for 28 years, the task of controlling recalcitrant tribes of the North West Frontier being its major role. It was not until its move to Dum Dum in December 1941 that its frontier duties were exchanged for those of a fighter squadron, its first commitment being the defence of Calcutta. Again the squadron records tell little of its activities and the story that nearly all the squadron records and silver were lost in the Indian Ocean, whilst being transported, could well be true. However, the following is an extract from the squadron history:

'*Dum Dum* 29 December 1941 – First Mohawk aircraft allotted to 5 Squadron was collected by Sergeant Campbell. Another Mohawk aircraft from Drigh Road was flown in by Sergeant Currin.

'*Dum Dum* 17 January 1942 – First Mohawk forced landing – Sergeant Bates force landed Mohawk AR677 at Basanti due to shortage of petrol. Squadron Leader Maling AFC, on landing at Basanti to give assistance to Sergeant Bates, struck a ridge on landing ground which caused his tailwheel to break off. 18th – Flight Lieutenant Fyson, Mohawk BJ438, landed at Dum Dum with his undercarriage partially lowered thereby causing considerable damage to aircraft. Three more Mohawks were collected during January and following added to strength: Flight Lieutenant J. H.

Mohawk under repair after undercarriage collapse. 5 Squadron Section, Dum Dum, early 1942.

Iremonger, Squadron Leader E. Sidey MO, Pilot Officer B. Fane-Saunders Admin.

'*Dum Dum* 21 February – Three Mohawks carried out first demonstration flight over Jamshedpur in aid of Tata's War Weapon Week. Eight Mohawks were collected from No 301 during February and five Audax were handed over to No 146 Squadron whose pilots flew them to Dinjan.

'*Dum Dum* 2 March 1942 – Squadron Leader J. H. Giles posted to 5 Squadron vice Squadron Leader J. R. Maling AFC. By end of month following were posted to No 5: Flight Lieutenants W. H. Pitt-Brown, A. K. MacEwan and D. O. Cunliffe; Flying Officers H. L. B. Girvan MO, C. S. Courtney-Clarke, Bedford; Pilot Officer W. J. N. Lee; and Sergeant Pilots C. E. Kron, B. S. Wipiti, Wood and E. W. J. Blake.

'*Dum Dum* 25 April – Wing Commander Stephens was forced to abandon Mohawk AR644 over Kasapara village due to failure of oil system. First abandonment.

'*Dum Dum* 5 May – Aircraft, pilots and approx fifty maintenance personnel of No 5 proceeded to Dinjan to join remainder of 146 Squadron to form No 5 Squadron at Dinjan. A like change-over of aircraft, pilots and personnel was carried out by 146 Squadron, the remainder of 5 Squadron at Dum Dum being absorbed into No 146 Squadron. Added to strength in May: Pilot Officers E. Cooper, J. T. May, B. Snowball, D. F. Bullen, B. R. Johnson Adjutant, S. Swaffer Admin; Sergeant pilots H. O. Seifert and B. Ferguson. 13th – R. W. Boyens, E. R. Worts and G. I. Baines arrived at Dinjan.

'*Dinjan* 16 June – First pamphlets/leaflets – Two aircraft of No 5 attempted pamphlet dropping Mainkwang, Shingwiyang, Tapapga but forced to return due to bad weather. Mohawks covered Audax (Sergeant Bates) which picked up messages at Shingwiyang and

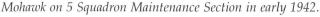

Mohawk on 5 Squadron Maintenance Section in early 1942.

dropped leaflets at Hkalak GA. 18th – ? First escort duty – six Mohawks of No 5, Group Captain Roberts leading, escorted by three Blenheim IVs of 113 Squadron RAF to attack target in Myitkyina area. 17th – Squadron Leader W. H. Pitt-Brown posted to 5 Squadron as CO.

'*Dinjan* (near Murkong Sellek) 19 June – First fatal accident. Two Mohawks reported missing AR641 Pilot Officer J. Trimble and BJ534 Sergeant Blake (785051) collided in the air. Last named aircraft dived into river and exploded. No trace of aircraft or pilot (Sergeant E. W. J. Blake).

Pilot Officer J. T. Trimble baled out and his aircraft exploded in hitting sandbank. Pilot Officer Trimble was uninjured. Accident occurred over Dibrugarh area.

'*Dinjan* 3 July – Flying Officer F. W. H. Russell (61083) posted as Adjutant vice Flying Officer P. P. Stares. Squadron Leader R. J. Walker posted to No 5 supernumerary for operations experience. Pilots posted to No 5: Acting Flight Sergeant A. R. Lawrence (Can 59882); Sergeants R. R. A. MacLauchlan (NZ404321), F. J. Tilley (NZ41964), W. W. Wood (NZ404440). 15th – Sergeant Ferguson force landed Mohawk AR646 at Daulatpur pm. He sustained no injuries. 7th – First ops from Tezpur. Four Mohawks attack BMP lines of Kalemyo … Green and Black sections of No 5 attack Myitkyina barracks, bashas & tents were burning fiercely. 19th – First death

Flight Sergeant R. W. Boyens gets a few final words of encouragement from Flying Officer J. R. Rashleigh before his first solo in a Mohawk at Dinjan.

(ground staff) Aircraftman 1st Class R. Giddings (1230659), Fitter 2E, deceased buried in Dibrugarh Cemetery. Died at 21:25 hours at Assam Oil Co Hospital, Digboi as result of haemorrhaegic purpura.

'*Tezpur* Sergeant W. S. Garnett first ever pilot to bring down Jap aircraft over India – 20 August 1942. Confirmed by Sergeant Ray MacLauchlan who acted as top cover during the combat.

'*Dinjan* 25 August – Pilots posted from 151 OTU: Pilot Officers D. R. Ryde, N. M. Beyts, W. M. Souter; Sergeants T. G. Smith (629168), D. St L. Parsons (1382250), W. G. Thomas (655513).

'*Dinjan* 27 September – Squadron move to Agartala begins. 29th – Air Maintenance Party left by DC-3 for Feni for Operation Bangor. 30th – Twelve Mohawks took off from Feni 08:55 hours to bomb and machine-gun. Eight enemy aircraft reported to be on Akyab Satellite. Mohawk Sergeant Thomas seen to crash on enemy occupied aerodrome, believed killed.

'*Agartala* 14 October – Squadron Leader P. M. Bond posted to command No 5 Squadron. Squadron-Leader Pitt-Brown proceeded to 169 Wing as Wing Leader. Squadron Leader Pitt-Brown and Flight Lieutenant Cunliffe in two aircraft of 5 Squadron took off from Imphal with eleven aircraft of 155 Squadron RAF (first joint operation of 5/155 Squadrons) in low level attack on Schwebo aerodrome.

'*Agartala* 24 November – Sergeant T. G. Smith after day practice flying Mohawk BJ446 belly landed, his undercarriage and flaps having jammed. He landed alongside runway in cloud of dust from Blenheims that had just landed. Sergeant Smith sustained facial injuries, having fractured jaw in two places and losing one eye. His aircraft was category III.

'*Agartala* 16 December – Ten aircraft of No 5 and two of No 155 provided escort for 21 bombers. Target – Buthidaung area.

'*Agartala* 4 January 1943 – Flight Sergeant Ferguson crashed on landing. His aircraft Mohawk BK580 came to rest nose down in middle of runway. Flying Officer Bellinger, Flight Sergeant Baines and Sergeant Worts continue 'Rhubarb' ops from Imphal. Mohawk BK572 (Flying Officer Bellinger) failed to return: believed hit by gunfire aircraft seen to make safe belly landing and immediately burst into flames at a point East of Bilumyo. Pilot was seen to jump out apparently unhurt and run towards a nearby house. 19th – Flight Lieutenant D. O. Cunliffe awarded DFC for successful ops against enemy from Tezpur during monsoon period of last summer. 28th – The Mohawk wing of nineteen aircraft made a fighter sweep of Akyab Island.

'*Agartala* 19 February – Flying Officer R. S. Tovey crashed near aerodrome approx 17:30 hours. He was flying Mohawk BB977 on air experience test. Aircraft spun into the earth and pilot was apparently killed instantly.

'*Agartala* 6 March – Flying Officer T. A. Scandrett Adjutant posted from No 1 R&R Party, Imphal. 5th – Squadron Leader P. M. Bond posted to 169 Wing RAF. 9th – Squadron Leader G. J. C. Hogan, ex-293 Wing, arrived to command 5 Squadron. Pilot Officer B. R. Johnson, Adjutant, sick in Calcutta posted to 224 Group. No 60 Squadron, RAF, consider No 5's escort very highly. The Intelligence Officer when at Chittagong, was in conversation with member of that Squadron who said they were always glad to have 5 Squadron in attendance. The Hurricane Squadron on the other hand did not look upon 5 Squadron so favourably as they found it difficult to distinguish our aircraft from Army 0I's of the enemy. Group found Mohawks so suitable for the work over Mayu Peninsula they would like to use them exclusively.

'*Agartala* 19 March – For first time during this war RAF used Vultee Vengeance dive bombers and 5 Squadron had the honour to be chosen to escort them.

'*Agartala* 6 April – First air raid. At 14:35 hours at least eighteen Army bombers escorted by twelve fighters attacked aerodrome. Main runway was damaged but made serviceable within the hour. Casualties – five British other ranks injured, one Indian other rank injured, approx 25 Indian civilians killed and fourteen injured. 18th – Flying Officers Lee and Chancellor went south to carry out offensive recce. At Hpaukyi-chaung four wall-less huts sheltering green-clad troops were seen. Flying Officer Lee made low level attack and saw Jap troops fleeing. He pulled up when below roof-top level and turned. It was then he saw Chancellor attacking huts and waited for him to pull up. This Chancellor never did – he hit the ground with all his guns firing. It is considered impossible he could have survived the crash.

'*Agartala* 4 May – Flying Officer Thomas flew a Mohawk against a Mosquito. In speed the Mosquito was master, but as experienced, it was beaten by the Mohawk in turning. 6th – Flight Lieutenant Rashleigh completed 200 hours operational flying. 12th – Squadron Leader Pitt-Brown awarded DFC. Some of his finest work was done when the squadron was at Dinjan during Monsoon of 1942. Flight Lieutenant "Doc" Skene's birthday coupled with news of move to Khargpur. A party is held with Jon Rashleigh behind the bar. 29th – Main party leave for Khargpur.

Line up of Mohawks at Agartala.

'*Khargpur* 1 June – No 5 Squadron arrives at its new location. 4th – First hill party left for Chakrata. 12th – Squadron Leader Hogan, Flight Lieutenant Courtney-Clarke, Flying Officer Mendizabel and Pilot Officer Lawrence left at dawn in a 31 Squadron C-47 transport bound for Allahabad to collect No 5's new aircraft – Hurricane IIds.'

* * *

On 15 October 1941, No 146 (Fighter) Squadron formed at Risalpur from a nucleus from 5 Squadron. Two days later Squadron Leader B. Barthold became Commanding Officer and the squadron strength was one flight ('B' Flight) of four Audax aircraft, three Sergeant pilots, one senior NCO, fifteen airmen and two coolies. No 146 Squadron moved to Dum Dum in the first week of December 1941, and by the end of the month had moved to Dinjan. No 146 (F) Squadron was destined to have only four Mohawk aircraft for a very short period and they were never used in combat. The four Mohawks arrived at the end of March 1942 and the following month the squadron diarist wrote:

'Dinjan 4 April 1941 – Orders received to hand over to No 5 Squadron the four Mohawks allotted to 146 Squadron. Instead, the squadron was to be given some Buffaloes for training. Very bitter disappointment. 6th-8th – The four Mohawks flown to Calcutta by

Slight mishap with the Mohawk at Agartala.

squadron pilots Flight Lieutenant Aitkens and Sergeant Gill, brought back two Buffaloes – very bad condition having been used in Burma. 24th – Flight Sergeant Sykes returned from Karachi with a Mohawk.'

* * *

The third Mohawk squadron was No 155 and this formed at Peshawar on 1 April 1942 and placed under No 233 Group Peshawar for no aircraft and equipment were available. As the weeks passed and still no aircraft the men became very restless and morale was at a low ebb. In early July four officers and 277 airmen left by train for Madras. At long last things were moving and on 24 August the first batch of six Mohawks, under the command of Flight Lieutenant P. Rathie, arrived at Madras. Two days later the second batch of Mohawks arrived with the exception of one aircraft left as unserviceable at Bhopal. The extracts from the squadron diary covering the Mohawk period from September 1942 to January 1943 which shows first hand their role and what it was like on a Mohawk squadron.

'*Madras* 3–11 September 1942 – Third batch of four Mohawks arrived. 17th – First Mohawk scramble for unidentified aircraft out to sea. Aircraft was friendly. 20th – First convoy patrol by two aircraft and first fly past by Mohawks for Air Force Day took place over town. Two aircraft arrived from Secunderabad bringing strength of aircraft to its total of twenty. 27th – Seven Mohawks led by Flight Lieutenant Rathie left for Vizagapatam for convoy patrol duties ("A" Flight).

'*Madras* 12 October 1942 – Preparations for move to Jessore. 13th – Main party of six officers and 243 airmen left for Avardi. Air party led by Squadron leader Stones w~th six officers and two Sergeant pilots proceeded via Vizagapatam, and "A" Flight detachment joined main party at that station. A Care and Maintenance party was left under Equipment Officer Pilot Officer Coleman. 15th – Fourteen airmen posted to squadron from 104 Squadron RAF. 30th – Eleven Mohawks made an attack on Schwebo aerodrome. All aircraft returned safely. Main party arrived Agartala 31 October 1942.

'*Calcutta* 1 November – Squadron Leader Stones posted and Flight Lieutenant Rathie took charge pending arrival of new CO. 10th – Flight Lieutenant Rathie, Flight Lieutenant Winton, Flying Officer Dawson-Squibb, Pilot Officers Buddle, McClumpha, Haley, Edmonds and Sergeant Boult escorted eight Blenheims to Akyab.

'*Agartala* 1 December – First wing formation practice with 5 and 155 Squadrons practising together. 25th – First Christmas with Mohawks. Christmas dinner served to airmen by officers and senior NCOs. The CO Squadron Leader Jeffries DFC thanked Flight Lieutenant D. Winton and Flying Officer Nicholson for fetching Christmas fare from Calcutta and also Pilot Weir for organizing the dinner and voluntary canteen.

'*Agartala* 1 January 1943 – Pilot Officer Haley believed to have been hit by ack-ack fire and posted missing. 14th – Six Mohawks

Flight Sergeant Ian Baines in his Mohawk, BS744, *with groundcrew Riley (left) and Carr.*

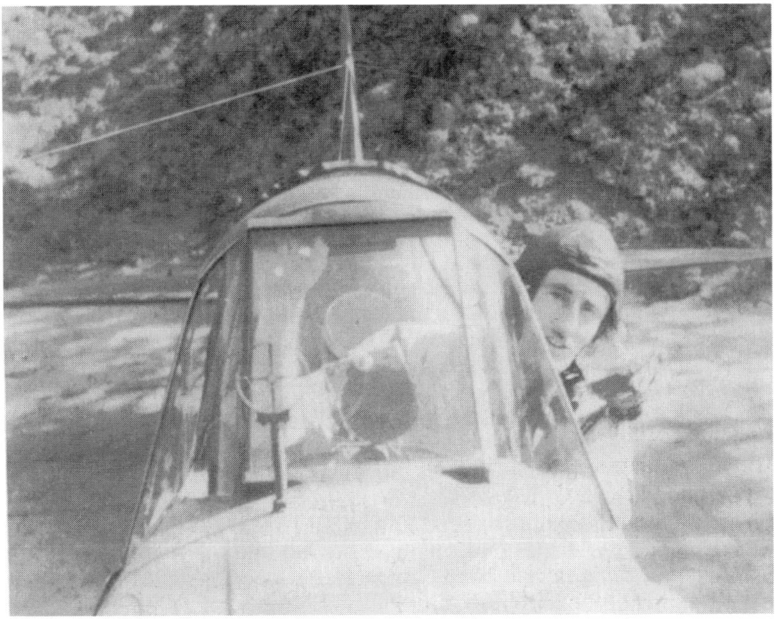

Flight Sergeant Ian Baines in Mohawk 'T' BS744.

flew to Dohazari for ops over Magwe. Flight Sergeant Potter and Sergeant Boult failed to return – believed to have collided mid-air in cloud. After searches crashed aircraft found near Comilla. Funeral took place as soon as possible after discovery. 29th – "A" Flight left for Imphal. Advance party left for Rajyespur, Squadron's new base.

'*Imphal* 4 February – General Scoones' 4th Army Corps met pilots and handed out bouquets to squadron. Army very pleased to have fighter aircraft working with them. 5th – Field Marshal Wavell met pilots and congratulated squadron, said – "he had heard" of us. 12th – The CO arrived this afternoon for pay parade!

'*Imphal* 11 April – Visit by Air Vice Marshal Williams, OBE, MC, DFC, AOC, Bengal Command and General Auchinleck. AVM advised that 155 Squadron would be staying at Imphal for Monsoon period and advised everyone to "dig in". His final observation was "keep up the good work and good luck!" 20th – Ten Mohawks "scrambled" to intercept bandits. After dogfights Flight Sergeant Freeman and Sergeant Simpson reported missing. 23rd – Sergeant Simpson's body and aircraft found many miles away.

'*Imphal* 11 May – Viceroy of India arrived to inspect Squadron. No 2 IAF and No 1 R&R Party were also present. His aircraft was

Maori Warrior painted on side panel of Mohawk 'T' BS744.

then escorted to Agartala by aircraft of the squadron. 16th – In a beat-up of Maungkan area Flying Officer Edmonds and Flight Sergeant Hick attacked village setting large huts afire. Herds of elephants and buffaloes were attacked at Maing

'*Imphal* 24 May – Squadron Leader Jeffries DFC and Flight Lieutenant Winton carried out first bombing raid of squadron using 20 lb bombs. 31st – Important bridge Hpaungzeik in Kalemyo area twice attacked with 20 lb bombs without result. A squadron concert party has been formed called "Ajax Revellers" and is in full swing preparing for a concert which it is hoped will be held at the beginning of next month. Third attack by Flying Officers Buddle and Edwards on bridge. In the afternoon Flying Officers Brinn and and Bishop made fourth attack without success. Last attacks on bridge made by Flying Officer MacGregor and Flight Sergeant Christison were successful, bridge being holed with three direct hits making it impossible for vehicles to cross. Flight Lieutenant Rathie posted to 261 Squadron, his post being filled by Flight Lieutenant F. J. Marshall from 261 Squadron.

'*Imphal* 1 June – Flying Officers MacGregor and Brinnand on 'Rhubarb', Kalemyo area, silenced gun position. MacGregor's aircraft was hit by two bullets and he force landed north of Kalemyo. He was seen to set fire to his aircraft and walk off westwards. 10th – 4 Corps advised that MacGregor had made contact and was able to reach squadron a few days later. 12th – during ops over Kalemyo area, bursts from slow-firing gun heard resembling sound of Chicago piano. 27th – Flying Officer Nicholson posted to No 151 OTU.

'*Agartala* 18 July – During "Rhubarbs" – Flying Officer Dunford and Flight Sergeant Christison – bridges at Hpaungzeik and Natkygon were seen to be unuseable former bridge washed away and centre span of latter missing. Move to Agartala – Air party 3rd and road/rail party on 5th.

'*Agartala* August 1943 – During month Flight Lieutenants Ford, Lawrie and Pilot Officer Prevezer arrived and Flight Lieutenant Winton left. At end of month it was decided to move squadron to Imphal and advance party under Flying Officer Prior left Agartala on 26th.

'*Imphal* September 1943 – Squadron move completed 2nd-l0th. Sergeant pilot Wolstenholme posted to squadron, 5 September. During month Flying Officers Hamilton and Brinnand were posted to AHQ Bengal and Base HQ Calcutta respectively.

'*Imphal* 5 October – Flying Officers Hunter and Dunford and Sergeant Parrish searched for missing Hurricane who was leading formation, but left behind with engine trouble. 6th – Flying Officers Edmonds, Dunford, Buddle and Sergeant Browne continue search for missing Hurricane. Weather very poor 7/10 ground level. All aircraft returned due to unsuitable weather. 9th – An air attack was made by Jap aircraft and a number of bombs fell on aerodrome, slight casualties and damage was caused.

'*Imphal* 3 November – Flight Lieutenant J. E. Meredith took over command of "A" Flight vice Flight Lieutenant J. V. Marshall promoted Squadron Leader. 9th – Squadron reverted to its original role as fighters and for the first time since 21 April 1943, came to grips with the enemy in the air.

'*Imphal* 9 November 1943 – Ten Mohawks scrambled by No 9 Fighter Ops Room at Imphal for two enemy formations of sixteen plus Salleys and six plus Oscars each. One attacked Imphal strip with 250/100 lb bombs and 40 lb AP bombs. The other formation attacked Palel strip. Few casualties were caused and certain damage to unserviceable aircraft on ground and installations. Four Mohawks intercepted two Oscars and one Oscar was claimed "destroyed" by Flying Officer Dunford. This aircraft was seen by Flying Officer Bishop to crash north-east of Palel. One Sally was shot down by heavy anti-aircraft fire. Hurricane IIes from Palel were also scrambled to intercept and unfortunately attacked one of our Mohawks mistaking it for an Oscar. Mohawk was damaged but able to force land at Palel; Sergeant pilot Tester was uninjured. 13th – Squadron Leader C. G. St. D. Jeffries DFC handed over squadron to Squadron Leader Winton. Support of the Army in the Chindwin Hills was carried out – thirteen sorties were made on Jap positions involving bombing and strafing runs. While taking off on one of these ops, a 25 lb bomb dropped off the port wing of Mohawk "V" AR677 – before it was above safety height. The aircraft caught fire and was totally destroyed. The pilot, Flight Lieutenant B. M. Ross-Magenty, was killed instantly. 20th – Three new pilots, Warrant Officer Holliday, Sergeants Willdey and Ottwell reported for duty. Concert party – "Scrambles" was shown in canteen and seen by over 1,000 troops.

'*Imphal* 4 December 1943 – Two Mohawks escorted Lockheed to Lake Indawgyi on a recce for Major General Wingate. 14th – Flying Officer MacGregor posted to Middle East. 19th – Flying Officer Dalrymple and Pilot Officer A. H. Wittridge reported for duty. 19th – Squadron to be re-equipped with Spitfires. 20th – Major-General G. E. Stratemeyer, USAAC, Air Commander Eastern Command ACSEA, visited station and decorated Squadron Leader D. Winton with the DFC. Flying Officer T. J. Buddle was also awarded DFC. 25th – Christmas fare was served to airmen at breakfast and tiffin, and at 19:30 hours officers and senior NCOs served Christmas dinner. Menu – Soup, duck, ham, veg, etc, Christmas pudding, biscuits, nuts and cigarettes...all appreciated by over 250 airmen.

'*Imphal* 1 January 1944 – New Year Message from CO was promulgated in DROs. 4th – Air party of fifteen Mohawks led by CO left for Alipore preparatory for re-equipping with Spitfires. Two messages received by 155 Squadron – (a) from Lieutenant General Scoones, No 4 Corps thanking officers and men for their excellent work and practical assistance over a long period... (b) from AOC 221 Group, farewelling 155 Squadron and acknowledging its record of achievement, low accident rate and high serviceability of aircraft which reflected great credit on the maintenance personnel, and thanking all ranks for the good work. 5th – New pilots reported for duty: Flying Officers N. Edwards, P. J. Cheverton, G. D. Brown, A. C. Tough, C. Entwistle; Pilot Officer D. Gillon; and Sergeants K. E. Pask and J. R. Clarke. 6th – Mohawks flown to their final resting place at Kanchrapara and the squadron turned its attention to the Spitfire VIIIs some of which had already arrived. 8th – Main body of squadron left for Alipore.'

The airfields used by the Mohawks were either all-weather or dirt strips, depending on location. Landing strips immediately to the rear of the front line were normally cleared paddy fields. At Dinjan airfield, located at the head of the Assam Valley, it was an all-weather macadam surface of 2,000 yd. From here North Burma was within range of the Mohawk. Tezpur was a grass field further west in the Assam Valley. 'A' Flight of No 5 Squadron was detached here to cover Imphal and Dimapur road area with their Mohawks.

Imphal was a short all-weather strip. However during the Mohawk period there were other grass strips around Imphal which were used by both transport, mostly DC-3s, and fighter aircraft as the density of air supply and defence grew to greater requirements. Agartala, in Eastern Bengal, had a 2,000 yd by 50 yd concrete runway and kutcha (grass) strip the latter used mainly for parking visiting bomber aircraft. Nos 5 and 155 formed No 169 Wing while at Agartala. Dum Dum had two macadam finished runways and Chittagong, situated at the head of the Bay of Bengal, was an all-weather runway while Ramu and Cox's Bazaar, south of Chittagong, were dirt strips.

The hangars were non-existent. A canvas cover to provide shade from the sun or waterproofing from Monsoon showers was the order of the day. At a few airfields, such as Dinjan and Agartala there may have been 'Hay-Barn' shelters. Major overhauls were mostly done at Kanchrapara on the northern outskirts of Calcutta. The ground facilities were very basic. Inspections were normally done at night in blast pens, although servicing sections did have a separate camouflaged location. Buildings were of bamboo 'basha', both for flights, Headquarters and accommodation huts. At Dinjan it was all tented accommodation.

The Mohawk was used solely as a day fighter and its gun armament was six .303 Browning machine-guns, two of which fired through the propellers. The Mohawk was also used as a fighter-bomber using 25 lb AP bombs and occasionally 30 lb incendiaries. The pilots termed the Mohawk a very nice aircraft to fly with a very good balance between aileron and elevator controls. It had a good rate of climb up to 12,000 ft for the tropical atmosphere experienced in India and Burma. One Mohawk pilot was Flight Sergeant Ian Baines: 'The supercharger was engaged at 11,000 ft and its ceiling was around 27,000 ft as I remember from my own experiences', he said. 'Spare parts were mostly at a premium, however, groundcrew did a wonderful job so that for "big shows" full serviceability was achieved normally.'

The Mohawks ranged over the whole Burma front. No 5 Squadron performed escort duties for the supply dropping, mainly with 31 Squadron, to the first Wingate expedition into North Burma – Ian Baines was on most of these duties: 'Some of these escort missions were our longest flights', he said. 'One such escort of eight Mohawks on 24 March 1943 involved one hour Agartala – Imphal, refuel; escort three DC-3s Imphal, area just north of Mandalay and on west bank of the Irrawaddy River – Imphal (45 minutes over the dropping area as troops in ambush and unable to display dropping signals), flight three hours and thirty five minutes. Imphal to Agartala was one hour and five minutes.'

CHAPTER TWENTY

Fighter Command's only VC

Extract from the London Gazette for 15 November 1940:

'The King has been graciously pleased to confer the victoria Cross on the undermentioned officer in recognition of most conspicuous bravery:

'Flight Lieutenant James Brindley Nicolson (39329)

'No 249 Squadron

'During an engagement with the enemy near Southampton on 16 August 1940, Flight Lieutenant Nicolson's aircraft was hit by four cannon shells two of which wounded him whilst another set fire to the gravity tank. When about to abandon his aircraft owing to flames in the cockpit he sighted an enemy fighter. This he attacked and shot down, although as a result of staying in his burning aircraft he sustained serious burns to his hands, face, neck and legs.

'Flight Lieutnant Nicolson has always displayed great enthusiasm for air fighting and this incident shows that he possesses courage and determination of a high order. By continuing to engage the enemy after he had been wounded and his aircraft set on fire, he displayed exceptional gallantry and disregard for the safety of his own life.'

James Nicolson was Fighter Command's only Victoria Cross of the last war. The reason why only one VC was awarded to a fighter pilot is because their valour, at high speed and altitudes was so seldom witnessed. They fought alone in the skies, where split seconds meant life or death. The Victoria Cross is awarded only on the evidence of reliable observers.

James Nicolson was born in 1917 in Hampstead and educated at Tonbridge School. He joined the Royal Air Force as a pilot in 1936. His father was a former member of the Royal Naval Air Service. He was 23 years old when he won his VC. On 16 August 1940, Red

Section of No 249 Squadron at Boscombe Down in Wiltshire were scrambled to patrol around Ringwood and Salisbury. Just after the three Hurricanes, piloted by Flight Lieutenant James Nicolson, Squadron Leader Eric King and Pilot Officer M. A. King, were airborne Gosport was attacked by twelve Ju 88s and eighteen Messerschmitt 110s. As the three Hurricanes sped to engage the enemy aircraft they were 'bounced' by Me 109s and all three of Red Section were hit, setting fire to both Nicolson's and Pilot Officer King's aircraft. Squadron Leader King broke away and made it back to Boscombe Down with his crippled fighter. Meanwhile Pilot Officer King had baled out of his blazing Hurricane but his parachute disintegrated, probably burnt, and he plunged to the ground.

While this was going on Nicolson, wounded and with his aircraft on fire, turned to evade the cannon fire and as he did so he got the 110 in his sights and shot it down. Having remained to fight the enemy the flames were now burning fiercely in the cockpit and Nicolson was sitting in the middle of the now raging inferno. With great difficulty he baled out, badly burned, especially his right hand. To add insult to injury an idiot from the Home Guard fired a shotgun at Nicolson as he approached the ground and dozens of lead pellets lodged in his legs. Peppered with gunshot and very badly burned, he lay on the ground in great pain. At this point a soldier with a rifle placed himself between the wounded fighter pilot and the lunatic Home Guard and shouted that he would shoot anyone who came near. The Home Guard was raving and shouting that the 'bloody' German should be killed. The soldier told him to shut up and menacingly brandished his rifle in a business-like manner to hold off the Home Guard, not knowing whether the injured pilot was friend or foe.

Eventually Nicolson was rushed to hospital and during the winter of 1940-41 was at the RAF Officers' Convalescent Hospital in Torquay, South Devon, where his wife Muriel came down from Yorkshire and joined him.

The Victorial Cross.

Nicolson said that he owed his life to that soldier and was hoping to learn his identity. Sadly it was not to be. He left hospital and eventually became a Wing Commander but he was lost in an aircraft that disappeared without trace on 2 May 1945 over the Indian Ocean. The aircraft took off at 13:00 hours, flew for 130 miles, and just disappeared.

Personal note: In April 1983 the Royal Air Force Museum at Hendon, North London, bought the dull bronze medal with its faded purple ribbon for a record £110,000. To the Government, Mrs Muriel Nicolson is worth around £44 a week, because her husband won the VC during the Battle of Britain – that is the pension price put on his valour.

Flight Lieutenant James Brindley Nicholson, No 249 Squadron.

* * *

Without a shadow of any doubt, one man who should have received the Victoria Cross posthumously was Flying Officer Fairbairn-McPhee of No 6 Squadron, Royal Air Force. The Victoria Cross is usually conferred for a single act of heroism and Fairbairn-McPhee lost his life by a most conspicuous act of heroism which called for valour of the highest order.

In 1942 Flying Officer Fairbairn-McPhee was with No 6 Squadron flying Hurricane IId 'Tankbusters' in the Western Desert. On one particular attack, when tanks were plentiful, Flying Officer 'Mac' Fairbairn-McPhee was coming in on a tank at zero altitude, when all of a sudden he saw a 'sprog pilot' directly overhead, engrossed in the same tank and losing altitude as he pressed home his attack.

The aircraft above him put Fairbairn-McPhee in a deadly situation and he had only seconds to make a choice. He had insufficient room to turn although some might have tried it in sheer desperation, and if he pulled up his aircraft would collide with the sprog pilot sitting above him. 'He was the bravest of the brave', said Squadron Leader Simpson. 'Mac had been known to fly low over German camps and wave to them – not firing at them, just waving. He said it was "to steel my soul against fear, and to show the Germans my contempt for death".' Flying Officer 'Masher' Maslyn, who was a very brave man, refused to fly with him again after that incident. He had been flying tail cover to Mac and they were on their way home from a reconnaissance mission.

Allan Simpson continues: 'Sensitive and artistic though he was, Fairbairn-McPhee was as tough as the rhinoceros he hunted, and delighted in mortal combat with man or beast. He justified it all with his philosophy.

We who knew him could imagine the method by which he reached his decision that fateful day. The sprog was going to get that tank anyway. It was sample. Either he and the sprog pilot would be killed, or else he alone. Two pilots and two aircraft, or one pilot and one aircraft – with that he nosed into the ground voluntarily, leaving a widow and two sons in Kenya.'

Flying Officer 'Mac' Fairbairn-McPhee ought to have received a Victoria Cross posthumously, but the truth behind Fairbairn-McPhee's death was not told at the regular debriefing. It was only later that the truth came out when, by chance, the Army Liaison Officer saw the sprog pilot sitting on the tailplane of his aircraft weeping his eyes out. Squadron Leader Simpson then had the true picture: 'From the thousands of details his eyes had seen that day, and the relatively few his mind could reconstruct, the memory of the fleeting form of Mac's wing below him told him the horrible truth', said Simpson. 'From his unofficial story we were able to reconstruct the processes by which Mac must have reached a mighty important decision in a split second. The only decision a man that brave could make.'

Index

Index of Units

Index Of Squadrons